Shadowmen 2

also by Jean-Marc & Randy Lofficier
Doctor Omega
(*adapted from Arnould Galopin*)

Shadowmen
Heroes and Villains of French Pulp Fiction

forthcoming from Black Coat Press:
Doctor Ardan: The City of Gold and Lepers
(*adapted from Guy d'Armen*)

The Man in Grey
(*adapted from Arnould Galopin*)

Sâr Dubnotal: Jack the Ripper

available from iUniverse:
The *Doctor Who* Programme Guide
The Nth Doctor
Into the Twilight Zone

available from McFarland & Company:
French Science Fiction, Fantasy, Horror and Pulp Fiction

Shadowmen 2
Heroes and Villains of French Comics

by
Jean-Marc & Randy Lofficier

A Black Coat Press Book

Acknowledgements: We are indebted to Alain Beyrand, Luciano Bernasconi, Claude J. Legrand, Pierre Liquois, Marc Madouraud, Félix Molinari, Michel Montbarbon, Thierry Mornet, Franco Oneta, Andrew Paquette, Daniel Riche, Edmond Ripoll, Gérard Thomassian, Dominik Vallet and David McDonnell for proofreading the typescript.

Copyright © 2004 by Jean-Marc & Randy Lofficier.
Cover illustration Copyright © 2004 by Andrew Paquette.

Visit our website at www.blackcoatpress.com

ISBN 0-9740711-8-8. First Printing. March 2004. Published by Black Coat Press, an imprint of Hollywood Comics.com, LLC, P.O. Box 17270, Encino, CA 91416. All rights reserved. Except for review purposes, no part of this book may be reproduced or transmitted in any form or by any means, electronic or mechanical, including photocopying, recording, or by any information storage and retrieval system, without permission in writing from the publisher. The stories and characters depicted in this book are entirely fictional. Printed in the United States of America.

Fantax

Table of Contents

Cool French Comics..7
Zig et Puce (1925)..13
Futuropolis (1937)..19
L'Epervier Bleu (1942)..23
Le Rayon U (1943)..29
Les Pionniers de l'Espérance (1945)..33
Fantax (1946) & Black Boy (1955)..45
Durga Rani (1946)...59
Fulguros (1946)...65
Guerre à la Terre (1946)...73
Kaza le Martien (1946) 79
Tom X (1946)..81
Salvator (1947)..87
Satanax (1948) 91
Stany Beulé (1949)...97
Arabelle, la Dernière Sirène (1950) 101
Les Conquérants de l'Espace (1953)...107

Monsieur Choc (Tif & Tondu) (1955) 121
Bibi Fricotin et les Martiens (1955) 131
Jacques Flash (1957) 137
Super Boy (1958) 145
Barbarella (1962) 159
Alain Landier (1962) 169
Zembla (1963) 175
Ténébrax (1963) 197
Les Naufragés du Temps (1964) 201
Titan (1963) 209
Lone Sloane (1966) 213
Jodelle (1966) 225
Luc Orient (1966) 229
Submerman (1967) 237
Olympio & Vincent Larcher (1967) 241
Wampus (1969) & L'Autre (1973) 249
Thorkael (1971) 259
Brigade Temporelle (1972) 263
Frankenstein (1972) 269
Tiriel (1974) 277
Kabur (1975) 281
Felina (1979) 289
Photonik (1980) 293
Mikros (1980) & Epsilon (1986) 299
Phénix (1980) 305
Index 310

Alain Landier

Cool French Comics

In a letter written in 1861 to the Baron de Chapuys-Montlaville, Paul Féval, the prodigious *feuilletoniste* and author of *Les Habits Noirs* [*The Black Coats*], defended popular literature by saying: "That insignificant literature sometimes has higher aspirations, but it never declares them, *and that is the secret of its power.*" The first volume of this series was therefore devoted not to famous French authors such as Balzac or Proust, who can be adequately researched in universities, but to the giants of French popular literature, a domain virtually unknown outside that country.

This companion volume is devoted to the equally wonderful field of comics, meaning comic books and comic strips, a medium that the French call *bandes dessinées*–illustrated strips–or *BD* for short. Again, instead of concentrating on renowned, mainstream characters, such as *Tintin*, *Spirou* and *Astérix*, we have chosen to focus our attention on lesser known heroes, four-color figures of the *fantastique*, in other words *Shadowmen* (and *Shadowomen*), both in terms of their characteristics as well as their place in the history of the medium.

To place these "Shadowmen" in their proper context, it is necessary to begin with a brief panorama of the history of comics. Comics are sometimes considered an indigenous American art form. Yet, they first took root in Europe, and have flourished there beyond the commercial and artistic limitations imposed upon them in the United States. Nowhere else in Europe have comics thrived and been so recognized as in France and Belgium, where they truly deserve the label of graphic novels–indeed, they are often called the "Ninth Art" by French academics.

Some scholars like to trace the ancestry of comics to medieval tapestries or the engravings used during the French Revolution to tell simple stories. However, most experts agree that the first, deliberate attempt at creating comics in a modern form should be credited to Swiss writer-cartoonist Rodolphe Topffer, whose first graphic story, *Histoire de M. Vieuxboix* [*The Story of Mr. Vieuxbois*], was published in Geneva in 1827, and in the United States in 1842 as *The Adventures of Mr. Obadiah Oldbuck*.

One of the first French comics creators was Christophe, who published fully illustrated children's books such as *Le Savant Cosinus* [*Prof. Cosine*] (1900) and *Les Malices de Plick et Plock* [*The Tricks of Plick and Plock*] (1904). Other luminaries of the period included cartoonist Caran d'Ache, the great animal artist Benjamin Rabier and science fiction writer-illustrator Albert Robida.

Soon, comics took off as a separate branch of children's literature, and appeared in a variety of illustrated magazines, such as *La Jeunesse Illustrée* [*Youth Illustrated Stories*] (1903-1935), *Le Petit Journal Illustré* [*The Little Illustrated Journal*] (1904-1914), *La Semaine de Suzette* [*Suzette's Weekly*] (1905-1940) (for which Joseph P. Pinchon made up the character of a naive, young housemaid from Brittany, *Bécassine*), *L'Epatant* [*The Wonderful*] (1908-1937) (in which Louis Forton created a trio of rogues and con artists, *Les Pieds Nickelés* [*The Nickel-Footed Gang*], the first comic strip to be adapted for animation by Emile Cohl in 1917) and *Fillette* [*Little Girl*] (1909-1942) (which published A. Vallet's classic *Espiègle Lili* [*Naughty Lili*]).

World War I had a severe impact on the budding French comics industry, both artistically and commercially. Nevertheless, the first *albums*–collections of comics stories previously serialized in magazines and sold in bookstores–began to appear on the children's bookshelves just after the War. This publishing practice enabled comics to achieve a degree of economic legitimacy in France which was denied to them in the United States.

The next revolution took place in 1925, when cartoonist Alain Saint-Ogan, following in the footsteps of Louis Forton, created the characters of *Zig et Puce* for *Le Dimanche Illustré* [*Illustrated Sunday*] (1924-1940). *Zig et Puce* was the first comics series to use word balloons and a clear, semi-caricatural drawing style.

Soon after *Zig et Puce*, Belgian cartoonist Hergé created the immortal character of *Tintin* in 1929 for *Le Petit Vingtième* [*The Little 20th Century*] (1928-1940), the illustrated weekly supplement to the local Catholic newspaper *Le Vingtième Siècle* [*The 20th Century*]. In 1938, French cartoonist Robert Velter, signing Rob-Vel, who had at one time been one of Martin Branner's assistants on *Winnie Winkle*, created the character of *Spirou* to compete with *Tintin*.

The 1930s were also marked by the importation of American comic strips, such as *Flash Gordon, Brick Bradford, Prince Valiant, Tarzan, Mickey, Popeye,* etc. These had a strong and lasting influence on French and Belgian artists.

Wampus (art by Bernasconi) (1969)

When the Nazis banned American strips during World War II, the French and Belgian comics industries were forced to replace them with local products, thus fostering local talent. Writer-artist Edgar P. Jacobs first finished the interrupted publication of *Flash Gordon*, then drew his own *Flash Gordon*-inspired series, *Le Rayon U* [*The U Ray*] (1943), before going on to create his own classic series, *Blake et Mortimer* in 1946.

After the War, artists such as Joseph Gillain a.k.a. Jijé (*Jean Valhardi*), Raymond Poïvet (*Les Pionniers de l'Espérance* [*The Pioneers of Hope*]) and Sirius (*L'Epervier Bleu* [*The Blue Hawk*]), created a variety of adventure series in the tradition of American artists Milton Caniff, Alex Raymond and Hal Foster. On the humor front, artists André Franquin (*Spirou*), Will (*Tif et Tondu*) and Peyo (*Johan* and, later, *Les Schtroumpfs* [*The Smurfs*]) crafted a number of Disney-inspired strips and eventually established a unique Belgian cartoony style, which still exerts its influence today.

In 1949, the political forces of the Catholic Church and the Communist Left combined to keep out American comics, deemed too violent for children by the former, and too imperialistic by the latter. This took the form of a law passed in France in July, which prevented the further exploitation of American strips and created a censorship review board of comics.

The French-Belgian comics industry was then comprised of a number of weekly children's magazines which published humor and adventure series, often inspired by, or derivative of, American series. These magazines were *Spirou* (created in 1938, still published today), *Tintin* (1946-1989), *Vaillant*, retitled *Pif* in 1969 (1945-1993) and *Pilote* (1959-1989).

Parallel to these socially respectable publications, cheaper comic books, which had come into existence after the War in order to satisfy the demand for harder-edged American-style comics, thrived. Known as *petits formats* [*small format*], these digest-sized comics published a mix of Westerns, crime stories, superheroes and science fiction. The small format publishers included Artima, later renamed Aredit, Editions Lug and Editions du Siècle, later renamed Imperia. All fought numerous battles with the state censors.

Three small format series made a lasting impression: Pierre Mouchot's *Fantax* (1946), a French superhero which was soon put out of business by the censors, R. Lortac and R. & R. Giordan's *Les Conquérants de l'Espace* [*The Space Conquerors*] (1953), Franco Oneta's jungle lord *Zembla* (1963) and Franco Frescura and Luciano Bernasconi's short-lived alien shapeshifter *Wampus* (1969), also felled by censorship.

In the 1970s, the French comics industry began to change. The readership grew older. The artists and writers were becoming tired of the limitations imposed on them by a juvenile market. The silver age eventually came to an end in 1972 when cartoonists Marcel Gotlib, Nikita Mandryka and Claire Brétécher left *Pilote* to create and self-publish an adult, underground humor magazine, *L'Echo des Savanes* [*The Echo of the Savanna*]. In 1974, artists Moebius, Philippe

Druillet and writer Jean-Pierre Dionnet did the same, creating *Métal Hurlant*, devoted to science fiction and fantasy.

Interestingly, the first adult comic book had been published in 1962. It was the daring science fiction epic *Barbarella*, by illustrator Jean-Claude Forest. *Barbarella* was soon followed by Druillet's *Lone Sloane* (1966), which migrated to *Pilote* in 1970, and Guy Pellaert's *Jodelle* (1966).

The mid-1970s saw the beginning of the decline of the traditional juvenile humor and adventure comics, with the exception of *Spirou*, and a rapid increase in the number of strips aimed at an older audience, published in magazines such as *Fluide Glacial* (1975-) and *À Suivre* (1978-1998). The small format publishers, who had introduced Marvel and DC Comics characters in 1969, followed suit with their own French-grown superheroes. Among the most fondly remembered were *Kabur*, *Mikros*, *Photonik* and *Phénix*.

As French comics entered the 1980s, they became increasingly respectable, attracting national attention, published in beautiful and expensive graphic novels. A certain conception of the popular nature of the medium was lost, which is why this survey stops in 1980.

Jean-Marc & Randy Lofficier

Zig et Puce – Futuropolis reedition (Vol. 4) (1988)

Zig et Puce (1925)

"All this would not have happened if we hadn't missed our train."
"And if the car we rented had worked, we would have caught our boat."
(Zig & Puce – *Zig et Puce et la Petite Princesse*)

Created by:

Writer-artist Alain Saint-Ogan (1895-1974). Saint-Ogan is, with Hergé, the founding father of French-language comics. The son of a newspaper editor, he started as a cartoonist in 1913, publishing in a variety of newspapers and magazines. In 1925, Saint-Ogan created *Zig et Puce* and was the first French artist to fully use word balloons. He continued producing *Zig et Puce*, as well as other, less memorable children's series, until the early 1950s. Alfred, Zig and Puce's pet  penguin, was for many years the name of a major French comics award. In 1945, Saint-Ogan co-wrote a fantasy novel with Camille Ducray, *Le Voyageur Immobile* [*The Motionless Traveller*]. He also created the character of *Monsieur Poche*, became a magazine editor and, later, hosted a radio show and produced a television series.

Story:

Zig and Puce, like most young pulp heroes of the time, are two teenagers without any inconvenient family ties. In their first adventure, anticipating the later exploits of *Tintin*, and reflecting the fascination of the era, they embark for America. A series of colorful, if wildly unrealistic, globe-trotting exploits follows. These include being sidetracked to Africa, crossing the Pacific by submarine and encountering a sea serpent. During a visit at the South Pole, the two heroes befriend a penguin which they name Alfred and who becomes their mascot.

In one of their most fantastic adventures, after rescuing Princess Yvette of Marcalance, Zig and Puce return to New York and decide to explore Earth's stratosphere in a hot-air balloon. In a mysterious, unexplained fashion, they land back on Earth in the year 2000. The future world they explore is a land of flying cars, rolling sidewalks, pneumatic trains, nutrition pills, artificial islands and interplanetary rockets–a future worthy of Jules Verne and Robida. Zig and Puce then take off in a rocket and journey to Venus, a planet inhabited by colorful natives and primeval beasts. They eventually return to their own time in another balloon trip. Saint-Ogan mentioned the possibility that it may all have been a dream.

Zig & Puce visit a floating island in the year 2000 (1935).

During the rest of the series, Saint-Ogan continued to alternate exotic yet mundane adventures with a few more fantastic stories, such as the discovery of Atlantis and an encounter with an Invisible Man. However, the context was always that of a harmless children's fantasy.

Zig & Puce on Venus (1935)

When writer-artist Greg (see *Luc Orient* entry) took over the series in 1963, he modernized the graphic style but was careful to preserve the spirit of *Zig et Puce*. At first, he only dealt with ordinary elements, such as a mysterious, vanishing thief. But then, he grew more daring, often drawing on ideas previously introduced by Saint-Ogan. In one of his stories, Zig and Puce prevent the sabotage of a super-powered, all-purpose vehicle dubbed Prototype 0-0. In another, they thwart a would-be world conqueror who uses an antigravity mineral to power a flying aircraft carrier, reminiscent of the flying ocean liners Saint-Ogan had depicted in the 21st century. In the last story, Zig and Puce rescue a young Princess in distress, not unlike young Yvette of Marcalance.

Zig & Puce drawn by Greg (1969)

Publishing History:
Zig et Puce is one of the oldest French adventure strips, predating the more famous *Tintin* by four years. *Zig et Puce* was created in 1925 by Alain Saint-Ogan for *Le Dimanche Illustré* [*The Illustrated Sunday*], a weekly newspaper that lasted from 1924 to 1940.

Zig et Puce reflected the influences of American cartoonists such as George McManus (*Bringing Up Father*) and Martin Branner (*Winnie Winkle*), both published with success in France at the time. It used word balloons exclusively, a clear, semi-caricatural drawing line and established modern comics storytelling conventions.

After their original publication in *Le Dimanche Illustré*, *Zig et Puce*'s adventures were collected in a series of graphic novels by publisher Hachette, starting in 1927 and establishing the tradition of the *album*. After World War II, Hachette continued the series, until Saint-Ogan moved on.

In 1963, Saint-Ogan agreed to entrust the characters to writer-artist Michel Greg, who then wrote and drew six new stories, serialized in the weekly magazine *Tintin* between 1963 and 1969. These were later collected in the graphic novel format by Editions du Lombard. However, Greg's many other professional commitments prevented him from continuing the series.

Finally, an almost complete, six-volume hardcover reedition of the original Saint-Ogan *Zig et Puce* was published by publisher Futuropolis from 1986 to 1992.

Zig et Puce was a serious rival to *Tintin*, which borrowed a number of its ideas. Certainly, Hergé publicly acknowledged his debt towards Saint-Ogan. While working on *Tintin in Congo* in 1930, the two artists met; Saint-Ogan encouraged Hergé and reportedly gave him a signed page of original art. However, *Tintin*'s stories were always more carefully constructed, its characters better defined, and ultimately Saint-Ogan did not redraw and adapt his earlier stories to suit the tastes of a more sophisticated post-War audience as Hergé did.

Bibliography:
Writer-Artist: Alain Saint-Ogan.
1. *Zig et Puce [En Route pour l'Amérique]* [*The Road to America*] (Hachette, 1927)
2. *Zig et Puce Millionnaires* [*Zig & Puce Millionaires*] (Hachette, 1928)
3. *Zig, Puce et Alfred* (Hachette, 1929)
4. *Zig et Puce à New York* [*Zig & Puce in New York*] (Hachette, 1930)
5. *Zig et Puce Cherchent Dolly* [*Zig & Puce in Search of Dolly*] (Hachette, 1931)
6. *Zig et Puce aux Indes* [*Zig & Puce in India*] (Hachette, 1932)

7. *Zig, Puce et Furette* (Hachette, 1933)
8. *Zig, Puce et la Petite Princesse* [*Zig, Puce and the Little Princess*] (Hachette, 1934)
9. *Zig et Puce au XXIème Siècle* [*Zig & Puce in the 21st Century*] (Hachette, 1935)
10. *Zig et Puce Ministres* [*Zig & Puce Ministers*] (Hachette, 1938)
11. *Zig et Puce et le Professeur Medor* [*Zig & Puce and Professor Medor*] (Hachette, 1941)
12. *Revoilà Zig et Puce* [*The Return of Zig & Puce*] (Hachette, 1947)
13. *Zig et Puce en Atlantide* [*Zig & Puce in Atlantis*] (1948; not originally collected by Hachette; reprinted in 1992 by Futuropolis)
14. *Zig et Puce et l'Homme Invisible* [*Zig & Puce and the Invisible Man*] (Hachette, 1949)
15. *Zig et Puce et le Complot* [*Zig & Puce and the Conspiracy*] (Hachette, 1950)
16. *Zig et Puce et le Cirque* [*Zig & Puce at the Circus*] (Hachette, 1951)
17. *Zig et Puce en Éthiopie* [*Zig & Puce in Ethiopia*] (Hachette, 1952)
18. *Zig et Puce sur Vénus* [*Zig & Puce on Venus*] (1954; not originally collected by Hachette; reprinted in 2000 by Glénat)
19. *Zig et Puce et Nenette* [*Zig & Puce & Nenette*] (1956; not originally collected by Hachette; reprinted in 2000 by Glénat)

Writer-Artist: Greg.
1. *Le Voleur Fantôme* [*The Phantom Thief*] (*Tintin* Nos. 759-780, 1963; rep. Ed. du Lombard No. 1, 1965)
2. *Le Vagabond d'Asie* [*The Asian Wanderer*] (*Tintin* Nos. 781-788, 1963; rep. Ed. du Lombard No. 1, 1965)
3. *S.O.S Sheila* (*Tintin* Nos. 789-818, 1964; rep. Ed. du Lombard No. 2, 1966)
4. *Prototype Zéro-Zéro* (*Tintin* Nos. 819-848, 1964; rep. Ed. du Lombard No. 3, 1967)
5. *Le Mystère de la Pierre qui Vole* [*The Mystery of the Flying Stone*] (*Tintin* Nos. 852-882, 1965; rep. Ed. du Lombard No. 4, 1968)
6. *Les Frais de la Princesses* [*The Expenses of the Princess*] (*Tintin* Nos. 1060-1085, 1969; rep. Ed. du Lombard No. 5, 1970)
7. *Zig et Puce contre le Légume Boulimique* [*Zig & Puce vs. the Bulimic Vegetable*] (collects various short stories by Greg originally published in *Tintin*) (Glénat, Volume 6, 1995)

Zig & Puce by Greg on the cover of Tintin (1969)

Film:
Zig et Puce Sauvent Nenette [Zig & Puce Rescue Nenette] (1952)
Dir: Georges Rollin.
Cast: Gilbert Forzano (Zig), Gérard Rosset (Puce), Stéphane Vander (Alfred)

Website:
http://www.coolfrenchcomics.com/zigpuce.htm

Futuropolis (1937)

*"There is no Unknown for our infallible Science.
Our reason must explain everything."*
(The Grand Master of the City – *Futuropolis*)

Created by:
Writer Martial Cendres and artist Pellos.

• Martial Cendres was one of the pseudonyms of renowned French science fiction writer René Thévenin (?-1967). Thévenin began his career penning such pulpish yarns as *La Cité des Tortures* [*The City of Tortures*] (1906) about an underground city where the Chinese secretly prepared to take over the world, *Le Collier de l'Idole de Fer* [*The Necklace of the Iron Idol*] (1912) about an idol of living metal worshipped by a Lost Tribe of Incas, *Le Maître des Vampires* [*The Master of Vampires*] (1923) and *Sous les Griffes du Monstre* [*The Claws of the Monster*] (1926). In the 1930s, however, Thévenin's production became more ambitious in terms of concept, and more literary in its execution. He wrote two classic genre novels, *Les Chasseurs d'Hommes* [*The Manhunters*] (1930), which tells the story of two superpowered mutants who keep men as pets or hunt them to feed on their lifeforce, and *Sur l'Autre Face du Monde* [*The Other Side of the World*] (1935) (written under the pseudonym of André Valérie), which became the basis for *Futuropolis*. Thévenin eventually retired from writing fiction after joining the staff of the Museum of Natural History in Paris.

• Pellos was the pseudonym of artist René Pellarin (1900-1998). After a prolific career as a sports cartoonist in the 1930s, Pellos began drawing a variety of children's comics. In 1937, he co-created *Futuropolis* for the magazine *Junior*. Pellos remained extremely prolific, both during and after World War II. He took over *Les Pieds Nickelés* in 1948, and continued the series until 1981. His other credits include *Electropolis* (1940), *Durga Rani* (1946) and a remarkable adaptation of J.H. Rosny Aîné's 1909 prehistoric novel, *La Guerre du Feu* [*Quest for Fire*] drawn in 1951. Pellos received the prestigious Grand Prize of Angoulême in 1977.

Story:
Futuropolis is the last city of men on Earth in the far future. It is ruled by a council of Elders, who command a powerful army of robots. But it is also a city without a soul. When the body of a primitive caveman is discovered, indicating that there is life beyond the City, the Elders dispatch Rao and Maia to investigate.

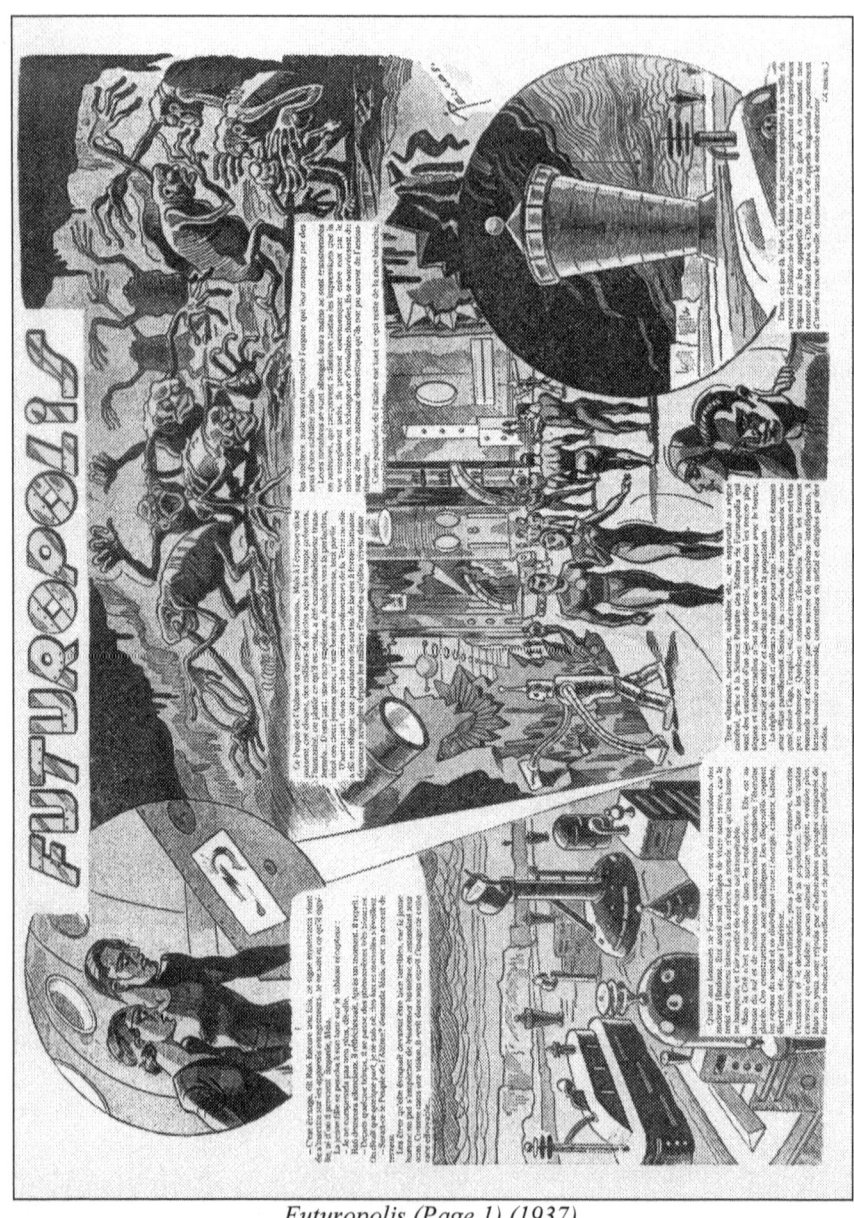

Futuropolis (Page 1) (1937)

After crossing a series of mutant-infested caves, the two City-dwellers discover a primitive tribe of cavemen. Upon their return, and after hearing their report, the Elders decide that the cavemen should be enslaved. But Rao, who in the meantime has fallen in love with one of the primitives, the beautiful Iaona, rebels and switches sides. Maia, feeling spurned, now savagely turns against him. Eventually, a fierce battle erupts between the two camps, at the end of which Iaona kills Maia. Futuropolis falls at last, and a new age dawns for mankind.

Publishing History:

Futuropolis was originally serialized in the magazine *Junior* in 1937 and 1938. A sequel of sorts, or rather a story tapping the same elements, *Electropolis*, followed in 1940, but was left unfinished because of the War. *Futuropolis* was finally collected in the graphic novel format by publisher Glénat in 1977, and again reprinted in 1999.

The text-beneath-the-art format was due to the fact that the story's publisher, Offenstadt, who also serialized many of Thévenin's novels, was aiming to publish something along the lines of an illustrated novel, as opposed to a pure comic.

Futuropolis is rightly considered one of the milestones of early French science fiction. It is, in many respects, a thinly-disguised adaptation of Thévenin's *Sur l'Autre Face du Monde* [*The Other Side of the World*] (1935), which strangely anticipates Arthur C. Clarke's *Against the Fall of Night* (1953). Its theme is the end of the sterile city of machines, a society without hope or progress, meant to be replaced by a new civilization, one which lives in harmony with nature, symbolized here by the union of Rao and Iaona. Graphically, Pellos was clearly inspired by Fritz Lang's *Metropolis* (1926), which provided the initial impetus for the project.

Website:
http://www.coolfrenchcomics.com/futuropolis.htm

L'Epervier Bleu (1942)

"This devilish girl has read too many adventure novels!"
(L'Épervier Bleu – *La Vallée Interdite*)

Created by:
Writer-artist Sirius. Sirius was the pseudonym of Max Mayeu (1911-1997), one of the first artists to join the editorial team of the weekly children's magazine *Spirou* in 1942. *L'Epervier Bleu* was Sirius' first creation for *Spirou* but, in 1951, after repeated problems with French censorship, Sirius decided to concentrate on a different and less controversial series. That series was the popular historical saga, *Timour*, which recounted the adventures of a family of heroes, starting in prehistoric times and moving forward in time with each book. Other creations by Sirius include the short-lived fantasy *Simon le Danseur* [*Simon the Dancer*] and the dark-humored and more cartoony *Pemberton*, created for *Pilote* in 1972.

Story:
L'Epervier Bleu [*The Blue Hawk*] is the nickname of a globe-trotting adventurer, entirely unconcerned about danger, whom his creator described as "always ready to throw himself into the most daring enterprise, defy the worst villains, and carve his own heroic saga." His real name is Eric, and he is proud and fearless, daring and gallant–in other words, a true hero.

Eric is not alone in his exploits. He is accompanied by his trusted friend, Larsen, a burly, red-haired Irishman whom he met during a bar fight in Palawang. Another sidekick is turbaned Hindu boy wonder Sheba. Finally, during his trip to the Moon, Eric is joined by the blonde Cristine Holiday.

The Blue Hawk's adventures began with a mundane action thriller, but quickly veered into a more fantastic direction with an Egyptian adventure, filled with lost tombs, secret treasures and exotic atmosphere.

Then, Eric fought a gang of air pirates who used a gigantic flying fortress

La Vallée Interdite (1950)

to ransom intercontinental traffic. From air pirates, it was a small leap to defying an evil underwater organization led by a mad scientist trying to take over the world.

Having crushed that villain, in *The Forbidden Valley*, Eric and his friend Larsen discovered the remains of a lost Aztec civilization and its buried treasure while exploring the Mountains of Central America.

But the final saga of *The Blue Hawk* was, by far, the most interesting and fantastic. In it, Eric learns of Professor Jonathan Holiday who built a rocket which took him to the Moon, but now needs to be rescued. However, before the heroes can do so, they first have to contend with the nefarious activities of two enemy spies, Vincente and Paco. Finally, Eric and his friends travel to the Moon, and explore its vast, underground caverns, where they are almost trapped by giant, indestructible mushrooms. They eventually free the Professor and return to Earth.

Publishing History:

L'Epervier Bleu was originally serialized in *Spirou*, starting in 1942. From the start, the series ran into trouble with the French censors because of its violence–in the best tradition of American comics, the hero was not afraid to use his fists and his guns–and its science fiction elements, such as mad scientists and other fantastic inventions, which were deemed far too extravagant for its youthful audience. As a result of this harassment, Sirius abandoned *The Blue Hawk* in 1951, but eventually returned to it, briefly, in the mid-1970s, before entrusting the character to fellow writer-artist Jean-Marie Brouyère.

The first eight *Epervier Bleu* stories were collected in the graphic novel format between 1948 and 1954 by *Spirou*'s Belgian publisher, Editions Dupuis. It is interesting to note that Volume 1 contained an additional 39 pages that had not been serialized in *Spirou* because of justified concerns about censorship. World War II forced Sirius to wrap up his first storyline. Volume 2 has since become extremely rare because of its low print run and only one printed copy of the original edition is known to exist today. Seven pages of Volume 3, initially censored, were eventually published in Volume 4. Volume 5 was eventually reprinted by Dupuis in 1979, and an Omnibus edition entitled *Territoires Interdits* [*Forbidden Territories*] containing Vols. 6-8 was finally published in 1986. None of the later *Epervier Bleu* stories were collected in graphic novel format.

Bibliography:
Writer-Artist: Sirius.
1. *L'Epervier Bleu* [*The Blue Hawk*] (*Spirou* Nos. 42/30-43/35, 1943; rep. as Vol. 1, 1948)
2. *Le Pharaon des Cavernes* [*The Pharaoh of the Caverns*] (*Spirou* Nos. 452-474, 1946; rep. as Vol. 2, 1950)
3. *L'Ile aux Perles* [*Pearl Island*] (*Spirou* Nos. 501-564, 1948; rep. as Vol. 3, 1950)
4. *Les Pirates de la Stratosphère* [*The Pirates of the Stratosphere*] (*Spirou* Nos. 565-600, 1949; rep. as Vol. 4, 1951)
5. *L'Ennemi sous la Mer* [*The Undersea Enemy*] (*Spirou* No. 601-648, 1949; rep. as Vol. 5, 1952)
6. *La Vallée Interdite* [*The Forbidden Valley*] (*Spirou* Nos. 649-690, 1950; rep. as Vol. 6, 1954)

7-8. *Point Zéro* [*Zero Point*] and *La Planète Silencieuse* [*The Silent Planet*] (serialized in *Spirou* under the single title of *La Planète Silencieuse*, Nos. 695-769, 1951; rep. as Vols. 7 and 8, 1954)

Writer: Jean-Marie Brouyère.
Artists: Sirius & J.-M. Brouyère.
9. *Le Puzzle de l'Au-Delà* [*The Puzzle From Beyond*] (*Spirou* Nos. 1854-1861, 1973)
10. *Le Cimetière de l'Infini* [*The Graveyard of Infinity*] (*Spirou* Nos. 1915-1922, 1975)

Writer-Artist: Sirius.
11. *Ce Bon Julius* [*Good Old Julius*] (*Spirou* Nos. 1926-1935, 1975)
12. *Les Guerriers des Solitudes* [*The Warriors of Solitude*] (*Spirou* Nos. 1989-1999, 1976)
13. *Ballade Irlandaise* [*The Irish Ballad*] (*Spirou* Nos. 2031-2046, 1977)

Website:
http://www.coolfrenchcomics.com/epervierbleu.htm

Eric and friends on the Moon (1951)

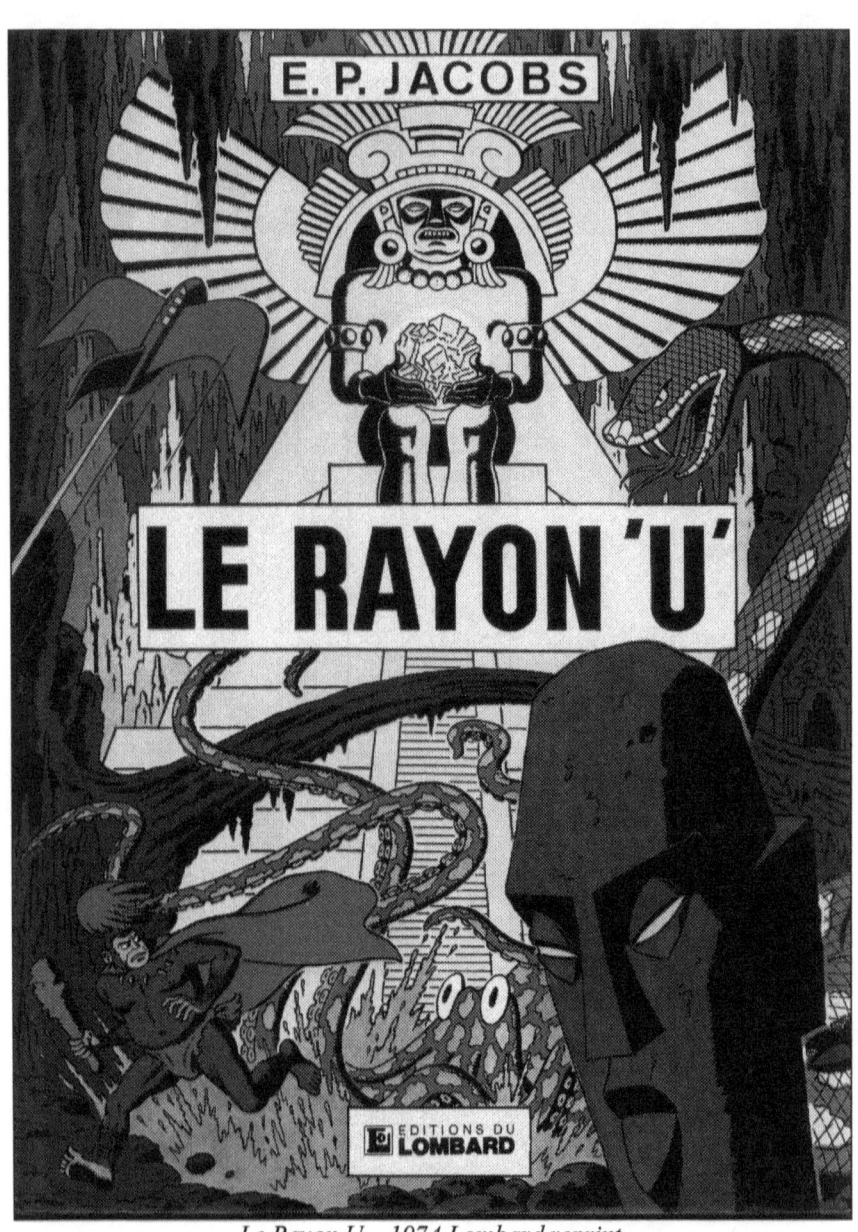
Le Rayon U – 1974 Lombard reprint

Le Rayon U (1943)

"Thanks to this mineral, science will make a prodigious leap forward, and the power of man shall be without limits!"
(Professor Marduk – *Le Rayon U*)

Created by:

Writer-artist Edgar-Pierre Jacobs (1904-1987). A commercial illustrator, fashion designer and even an opera baritone, Jacobs entered the field of comics during World War II, when, in 1942, he was asked by Belgian weekly magazine *Bravo* to continue the adventures of *Flash Gordon*. *Flash Gordon* had first appeared in France under the title *Guy l'Eclair* in the French weekly magazine *Robinson*, from April 1936 to June 1940. *Robinson* was owned by Paul Winkler's comics syndicate Opera Mundi which imported most of the classic American comic strips in France.

After the forced cancellation of *Robinson*, due to the invasion of France by the Nazis, *Flash Gordon* migrated to *Bravo* in occupied Belgium, where it was retitled *Gordon l'Intrepide* [*Gordon the Fearless*]. But in early 1942, after the U.S. entered World War II, the Nazis ordered the cancellation of all American comic strips. Eventually, in mid-1942, the *Bravo* editors ran out of original *Flash Gordon* pages and asked Edgar P. Jacobs to continue the series as a ghost artist, which he did for a few weeks. But the Nazis were not pleased, and gave *Bravo* an ultimatum: they had one week to stop the series, or else. The editors were forced to ask Jacobs to draw a final page, bringing the series to a quick conclusion. Immediately thereafter, *Bravo* asked Jacobs to create a similar series, which he did. It was *Le Rayon U*.

In 1943, Jacobs joined Hergé's studio and collaborated on some of the *Tintin* stories, redrawing backgrounds and costumes for the revised editions of *The Blue Lotus* and *King Ottokar's Sceptre* that were to be republished in the graphic novel format. He also contributed to *The Seven Crystal Balls* and *The Temple of the Sun*.

In 1946, when publisher Raymond Leblanc licensed the right to launch a weekly *Tintin* magazine in Belgium (a French edition followed in 1948), Jacobs chose to slightly revamp the two heroes of *Le Rayon U*. The blond, aristocratic Lord Calder became Captain Francis Blake of MI6, and the genial, bearded Professor Marduk, Professor Philip Mortimer. Calder and Marduk's arch-enemy Dagon became the mustachioed Olrik.

Blake & Mortimer became Jacobs' lifework. He produced only eight stories in total, but they all became classics of French comics. Edgar P. Jacobs, almost as much as Hergé, is responsible for the so-called "clear line" style of Belgian comics.

Flash Gordon by Edgar P. Jacobs

Story:

Le Rayon U takes place on a pseudo-Earth divided between the enemy states of Norlandia and Australia. In peaceful Norlandia, Professor Marduk and his assistant, the beautiful Sylvia Hollis, have devised the ultimate weapon, the powerful *U Ray*, but they need the mineral uradium to power it.

With the help of famed explorer Lord Calder and his faithful Adji, Marduk embarks on an expedition through the savage lands of Norlandia to find it. Their journey is imperiled by dinosaurs, giant snakes and tigers, a tribe of man-apes and the evil schemes of Australian spy Dagon. They eventually find the uradium on the volcanic island of Urakowa, inhabited by an Aztec-like race.

Publishing History:

The first version of *Le Rayon U* featured captions, but no dialogue or word balloons, as was often the case in comics of that period. Its coloring was muted in order to accommodate the newsprint medium. It was also formatted in what later was called the Italian format, i.e.: horizontal rather than vertical, just like *Futuropolis*.

Le Rayon U was first reprinted in black & white serial form in Nos. 5-7 of the magazine *Phénix* in 1966, and was then collected in the graphic novel format (including the last *Flash Gordon* page) by publisher RTP in 1967.

Le Rayon U – 1943 version

In 1974, Jacobs reformatted *Le Rayon U* to fit the traditional French graphic novel format, recolored it and replaced some of the captions with dialogue. This new version was serialized in *Tintin* in 1974, and was then collected as a graphic novel by Editions du Lombard the same year. In 1991, a new edition was published by Editions Blake & Mortimer.

Le Rayon U – 1974 version

Website:
http://www.coolfrenchcomics.com/rayonu.htm

Les Pionniers de l'Espérance (1945)

The eyes of the Pioneers remained fixed far above the city, upon what was to them the most beautiful star of all, a soft shining blue light–Earth.
(*Les Pionniers de l'Espérance – Kataraz la Maudite*)

Created by:
Writer Roger Lecureux and artist Raymond Poïvet.

- Roger Lecureux (1925-1999) was a prolific writer who joined the editorial team of *Vaillant* in 1945 and later became its editor-in-chief from 1958 to 1963. There, he created adventure series, such as *Les Pionniers de l'Espérance* with Poïvet, *Nasdine Hodja* with René Bastard, *Teddy Ted* with Gérald Forton, *Lynx* with Bob Sim, *Fils de Chine* with Paul Gillon, *Le Grêlé 7/13* with Christian Gaty, *Rahan* with André Chéret, *Les Robinsons de la Terre* with Alfonso Font and others. During that time, Lecureux also contributed many stories to a variety of digest-sized comics magazines, including the popular space opera, *Galax*. Lecureux died on December 31, 1999.

- Raymond Poïvet (1910-1999) worked as a fashion artist in the 1940s and contributed to *Le Téméraire* during World War II, before joining the editorial team of *Vaillant* in 1945 where he and Lecureux created *Les Pionniers de l'Espérance*. During that period, he also co-created *Colonel X* with Marijac in 1947 and a *Tarzan*-like series, *Tumak*, in 1948. In 1961, he and writer Jean-Michel Charlier co-created *Guy Lebleu* for *Pilote*. In 1964, Poïvet contributed *P'tit Gus* to the short-lived magazine *Chouchou*. With writer Jean-Pierre Dionnet, Poïvet created the remarkable fantasy *Tiriel*. Poïvet passed away in July 1999.

Story:
The saga of the Pioneers takes place in a future when Earth has just begun to enter a period of space exploration. Episode 10 mentions the date of 2205, while Episode 20 states 2066, so the exact year remains uncertain. The first episode opens when Earth is threatened by the appearance of a mysterious new planet, Radias. The planetary government gathers a team comprised of seven of the best men and women they can find: dark-haired Tangha from Russia, blond Rodion, Tom from Martinique, Neo, kindly Professor Wright, beautiful Maud and Tsin-Lu from China. This team is dispatched to Radias in a rocket named *Espérance* [*Hope*], and is therefore called the *Pioneers of Hope*.

Radias, very much like Mongo, is a mosaic of warring cultures. The Pioneers first help the natives of Bangra, then overthrow Torg, the tyrant of Kataraz. But during their adventures, Neo dies when his airship crashes on Radias' snowy wastes, and Tom is killed during the revolution in Kataraz. Later, as they explore a mysterious prehistoric planet, Professor Wright is crushed in a volcanic explosion. Only four of the original team return to Earth: Tangha, Rodion, Maud and Tsin-Lu.

Inaccessible 7 (1960)

The Pioneers' next adventure took them to the underwater city of Aquatide, the modern-day creation of a new Nemo. After two Earthbound thrillers, the Pioneers embarked on their greatest saga, a story that struck the readers' imagination and has since become a science fiction classic.

Known as *The Fantastic Garden*, it chronicled the adventures of the Pioneers, miniaturized to insect-size by Professor Dickens, in an ordinary country garden, replete with insects and natural challenges.

Next, Tangha, Maud and Tsin-Lu thwarted invasions from golden-eyed aliens from Caluda and the diminutive Zions. This was followed by another cosmic journey to a far-off world with six artificial satellites. It is at that time that Lecureux began to add details to his universe. The Pioneers were now described as extraordinary space captains; they acted as top troubleshooters and investigators for an organization called EMC (*Etat-Major Cosmique*), or Cosmic High Command, a term first used in Episode 20, which monitored the security of Earth and loosely associated planets in a context not too different from the early days of *Star Trek*'s Federation.

Kataraz la Maudite (1949)

The Fantastic Garden (1952)

The long sagas of the past were replaced by self-contained 12- or, from 1969 onward, 20-page stories, small galactic puzzles, like a futuristic *X-Files*.

Publishing History:

Les Pionniers de l'Espérance was the first modern French science fiction comics series. It was originally serialized in the weekly magazine *Vaillant* (later retitled *Pif*) between 1945 and 1973. *Vaillant*'s policies rarely included the reprinting of its contents in the graphic novel format, so only the first six episodes of *Les Pionniers* were collected as albums.

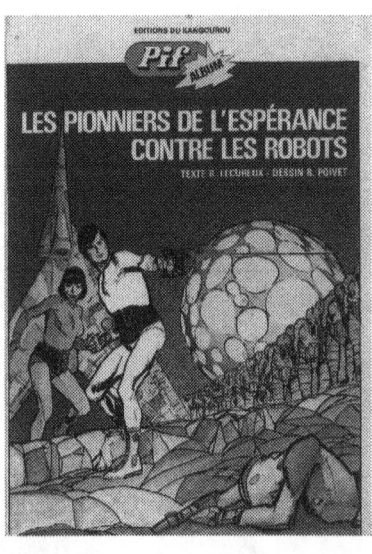

In 1974, Editions du Kangourou released one graphic novel, *Les Pionniers de l'Espérance contre les Robots* [*The Pioneers of Hope vs. The Robots*]. In 1979, Editions du Fromage reprinted Episodes 6 and 9 which had become classics.

Finally, the *Pioneers*' first twelve adventures were collected in a handsome, hardcover five-volume set by Futuropolis between 1984 and 1989. Two more volumes were then issued by publisher Soleil in 1994 and 1995.

Bibliography:

1. *Les Pionniers de l'Espérance* [*The Pioneers of Hope*] (52 p.) a.k.a. *Vers l'Ourang Mystérieux* [*Towards Mysterious Ourang*] and *Radia, La Planète aux 1000 Secrets* [*Radia, The Planet of 1000 Secrets*] (*Vaillant* Nos. 45-96, 1945-47; rep. *Vaillant* graphic novel No. 1, 1947; incl. in Futuropolis Vol. 1, 1984)
2. *La Cité de Bangra* [*The City of Bangra*] (42 p.) (*Vaillant* Nos. 97-138, 1947-48; incl. in Futuropolis Vol. 1, 1984)
3. *Le Désert Blanc* [*The White Desert*] (12 p.) (*Vaillant* Nos. 139-151, 1948; incl. in Futuropolis Vol. 2, 1984)
4. *Kataraz la Maudite* [*Kataraz the Accursed*] (55 p.) (*Vaillant* Nos. 152-206, 1948-49; rep. *Vaillant* graphic novel No. 2, 1960; incl. in Futuropolis Vol. 2, 1984)

Les Pionnièrs de l'Espérance – Futuropolis reedition (Vol. 3) (1984)

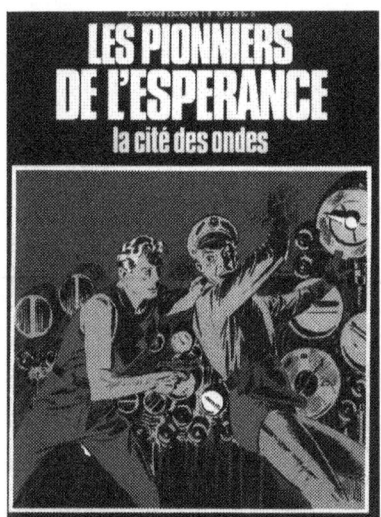

5. *500,000 Ans Avant* [*500,000 Years Before*] a.k.a. *C'était il y a 50.000 Ans* [*It Happened 50,000 Years Ago*] (25 p.) (*Vaillant* Nos. 207-230, 1949; rep. *Vaillant* graphic novel No. 5, 1961; incl. in Futuropolis Vol. 2, 1984)
6. *Aquatide, la Cité des Ondes* [*Aquatide, City of Waves*] (47 p.) (*Vaillant* Nos. 255-301, 1950-51. rep. *Vaillant* graphic novel No. 3, 1961; incl. in Futuropolis Vol. 3, 1984)
7. *Le Secret de Jacques Ferrand* [*The Secret of Jacques Ferrand*] a.k.a. *On a volé les Plans du Satellite Artificiel* [*Someone Stole the Artificial Satellite's Blueprints*] (25 p.) (*Vaillant* Nos. 302-326, 1951; rep. *Vaillant* graphic novel No. 6, 1962; incl. in Futuropolis Vol. 3, 1984)
8. *Le Professeur Marvel a Disparu* [*Prof. Marvel Has Vanished*] (27 p.) (*Vaillant* Nos. 335-362, 1951-52; rep. *Vaillant* graphic novel No. 6, 1962. incl. in Futuropolis Vol. 3, 1984)
9. *L'Etang des Solitudes* [*The Pond of Loneliness*] a.k.a. *Le Jardin Fantastique* [*The Fantastic Garden*] (50 p.) (*Vaillant* Nos. 363-412, 1952-53; rep. *Vaillant* graphic novel No. 4, 1961; incl. in Futuropolis Vol. 4, 1988)
10. *Les Hommes aux Yeux d'Or* [*The Men With Golden Eyes*] a.k.a. *Caluda* (63 p.) (*Vaillant* Nos. 622-684, 1957-58; incl. in Futuropolis Vol. 4, 1988)
11. *Echec aux Zions* [*The Zions in Check*] (80 p.) (*Vaillant* Nos. 685-764, 1958-59; incl. in Futuropolis Vol. 5, 1989)
12. *Inaccessible 7* [*Unreachable 7*] (36 p.) (*Vaillant* Nos. 767-802, 1960; incl. in Futuropolis Vol. 5, 1989)
13. *Nibor* (49 p.) (*Vaillant* Nos. 803-851, 1960-61)
14. *Les Forbans de l'Espace* [*The Space Pirates*] (55 p.) (*Vaillant* Nos. 879-933, 1962-63)

12-page episodes:
15. *Il n'est Jamais Trop Tard* [*It's Never Too Late*] (*Vaillant* No. 1053, 1965; incl. in Soleil Vol. 6, 1994)
16. *L'Otage des Profondeurs* [*The Hostage of the Deep*] (*Vaillant* No. 1058, 1965; incl. in Soleil Vol. 6, 1994)
17. *La Première Fugue* [*The First Flight*] (*Vaillant* No. 1063, 1965; incl. in Soleil Vol. 6, 1994)
18. *La Terre Sautera Ce Soir* [*Earth Will Explode Tonight*] (*Vaillant* No. 1068, 1965; incl. in Soleil Vol. 6, 1994)
19. *Les Buveurs de Mer* [*The Sea Drinkers*] (*Vaillant* No. 1073, 1965; incl. in Soleil Vol. 6, 1994)
20. *Prisonniers du Temps* [*Prisoners of Time*] (*Vaillant* No. 1079, 1966; incl. in Soleil Vol. 6, 1994)
21. *Le Paradis du Professeur. Danvers* [*The Paradise of Prof. Danvers*] (*Vaillant* No. 1084, 1966; incl. in Soleil Vol. 6, 1994)
22. *Les Naufragés de l'Espace* [*The Castaways of Space*] (*Vaillant* 1088, 1966; incl. in Soleil Vol. 6, 1994)
23. *Le Cas du Dr. Kitt* [*The Case of Dr. Kitt*] (*Vaillant* No. 1094, 1966; incl. in Soleil Vol. 7, 1995)
24. *4 - 2 = 1* (*Vaillant* No. 1100, 1966; incl. in Soleil Vol. 7, 1995)
25. *Les Mirages d'Or* [*The Golden Mirages*] (*Vaillant* No. 1106, 1966; incl. in Soleil Vol. 7, 1995)
26. *Destination Infini* [*Destination Infinity*] (*Vaillant* No. 1111, 1966; incl. in Soleil Vol. 7, 1995)
27. *L'Etrange Fin du Capitaine Jork* [*The Strange End of Captain Jork*] (*Vaillant* No. 1116, 1966; incl. in Soleil Vol. 7, 1995)
28. *Une Chaude Affaire* [*A Hot Affair*] (*Vaillant* No. 1122, 1966; incl. in Soleil Vol. 7, 1995)
29. *Une Conquête Silencieuse* [*A Silent Conquest*] (*Vaillant* No. 1128, 1966; incl. in Soleil Vol. 7, 1995)
30. *L'Invulnerable X* [*The Invulnerable X*] (*Vaillant* No. 1133, 1967; incl. in Soleil Vol. 7, 1995)
31. *L'Affaire des Héros* [*An Affair of Heroes*] (*Vaillant* No. 1139, 1967)
32. *La Tête d'Épingle* [*The Head of a Pin*] (*Vaillant* No. 1144, 1967)
33. *L'Homme de Chair* [*The Man of Flesh*] (*Vaillant* No. 1146, 1967)

Le Cas du Dr. Kitt (1966)

34. *Les Esclaves du Cosmos* [*The Cosmic Slaves*] (*Vaillant* No. 1150, 1967)
35. *Un Soleil a Disparu* [*A Sun Has Disappeared*] (*Vaillant* No. 1153, 1967)
36. *Les Hommes Papillons* [*The Butterfly Men*] (*Vaillant* No. 1156, 1967)
37. *La Mort de Tangha* [*The Death of Tangha*] (*Vaillant* No. 1159, 1967)
38. *La Planète Diamant* [*The Diamond Planet*] (*Vaillant* No. 1165, 1967)

39. *Les Grands Monstres* [*The Great Monsters*] (*Vaillant* No. 1171, 1967)
40. *L'Armada Fantôme* [*The Phantom Armada*] (*Vaillant* No. 1176, 1967)
41. *Les Oiseaux Poignards* [*The Dagger Birds*] (*Vaillant* No. 1182, 1968)
42. *Le Fléau d'Or* [*The Golden Plague*] (*Vaillant* No. 1188, 1968)
43. *Les Robinsons de la Planète X* [*The Robinsons of Planet X*] (*Vaillant* No. 1193, 1968)
44. *Le Jour où la Terre se rendit* [*The Day Earth Surrendered*] (*Vaillant* No. 1199, 1968)
45. *Les Garrots Vivants* [*The Living Garrotes*] (*Vaillant* No. 1203, 1968)
46. *L'Homme Poussière* [*The Man of Dust*] (*Vaillant* No. 1209, 1968)
47. *Le Hérisson de Métal* [*The Metal Hedgehog*] (*Vaillant* No. 1215, 1968)
48. *Un Simple Cauchemar* [*A Simple Nightmare*] (*Vaillant* No. 1219, 1968)
49. *La Pierre de Joie* [*The Stone of Joy*] (*Vaillant* No. 1224, 1968)
50. *La Créature du 2/10/2069* [*The Creature of 10/2/2069*] (*Vaillant* No. 1229, 1968)

20-page episodes:
51. *Les Gladiateurs de Tarengo* [*The Gladiators of Tarengo*] (*Pif* No. 1240, 1969)
52. *Ceux qui Prévoyaient Tout* [*Those Who Predicted Everything*] (*Pif* No. 1248, 1969)
53. *Les Hommes d'En Bas* [*The Men from Below*] (*Pif* No. 1252, 1969)
54. *La Nuit des Horreurs* [*The Night of Horrors*] (*Pif* No. 1259, 1969)
55. *Le Cerveau de Secours* [*The Spare Brain*] (*Pif* No. 1266, 1969)
56. *Commando sur l'EMC* [*Commando EMC*] (*Pif* No. 1272, 1969)
57. *Les Hommes Squales* [*The Shark Men*] (*Pif* No. 1278, 1969)
58. *Le Tremblement de Fleurs* [*Flower Quake*] (*Pif* No. 1283, 1970)
59. *17 Minutes à Vivre* [*17 Minutes to Live*] (*Pif* No. 1289, 1970)
60. *Le Sanctuaire de Glace* [*The Ice Sanctuary*] (*Pif* No. 1294, 1970)
61. *La Mousse Verte* [*The Green Moss*] (*Pif* No. 1300, 1970)
62. *L'Arche de Noé* [*Noah's Ark*] (*Pif* No. 1308, 1970)
63. *Les Voleurs de Pensée* [*The Mind Stealers*] (*Pif* No. 1318, 1970)
64. *Une Surprise de Taille* [*A Big Surprise*] (*Pif* No. 1324, 1970)
65. *Le Monstre Invisible* [*The Invisible Monster*] (*Pif* No. 1331, 1970)
66. *L'Éponge de l'Espace* [*The Space Sponge*] (*Pif* No. 1340, 1971)
67. *Station 67* (*Pif* No. 1351, 1971)
68. *Les Mandraghommes* [*The Mandramen*] (*Pif* No. 1359, 1971)
69. *Les Creatures de Chahawa* [*The Creatures of Chahawa*] (*Pif* No. 1366, 1971)
70. *Le Sarcophage Zorien* [*The Zorian Sarcophagus*] (*Pif* No. 1374, 1971)
71. *Les Sept Derniers Jours* [*The Seven Final Days*] (*Pif* No. 1383, 1971)
72. *Angoisse à l'EMC* [*Terror at EMC*] (*Pif* No. 1392, 1972)
73. *Le Paradis du Diable* [*The Devil's Paradise*] (*Pif* No. 1403, 1972)

74. *La Désertion de Tangha* [*Tangha's Desertion*] (*Pif* No. 1411, 1972)
75. *Le Robot Invulnérable* [*The Invulnerable Robot*] (*Pif* No. 1418, 1972)
76. *Commando T* (*Pif* No. 1424, 1972)
77. *Les Bracelets G* [*The G Bracelets*] (*Pif* No. 1435, 1972)
78. *Les Explorateurs du Temps* [*The Explorers of Time*] (*Pif* No. 1444, 1973)
79. *Un Trou dans les Archives* [*A Hole in the Archives*] (*Pif* No. 1456, 1973)
80. *La Chute d'un Tyran* [*The Fall of a Tyrant*] (*Pif* No. 1466, 1973)
81. *La Grande Sépulture* [*A Great Burial Site*] (*Pif* No. 1477, 1973)

Website:
http://www.coolfrenchcomics.com/pionniers.htm

Fantax No. 1 (1946)

Fantax (1946) & Black Boy (1955)

"I am always ready to stand in the way of evil-doers. Tell me at once where they took Patricia or I shall not be responsible for my wrath!"
(Fantax – *Fusillade à Brooklyn*)

Created by:
Writer J.K. Melwyn-Nash and artist Chott.

- J.K. Melwyn-Nash was one of the pseudonyms of the prolific writer Marcel Navarro (1922-). (Another of Navarro's *noms-de-plume* was "Malcolm Naughton.") Navarro was a journalist in Lyon during World War II; he also moonlighted writing and translating Italian comics for publisher S.A.G.E. There, he met Robert Bagage, the future founder of Editions Imperia, and artist Pierre Mouchot who, in September 1944, asked him to create a new superhero character. That character was *Fantax*. At first, *Fantax* was rejected by several publishers before Navarro and Mouchot managed to get it published in 1946. In addition to *Fantax*, Navarro created and wrote the Western superhero *Big Bill le Casseur* [*Big Bill the Wrecker*] and *Robin des Bois* [*Robin Hood*] for Mouchot's newly-formed publishing company. But the two men parted ways in 1948 over the issue of Navarro's ownership of his creations. Navarro then met another former French Resistant, Auguste Vistel, and together they created a new publishing company, Aventures & Voyages, with Bernadette Ratier, in 1948. For Aventures & Voyages, Navarro created *Marco Polo*, *Diavolo*, *Brik* and *Yak*. But after starting yet another company with Vistel, Editions Lug in 1950, Navarro eventually sold his shares in Aventures & Voyages to Ratier in 1955.

At Editions Lug, Navarro used his extensive Italian contacts to make the new company the leading publisher of French and Italian digest-sized comics and, starting in 1969, of French editions of Marvel Comics. At Lug, Navarro co-created and edited a number of popular characters such as *Zembla*, *Rakar*, *Dick Demon*, *Wampus* and, later, *Kabur*, *Waki*, *Mikros*, *Photonik* and *Phénix*. Navarro also wrote a special episode of *The Silver Surfer* drawn by Jean-Yves Mitton for the French market. In 1989, Marcel Navarro retired and Editions Lug was sold to Semic.

- Chott was the pseudonym of artist Pierre Mouchot (1911-1966), who drew a number of children's adventure strips for publisher S.A.G.E. during World War II. There, Mouchot met Marcel Navarro and, together, the two men created *Fantax*. In 1945, Mouchot, who had been a leader in the French Resistance, launched his own publishing company, Editions Pierre Mouchot, renamed Société d'Editions Rhodaniennes (or S.E.R.) in 1951. In 1946, Mouchot began to publish a line of adventure comics, starting with *Fantax*, which was an immediate success, following with *Big Bill le Casseur* and *Robin des Bois* in 1947.

Mouchot and Navarro parted in 1948, but other collaborators continued to assist Mouchot with his creations. These included Robert Rocca (1927-) who later became a fine artist and sculptor, and Rémy Bordelet (1931-2003), who went on to work for Lug in the 1960s.

With the adoption, in July 1949, of a law establishing a board of censors to monitor children's magazines, Mouchot was forced to discontinue *Fantax*. He began to experience recurring problems with the censors. In 1955, he was prosecuted by the State, supported by a conservative family defense organization, over the contents of his magazines, deemed to have a deleterious effect on children. During the next six years, Mouchot won four judgments, but ultimately lost the final appeal in 1961. S.E.R. was driven into bankruptcy. Mouchot died in 1966. (Left page: *Fantax* No. 10 (1947) – art by Mouchot.)

Story:

Fantax is the alter ego of Lord Horace Neighbour, who works during the day as attaché at the British Embassy in Washington, and fights crime at night as the caped crusader Fantax. Like Batman, Fantax has no superhuman powers, and is merely an athlete in peak condition. Lord Neighbour wears a monocle and is as suave and refined as Fantax is tough and merciless.

Fantax's fiancée, and later wife, is the beautiful Patricia, née Bennett. They have two children, a son, Horace Jr., who grows up to become a fearless G-man known as Black Boy, and a daughter, Barbara. At one point, Barbara was believed to be dead, murdered by Fantax's arch-enemy, the gangster Al Capy. But she was later revealed to be alive.

As was the case with Fantax's son, Mouchot once intended to spin-off a grown up Barbara in her own series, *Barbara Tiger*, but that did not happen.

Fantax's trusted butler, Murph, occasionally assists his master; another helper is the burly Frenchman, P'tit Louis.

The first *Fantax* story pits the masked avenger against Al Capy's gang, responsible for the kidnapping of Senator O'Berley's daughter. Al Capy returned to plague Fantax in Nos. 3, 4, 9, 10, 38 and 39, the last issue of the first comics series, in which he became responsible for Barbara's then-presumed death, and was killed by Fantax. The comic ended with Fantax mourning over his daughter's grave.

Other villains included the Mikado (No. 2), the Nazi Werewolves (Nos. 5 and 6), the Ku-Klux-Klan (Nos. 13 and 14), the gun-smuggling gang of the Black Tigers (Nos. 23), the Cobra (No. 29) and many more. In Nos. 15 and 16, Fantax discovered a Lost City of the Incas. Its priestess, Maya, fell in love with him, but was murdered by a jealous priest, Uxmal. Fantax killed Uxmal, and the Lost City was destroyed in a volcanic eruption.

Fantax drawn by Robert Rocca (1948)

As was the case with the early *Batman*, *Fantax* owed more than a passing debt to American pulps like *The Shadow*, *The Spider* and *The Avenger*. Navarro credited *The Phantom* as being his inspiration, but the stories themselves were often more evocative of Dashiell Hammett than Lee Falk or Jerry Siegel. Fantax, and later his son, Black Boy, are tough, brutal crime-fighters, who are not afraid of dealing vigilante justice, like *The Saint*, who was also very popular in France at the time. Fantax gets impaled (No. 7), whipped to the point of near-death (No. 19), has his leg crushed by a bear trap (No. 27), but he always returns and never hesitates to condemn the villains to the same grisly, always fatal, fate.

The visual look of *Fantax* was almost certainly borrowed from the DC comics superhero *The Hourman*, two stories of which had been translated and published by Editions Mondiales (which also published *The Phantom* in France) in March 1945 and April 1946. Mouchot and his collaborators also swiped from Alex Raymond's *Flash Gordon* and Burne Hogarth's *Tarzan*.

Black Boy, Horace Neighbor, Jr., rode a souped-up red motorbike and fought crime as an FBI agent. By removing the mask and the vigilante element and focusing on more mundane stories–many plots involved crime rings, spies and saboteurs–Mouchot thought he might escape the censors' wrath. His father, Fantax, drawn to look older, made occasional guest appearances in the series. The models for Black Boy were actors Lino Ventura and, to a lesser degree, Eddie Constantine, who starred in the *Lemmy Caution* movies.

Publishing History:

Fantax first appeared as a series of 20 strips serialized in the newspaper *Paris Monde Illustré* in early 1946.

Then, the first series of *Fantax* comics were published by Editions Pierre Mouchot, starting in July 1946. Because of its violence and mature contents, mild by today's standards but deemed rather prurient at the time, *Fantax* quickly drew the wrath of conservative organizations and the censors. It was discontinued with issue No. 39 around the time of the adoption of the Law of July 1949.

*First apperarance of Fantax
in Paris Monde Illustré (1946)*

Almost immediately, Mouchot launched *Fantax Magazine*, devoted to text short stories (as opposed to comics), including a *Fantax* novella, *La Perle de Manille* [*The Manila Pearl*], written by science fiction writer Max-André Dazergues under the pseudonym of J.-F. Ronald-Wills. *Fantax Magazine* was cancelled after six issues in November 1949.

In October 1950, *Fantax* returned to the comics in *The New Adventures of Lord Horace Neighbour*, serialized in *Reportages Sensationnels*, but that magazine lasted only five issues.

Mouchot then introduced *Black Boy*, the son of *Fantax*, in *Rancho* No. 5 in 1955. The series also appeared in *Rancho Special* and *Fantasia* until 1961, when S.E.R. went out of business. After the character was launched, Mouchot entrusted it to the talented Rémy Bordelet and Francis Péguet, and often reused redrawn versions of *Fantax* stories.

In the meantime, in 1959, Mouchot tried relaunching a second *Fantax* comic, in a squarebound format, but that lasted only nine issues.

One had to wait until 1986 to see Lord Neighbour again when fan publisher Bedesup reprinted a *Fantax* collection entitled *Fantax est de Retour* [*Fantax Returns*].

Because of its success, a rather blatant imitation of *Fantax* was published in Italy under the name of *Maskar*.

Bibliography:

A. *Paris Monde Illustré* Nos. 28-47, 1946.
Wri: J.K. Melwyn-Nash; **Art**: Chott.
Fantax contre les Gangsters [*Fantax vs. The Gangsters*] (20 p.)

B. *Fantax* (1st Series) Nos. 1-39, 1946-49.
Wri: J.K. Melwyn-Nash; **Art**: Chott.
1. *Le Gentleman Fantôme* [*The Gentleman Ghost*] (1946)
2. *Fantax contre le Mikado* [*Fantax vs. The Mikado*] (1946)
3. *Fantax chez les Gangsters* [*Fantax vs. The Gangsters*] (1946) (redrawn version of the *Paris Monde Illustré* story)
4. *Fantax contre l'Homme qui Terrorisait New York* [*Fantax vs. The Man Who Terrified New York*] (1946)
5. *Fantax contre le Werewolf* [*Fantax vs. The Werewolf*] (1946)
6. *Les Pirates de l'Edelweiss* [*The Pirates of the Edelweiss*] (1946)
7. *La Torture du Corbeau* [*The Torture of the Raven*] (1946)
8. *Le Vautour de la Jungle* [*The Vulture of the Jungle*] (1947)
9. *Le Gang de la Mort* [*The Gang of Death*] (1947)
10. *Fusillade à Brooklyn* [*Gunfight in Brooklyn*] (1947)
11. *La Mort Noire* [*The Black Death*] (1947)
12. *Les Six Gardiennes de l'Enfer* [*The Six She-Guardians of Hell*] (1947)

13. *Fantax contre le Ku-Klux-Klan* [*Fantax vs. the KKK*] (1947)
14. *La Maison des 7 Géants* [*The House of the 7 Giants*] (1947)
Wri: J.K. Melwyn-Nash; *Art*: Robert Rocca.
15. *Le Monde du Silence* [*The Silent World*] (1947)
16. *La Prêtresse du Soleil* [*The Priestess of the Sun*] (1947)
17. *Les Ecumeurs de Londres* [*The Reavers of London*] (1947)
18. *Le Château de l'Épouvante* [*The Castle of Terror*] (1947)
Wri: J.K. Melwyn-Nash; *Art*: Chott.
19. *Le Désert de la Peur* [*The Desert of Fear*] (1947)
20. *Terre de Feu* [*Land of Fire*] (1947)
Wri: J.K. Melwyn-Nash; *Art*: Robert Rocca.
21. *Les Buveurs de Sang* [*The Blood Drinkers*] (1947)
22. *La Jungle en Délire* [*The Mad Jungle*] (1947)
23. *Les Tigres Noirs* [*The Black Tigers*] (1947)
24. *La Rose du Levant* [*The Rose of Sunrise*] (1947)
25. *Coupeurs de Têtes* [*The Head Shrinkers*] (1947)
26. *La Tour de la Faim* [*The Tower of Hunger*] (1948)
Wri: J.K. Melwyn-Nash; *Art*: Chott.
27. *Dans le Grand Silence Blanc* [*In the Great White Silence*] (1948)
28. *La Proie du Monstre* [*The Monster's Prey*] (1948)
Wri: J.K. Melwyn-Nash; *Art*: Robert Rocca.
29. *Sous le Signe du Cobra* [*The Mark of the Cobra*] (1948)
Wri: Chott; *Art*: Robert Rocca.
30. *Evadés de l'Enfer* [*Escape From Hell*] (1948)
Wri/Art: Chott.
31. *Le Spectre de la Mine* [*The Spectre of the Mine*] (1948)
32. *Le Monstre de l'Abîme* [*The Monster from the Abyss*] (1948)
33. *L'Atoll Mystérieux* [*The Mysterious Atoll*] (1948)
34. *Le Jockey Sans Nom* [*The Nameless Jockey*] (1948)
Wri: Chott; *Art*: Robert Rocca.
35. *Le Bolide Noir* [*The Black Racer*] (1948)
36. *La Piste Tragique* [*The Tragic Trail*] (1949)
37. *Echec à Banserman* [*Banserman in Check*] (1949)
Wri/Art: Chott.
38. *Le Retour d'Al Capy* [*The Return of Al Capy*] (1949)
39. *Fantax Joue... et Perd!* [*Fantax Plays... And Loses!*] (1949)

(right: *Fantax* (2nd Series) No. 7 drawn by Rémy Bordelet.)

C. *Fantax Magazine* Nos. 1-6, 1949.
Wri: J-F. Ronald-Wills (Max-André Dazergues).
La Perle de Manille [*The Manila Pearl*]

D. *Reportages Sensationnels* Nos. 1-5, 1950-51.
Wri: Chott; ***Art***: Rémy Bordelet.
Les Nouvelles Aventures de Lord Horace Neighbour [*The New Adventures of Lord Horace Neighbour*]

E. *Fantax* (2nd Series) Nos. 1-9, 1959.
Wri: Chott; ***Art***: Rémy Bordelet.

1. *L'Homme Noir Prend la Main* [*The Dark Man Returns*] (1959)
2-3. *L'Ange Noir* [*The Dark Angel*] (1959)
3-4 & 6. *L'Enfer Blanc* [*The White Hell*] (1959)
5. Reprint of *Fantax* (1st Series) Nos. 9, 10, 38 and 39
7-8. *Fantax contre les Tigres Noirs* [*Fantax vs. The Black Tigers*] (redrawn version of *Fantax* (1st Series) No.23) (1959)
9. Reprint of *Les Nouvelles Aventures de Lord Horace Neighbour* [*The New Adventures of Lord Horace Neighbour*] with 3 new pages by Bordelet to complete the story.

A. *Rancho* Nos. 5-24, 1955-56
Wri/Art: Chott.
1. *Black Boy, G-Man* (Nos. 5-9, 11, 1955)
Wri/Art: Rémy Bordelet.
2. Redrawn version of *Fantax* (1st Series) Nos. 11-12 (No. 17, 1956)

3. Redrawn version of *Fantax* (1st Series) Nos. 7-8 (Nos. 20-22, 1956)
4. Redrawn version of *Fantax* (1st Series) No. 15 (Nos. 23-24, 1956)

Black Boy drawn by Mouchot (1955)

B. *Rancho Special* Nos. 1-33, Hors-Série, 1955-61
Wri/Art: Chott.
1. Redrawn version of *Fantax* (1st Series) Nos. 32-33 (1955)
2. Redrawn version of *Fantax* (1st Series) Nos. 27-28 (1956)
Wri/Art: Rémy Bordelet.
3. Redrawn version of *Fantax* (1st Series) Nos. 13-14 (1956)
4. Redrawn version of *Fantax* (1st Series) Nos. 34-37 (1956)
5. Redrawn version of *Fantax* (1st Series) Nos. 3-4 (1956)
6. Redrawn version of *Fantax* (1st Series) Nos. 30-31 (1957)

7-8. *L'Affaire des Soucoupes* [*The Saucer Case*] (1957)
Wri/Art: Francis Péguet.
9. *L'Affaire Bentley* [*The Bentley Case*] (1957)
10. *Le NWB 505 Ne Répond Plus* [*NWB 505 Does Not Answer*] (1958)
11. *Trafic* [*Traffic*] (1958)
12. *Johnny Brent s'est évadé!* [*Johnny Brent Escaped!*] (1958)
Wri/Art: Rémy Bordelet.
13. *L'Étoile à Six Branches* [*The Six-Pointed Star*] (1958)
Wri/Art: Francis Péguet.
14. *X18 ne décollera pas* [*X18 Won't Take Off*] (1958)
15. *Les Rescapés du Mont Murud* [*Escape from Mount Murud*] (1959)
16. *Objectif Siang-Tan* [*Target Siang-Tan*] (1959)
Wri: E. Roos; ***Art***: Rémy Bordelet.
17. *Ténébreuse Enquête* [*Dark Investigation*] (1959)
Wri/Art: Francis Péguet.
18. *La Caragaison de Taka-Maru* [*The Cargo of Taka-Maru*] (1959)
19. *Les Sous-Marins Pirates* [*The Pirate Submarines*] (1959)
20. *Le Monstre du Tchad* [*The Monster of Tchad*] (1959)
21. *La Cité sous les Glaces* [*The City Beneath the Ice*] (1960)
22. *Les Contrebandiers du Lac Toronto* [*The Smugglers of Lake Toronto*] (1960)
23-24. *Black Boy contre X* [*Black Boy vs. X*] (1960)
25. *Dans l'Ombre de l'ONU - 1* [*In the Shadow of the UN - 1*] (1960)

Wri/Art: Rémy Bordelet.
26. *Mystère au Cirque* [*Mystery at the Circus*] (1960)

Wri/Art: Francis Péguet.
27. *Dans l'Ombre de l'ONU - 2* [*In the Shadow of the UN - 2*] (1960)
28-29. *Le FBI en Echec* [*The FBI in Check*] (1960)
30-31. *Le Disque Rouge* [*The Red Disk*] (1961)
32. *En Week-End à Paris* [*A Week-End in Paris*] (1961)
33. *Le Fantôme d'Alexander Krown* [*The Ghost of Alexander Krown*] (completed in *Rancho Special Hors-Série*) (1961)

Black Boy drawn by Bordelet

B. *Fantasia* Nos. 1-48, Hors-Série, 1957-61
Wri/Art: Rémy Bordelet.
1-3. *Le Cercle Vert* [*The Green Circle*] (1957)
3-4, 6. *Trafic d'Armes* [*Gun Smuggling*] (redrawn version of *Fantax* (1st Series) Nos. 5-6) (1957)
Wri/Art: Chott.
5. *Altitude 3000* (1957)
Wri/Art: Rémy Bordelet.
7-9. *Chasse à l'Homme* [*Man Hunt*] (1957-58)
9-11, 12. *Région Interdite* [*Forbidden Area*] (1958)
Wri/Art: Francis Péguet.
12-13. *Le Vaisseau Fantôme* [*The Ghost Ship*] (1958)
14-16. *Black Boy contre les Kidnappers* [*Black Boy vs. the Kidnappers*] (1958)

17-18. *Le Rendez-Vous d'Istambul* [*Rendezvous in Istambul*] (1958)
19-20. *Le Gang des Secrets Atomiques* [*The Atomic Secrets Gang*] (1958)
21-22. *Vacances Napolitaines* [*Neapolitan Holidays*] (1959)
23-25. *Les Conspirateurs* [*The Conspirators*] (1959)
26-28. *Les Fantômes* [*The Ghosts*] (1959)
28-30. *Les Faux-Monnayeurs* [*The Counterfeiters*] (1959)
30-31. *Le Retour de Manco Pacac* [*The Return of Manco Pacac*] (1959)
31. *Le Dragon Rouge* [*The Red Dragon*] (1959)
32-33. *Le Bouddha de Jade* [*The Jade Buddha*] (1960)
33-35. *La Déesse Kali* [*The Goddess Kali*] (1960)
35-40. *Course contre la Mort* [*Race Against Death*] (1960)
41-45. *L'Affaire des Bases US en Italie* [*The Affair of the US Bases in Italy*] (1960)
46-47. *Au Pays du Soleil Levant* [*In the Land of the Rising Sun*] (1961)
48. *Espionnage à Cap Canaveral* [*Spying at Cape Canaveral*] (1961) (completed in *Fantasia Special Hors-Série*) (1961)

Websites:
http://www.coolfrenchcomics.com/fantax.htm
http://www.coolfrenchcomics.com/blackboy.htm

Durga Rani (1946)

*"You are, like myself, a free child of the Free People,
who have sworn to live in accordance with the Laws of Nature."*
(Durga Rani to Nour-Djahan – *Durga Rani*)

Created by:
Writer Martial Cendres and artist Pellos (see *Futuropolis* entry).

Story:
It is unclear whether *Durga Rani* takes place in the ancient past, the far future or on another planet altogether. Her world is an India or Asia that has no connection to any historical reality. Durga Rani, the so-called "queen of the jungle," lives in peace with all the animals of the jungle. Her companions include Hanuman the ape and Hogh the elephant. She is the daughter of a secret race of mystics who live on a hidden island, the Island of Silence, located in the middle of a great lake, in a lost valley in the fearsome Black Mountains. That Shangri-la is ruled by a wise and ancient Master, who dispatches Durga Rani to help the less civilized people of the world.

First, Durga thwarts the machinations of the tyrant Daiki Khan of Islar Nabo. But his successor, Queen Balkis, and her advisor, the dervish Gartok, plan to get rid of the meddling Durga. Their schemes fail; Gartok is crushed by the metal idol he worshipped, and Balkis is forced to flee into exile.

Durga then returns to her jungle kingdom. But she is summoned by the Master. Before she reaches the Island of Silence, she travels through the kingdom of Asoka. There, Durga meets the handsome tribe chieftain Anang-Pal, but runs afoul of jealous Queen Nour-Djahan. Working with the evil Banou, Nour has Durga framed and arrested, but she escapes. After a perilous journey, she reaches the Island of Silence where the Master reveals that Nour-Djahan is one of their people, who has become corrupted by the wealth of the kingdoms of men. Durga is instructed to set her right.

Durga Rani – SERG reedition (1976)

Durga Rani

Durga kidnaps Nour and, eventually, in the wilderness, the young woman comes to her senses and renounces her evil ways. But Banou is now intent on bringing down the two women who are a threat to his plan to take over Asoka from its rightful ruler, Prince Surabai. In the end, with the help of her faithful animals, Durga defeats Banou. Nour goes on to marry Surabai and become an enlightened queen. Durga rides on towards new adventures.

Publishing History:

Durga Rani was originally serialized in 1946 in a popular girls' comic magazine entitled *Fillette*. The 126-page saga was later collected as three graphic novels by Société Parisienne d'Edition, *La Reine des Jungles* (two volumes) [*The Queen of the Jungle*] in 1948 and *L'Appel du Maître* [*The Call of the Master*] in 1949.

These three volumes were reprinted in a two-volume set by SERG in 1976, and again by Les Amis de Pellos [*The Friends of Pellos*] in 1992-94.

Website:
http://www.coolfrenchcomics.com/durgarani.htm

À bord de la barque aux blanches ailes, Durga traverse de nouveau le lac, sur le chemin du retour. Le ciel n'est plus celui qui l'accueillit à son arrivée. De lourdes nuées d'orage s'y accumulent. Le vent souffle et soulève de grosses lames écumantes. Est-ce le présage de la lutte douloureuse et tragique qu'il va falloir soutenir?

Mais la fière reine des jungles n'est pas de celles qu'effraient ces fureurs de la nature. Au contraire, il semble qu'elle y puise des forces neuves.

Et la rive est enfin atteinte, sous la lueur tragique des éclairs et le grondement de la foudre. Les serviteurs du Maître sont là, qui ont ramené à Durga son cheval. Elle le retrouve avec joie, saute sur son dos, tandis que la noble bête hennit et se cabre. Et après un cordial adieu à ses compagnons elle s'élance, ardente, comme si elle courait vers de nouveaux combats!

Bientôt voici de nouveau l'âpre région des montagnes, dans leur primitive sauvagerie. On pourrait croire que la fureur des éléments, dont l'espace continue d'être agité, s'est communiquée aux êtres qui le hantent, car, de tous côtés, apparaissent et disparaissent des bêtes de proie, hargneuses ou hurlantes, en quête de tuerie.

Troublée par ces présages, Durga, quand elle arrive aux frontières de l'immense domaine, abandonné par celle qui en avait la garde, décide d'y pénétrer, pour voir ce qui s'y passe. Malgré la résistance de son cheval qui s'effare, elle le maîtrise et le pousse en avant, sous la nuit épaisse des arbres millénaires.

Bientôt, elle comprend. Tout ce qui vit là dedans est retourné à la haine, à la férocité, à la guerre perpétuelle et sans merci. Non seulement les grands fauves chasseurs poursuivent avec acharnement leur pitoyable gibier, mais ils se battent entre eux, dans une rivalité implacable.

Durga surprend deux panthères qui s'entr'égorgent sur le cadavre d'un cerf. Elle bondit entre elles, les sépare en lançant le vibrant cri d'appel des jungles. Mais il lui faut longuement lutter avant qu'elles s'apaisent, et elle-même n'est pas épargnée par leurs griffes et par leurs dents. Tout, dans cet antique royaume de paix, est revenu à la barbarie et à la cruauté!

Durga Rani

Fulguros in Audax No. 63 (1959)

Fulguros (1946)

"I thought my machines could save Man from the plague of War. I was wrong!"
(Fulguros – *La Fin d'un Rêve*)

Created by:
Writer R. Lortac and artist René Brantonne.

- R. Lortac was the pseudonym of Robert Colliard (1884-1973), a pioneer filmmaker and animator, who owned and operated France's largest animation studio in the 1920s. Lortac studied art at the Ecole des Beaux-Arts in Paris. From 1906 to 1914, he worked as a cartoonist for a number of Parisian newspapers, doing sketches of stage actors to illustrate reviews of their plays. In 1914, Lortac produced and directed *Le Savant Microbus et son Automate* [*Scientist Microbus and his Automaton*], a humoristic science fiction short feature. Lortac was wounded at the front during World War I and embarked on the making of short animated puppet films to help sell National Defense bonds. He met animation pioneer Emile Cohl and collaborated with him. Lortac was sent by the French Government to the United States to present an exhibit of French Artists to help raise money for the war effort, and there, he discovered the works of Winsor McCay. Back in France, in 1919, Lortac launched his own production company, and began producing hundreds of animated shorts. His total output remained the largest single production of cartoons in French animation history. He also made documentaries, educational films, etc.

By the mid 1920s, Lortac's Montrouge studio was the largest in Europe, with 10 to 15 full-time assistants, and five cameras. In 1922, Lortac launched the *Canard en Ciné* [*Cine Paper*], a series of short animated features distributed by Pathé, commenting and satirizing popular news items. He also made adaptations of Jean de La Fontaine's animal fables, and a number of shorts featuring funny characters such as *Toto*, *Toby*, *Mistoufle* and *Joko the Monkey*. Lortac's most ambitious production was a 35-minute, three-part animated adaptation of the early comic book story *Monsieur Vieuxbois* by Rodolphe Topffer, made in 1921. In 1936, business began to slow because of the Depression, and with the advent of World War II, Lortac sold his film and animation business.

Lortac then began a new, prolific career as a writer, contributing numerous stories (both prose and comics) and novels to various magazines and publishers from the 1930s to the 1960s. His genre contributions include *Démonax* (1938) and *Les Bagnards du Ciel* [*The Convicts of Space*] (1954), and in the field of comic books *Tetar-Zan* with Mat, *Démonax*, an adaptation of his novel for *Gavroche* in 1941, and numerous scripts for the *Bibi Fricotin* series drawn by Pierre Lacroix. His most remarkable contribution, however, was the haunting saga of *Les Conquérants de l'Espace* [*The Space Conquerors*] and its companion series, *Les Francis*, both drawn by R. & R. Giordan, for the magazine *Meteor* from 1953 to 1964.

• René Brantonne (1903-1979) was one of the foremost French science fiction illustrators. Brantonne began his career as a commercial artist in the mid-1920s, drawing French film posters for MGM, Universal, Disney and other French divisions of major U.S. studios. Brantonne claimed to have left France in 1942, but may have in fact continued to live in Paris. After the War, Brantonne began working as a popular illustrator, cover artist and comics artist on a vast number of adventure series for a variety of digest-sized magazines: *Fulguros* and *Johnny Speed* for Artima (later Aredit), *Praline*, *Buffalo Bill* for Editions des Remparts, *Radarex*, etc. He illustrated a comic book version of *Gulliver's Travels*, and even drew short-lived French versions of *Brick Bradford* and *Batman*.

During that time, he also became the cover artist *par excellence* of the *Anticipation* imprint of Editions Fleuve Noir, drawing the covers of Nos. 1-273 (1954-1965) (right page), and Nos. 562-792 (1973-1977), influencing virtually every French science fiction reader of the 1950s and 1960s. He also illustrated the novels of Jean de La Hire, creator of *The Nyctalope*. Brantonne died from cancer in 1979. An *Art of Brantonne* book was published by Le Dernier Terrain Vague in 1983.

Story:

The origins of Fulguros remain shrouded in mystery, and whatever superhuman powers he exhibited (strength, speed, energy control) were clearly the product of his science, not some freak accident of nature.

Fulguros began his crime-fighting career as a regular superhero, dressed in a red costume, battling a balding mad scientist, Professor Klabus. During what we may call his "costumed period," he went on to clash with giant robots and a few other world-threatening menaces.

The science fiction art of René Brantonne

Fulguros (1946)

Then, for reasons which were never explained within the series continuity, readers were suddenly re-introduced to an 18-year-old Fulguros, a scientific genius, who was also a homeless man sleeping on a sewer grate. That Fulguros (who claimed that his last name really was "Fulguros") was taken in by Nobel-like billionaire Max de Simiane, a retired weapons manufacturer seeking to atone for his past activities. Two years later, Simiane died, bequeathing his vast fortune to Fulguros.

The story then jumped forward in time by 20 years. Fulguros is said to have married, lost his wife, and now has a 20-year-old son, Jean. From that point onward, Fulguros never again wears a costume. Whether his costumed adventures took place in the intervening years (which is more likely), or after what we may call his "civilian period," is unclear.

At that point in his life, Fulguros has built a giant, weather-controlling machine in his Alpine castle. He becomes known as the "Master of Thunder." His goal is to blackmail the world's governments into disarming to honor a promise he made to Simiane, or else he will use his powers to cause untold havoc. Indeed, he destroys the Eiffel Tower as a demonstration of his superiority.

But Fulguros' path crosses that of the gangster Murdock, the so-called Public Enemy No. 1, who takes over the castle and hijacks the weapon for his own, mercenary ends. Fulguros is forced to blow up the castle with an atomic explosion, but the wily Murdock escapes.

Fulguros then becomes a science pirate, an outlaw Captain Nemo-like scientist determined to save the world in spite of itself, even though people fear him and governments treat him as an enemy. His new base of operations is a giant rocket-propelled flying fortress, the *Kronexa*. We meet Fulguros' brother-in-law, aviator Paul Duran. But Murdock has not disarmed, and tries to take over the *Kronexa*.

Publishing History:

Fulguros was a promising series that never achieved the success it deserved, perhaps because of Brantonne's other commitments, which forced him to hire various uncredited assistants. Also, censorship struck soon after its creation, and Fulguros was forced to abandon his superhero costume to become a more ordinary-looking scientist.

Fulguros reportedly made its debut in 1946 in a magazine named *Andax*, although that information has never been verified. It is, however, certain that the first story, pitting Fulguros against Klabus, was published (possibly reprinted?) in 1947 in Nos. 37-48 of the magazine *Pic-Nic*, published by SAETL.

Then Fulguros, now dressed in civilian clothes, reappeared in 1954 in a young girl's comics magazine called *Sylvie*, published by French comics publisher Artima. This was the "Master of Thunder" sequence. To no one's surprise–except perhaps the publisher–that story did not reach its intended audience.

Fulguros then made a return appearance in 1959, this time back in his red superhero costume, in three issues of *Audax* (Second Series), also published by Artima. Again, it failed to prove popular. Finally, in 1967, five years after Artima had become Aredit, nine episodes of *Fulguros*, including six never printed before, which had obviously been written and drawn to follow the *Sylvie* 1954 "civilian" sequence, appeared in *Meteor*.

Bibliography:
Fulguros le Surhomme [*Fulguros the Superman*] (*Andax* Nos. ??, 1946; *Pic-Nic* Nos. 37-48, 1947).
Sylvie: *Le Maître du Tonnerre* [*The Master of Thunder*]
La Maison Mystérieuse [*The Mysterious House*] (2 x 6 p.) (No. 7-8, 1954)
L'Ultimatum [*The Ultimatum*] (2 x 6 p.) (Nos. 9-10, 1955)
Fulguros contre Murdock [*Fulguros vs. Murdock*] (12 p.) (No. 11, 1955)
La Fin d'un Rêve [*The End of a Dream*] (12 p.) (No. 12, 1955)
Audax:
Les Robots Géants [*The Giant Robots*] (No. 55, 1959)
L'Elixir de Jeunesse [*The Elixir of Youth*] (No. 59, 1959)
Le Fils du Radjah [*The Rajah's Son*] (No. 63, 1959)
Meteor:
La Maison Mystérieuse (reprint) (No., 160, 1967)
L'Ultimatum (reprint) (No. 161, 1967)
Fulguros contre Murdock / La Fin d'un Rêve (reprint) (No. 162, 1967)
Fulguros et sa Kronexa [*Fulguros and his Kronexa*] (No. 163, 1967)
L'Ennemi Public No. 1 [*The Public Enemy No. 1*] (No. 164, 1967)
Fulguros contre le Dragon Vert [*Fulguros vs. The Green Dragon*] (No. 165, 1967)
Le Gaz Alpha et la Poudre Omega [*The Alpha Gas and the Omega Powder*] (No. 166, 1967)
Aventures Extraordinaires [*Amazing Adventures*] (No. 167, 1967)
La Fuite de Murdock [*Murdock's Escape*] (No. 168, 1967)

Website:
http://www.coolfrenchcomics.com/fulguros.htm

Fulguros – The Master of Thunder (1954)

Guerre à la Terre – Glénat reedition (1976)

Guerre à la Terre (1946)

"The War of the Worlds has begun!"
(Radio Announcer – *Guerre à la Terre*)

Created by:

Writer Marijac and artist Auguste Liquois.

• Marijac, a pseudonym of Jacques Dumas (1904-1994), began his career in 1926. In 1931, he created the humorous cowboy *Jim Boum*, which was followed by *Césarin Pitchounet* and *Capitaine Pat'Folle* in 1935, and *Jules Bariboule* in 1936. Starting in 1934, Marijac created *Rouletabosse Reporter*, *Costo Chien Policier*, *Onésime Pellicule*, *Jim et Joe*, *Le Chasseur de Monstres* [*The Monster Hunter*] and *François Veyrac* for *Pierrot*. During the War, Marijac served in the Army where he managed to produce *La Vie est Belle* [*Life is Beautiful*] (1939-40) and *Le Chéval Mécanique* [*Mechanical Horse*] (1940). He was taken prisoner, but escaped and joined the Resistance. During this period, he created one of his most popular series, *Les Trois Mousquetaires du Maquis* [*The Three Musketeers of the Resistance*]. After the War, he launched his own magazine, *Coq Hardi*, which ran from 1945 until 1963. His other creations include *Capitaine Fantôme*, *Colonel X* and *Guerre à la Terre*. For his tremendous contribution as an artist, writer and editor, Marijac received the prestigious Grand Prize of Angoulême in 1979.

• Auguste Liquois (1902-1969) was a comic book artist and illustrator from the 1930s and 1940s who took over *Tarzan* after the Nazis banned the import of American strips in Occupied France. Today, Liquois is remembered for his science fiction series, *Vers les Mondes Inconnus* [*Towards The Unknown Worlds*] (1943), a *Flash Gordon* imitation serialized in *Le Témeraire*. After the War, Liquois drew *Guerre à la Terre* [*War against Earth*] for *Coq Hardi* in 1946-47, *Salvator* and *Satanax* in 1947. Auguste Liquois retired from comics in 1959 to devote his time to painting and fine arts.

• After Marijac and Liquois parted company, *Guerre à la Terre* was completed by artist Pierre Duteurtre, a.k.a. Dut (1911-1989). Duteurtre began his comics career in *L'As* in 1937. After the War, he worked on *Vigor* for Artima then on *Sitting Bull* (1948-53) for *Coq Hardi*. Duteurtre then went on to draw various historical newspaper strips in the 1960s.

Story:
War Against Earth is the tale of a merciless future war between the invading Martian armies and the forces of Earth. The resistance effort is led by French Captain Jean Veyrac, later promoted to the rank of General, and his various heroic companions, including American Air Force ace Glenn Martin, Russian pilot Boris Rasdoloff and British rocketeer Tom Buster. The Martians, small, green-

Guerre à la Terre drawn by Liquois

Guerre à la Terre drawn by Duteurtre

skinned humanoids with big heads, use deadly, spherical war machines and hordes of savage ape-like warriors in their war effort. They also ally themselves with renegade Japanese military out for revenge after their bitter defeat in World War II.

Eventually, the united Earth forces use the power of atomic explosions to modify the angle of the Earth's rotation, wiping out most of the invading armies. A Martian peace faction triumphs after the death of their former bellicose leader, and negotiates a peace treaty with Earth.

Guerre à la Terre drawn by Liquois

Publishing History:
War Against Earth was originally serialized in *Coq Hardi* in 1946 and 1947. The first part of the story was drawn by Auguste Liquois; the second part was entrusted to Pierre Duteurtre.

War Against Earth was republished in two volumes by Glénat in 1975 and 1976, and again in an omnibus edition in 1999.

Website:
http://www.coolfrenchcomics.com/guerreterre.htm

Kaza le Martien by Kline (1946)

Kaza le Martien (1946)

"I am not yet ready to be stopped by you!"
(Prince Kaza – *Kaza le Martien*)

Created by:
Writer-artist Kline. Kline was the pseudonym of Roger Chevallier (1922-?). *Kaza le Martien*, obviously inspired by Alex Raymond's *Flash Gordon*, was Kline's first comic series. He then went on to create and/or work on numerous juvenile adventure series, such as *Stany Beule dans la Lune* [*Stany Beule on the Moon*] (1949) and *Magda* (1956-60), both published in *Fillette*, and took over the art chores on Marijac's spy series *Colonel X* for a fantasy-laden Tibetan adventure (1954) published in *Coq Hardi*. For *Vaillant*, Kline drew *Davy Crockett* (1960-69) and finally created the saga of a brave Sioux warrior called *Loup Noir* [*Black Wolf*] (1969-83).

Story:
An elderly Earth scientist, his daughter Jane, and his assistant Jacques, travel to Mars, where they meet the handsome Prince Kaza, the legitimate emperor of the red planet. Kaza has been overthrown by the tyrant Agold. With the help of his Earth friends, Kaza launches a revolution, and eventually retakes his home city of Liberapolis. During the course of their adventures, the four heroes encounter colorful Martian races such as the Triangle-Heads and the People of Yog.

Publishing History:
Kaza le Martien was originally serialized in *OK* magazine from 1946 to 1948. The series ended with Agold's defeat and Kaza's retaking of Liberapolis. It was

partially reprinted in 1980 and 1981 by publisher Michel Deligne in his imprint *Aventures de l'Age d'Or* [*Adventures of the Golden Age*].

Website:
http://www.coolfrenchcomics.com/kaza.htm

Tom X (1946)

"So you're the mighty Tom X, who single-handedly defied all our forces."
(Tara to Tom X – *La Vénus de Tarawa*)

Created by:

Writer-artist Robert Bagage. After starting as a sports illustrator in the 1930s, Robert Bagage (?-2002) went to work for the Lyon-based comic book publisher S.A.G.E. during World War II. His first comic book series was *Yvon et Toni*, a *Tim Tyler's Luck*-type of jungle adventure, which began in 1942 in the magazine *Jumbo*, which he signed using the pseudonym of "Robba." In 1943, Bagage also worked for *Pic & Nic*, *Cendrillon* and *Coeurs Vaillants*.

It was at that time that Bagage met Marcel Navarro, the writer of *Fantax* and future co-founder of Editions Lug, and Pierre Mouchot, the artist of *Fantax*. These three men eventually were almost single-handedly responsible for the small format publishing phenomenon of the 1950s and 1960s.

After the war, Bagage drew the character of *Secret Agent Z.302*, written by Navarro, for Éditions Sprint. Then, in 1946, Bagage left Sprint to launch his own publishing company, the Éditions du Siècle, which were renamed Imperia in 1952.

Also based in Lyons, Imperia published a mix of colorful adventure titles, many of Italian and Spanish origin, with a few French series thrown in, such as *Tom X*, *Radar*, *Targa* and *Super Boy*. Imperia led an uneventful life throughout the 1960s, 1970s and 1980s, and eventually went out of business in 1986 after Bagage retired. Robert Bagage passed away on October 3, 2002.

Story:

Tom X is the code-name of Tom Hall, a *Doc Savage*-like hero, an intrepid explorer, polymath and adventurer who secretly works as a special agent for Admiral Brandy of U.S. Intelligence. Tom X fights former Nazis and evil Japanese who seek revenge for their defeat at the hands of the Allies; he even comes face-to-face with Adolf Hitler in No. 35.

Other missions involve mad scientists such as the Blue Dragon, criminal empires such as the 13 Hoods and various science fiction and fantasy elements such as the discovery of Atlantis (No. 25), Lost Incas (No. 23), etc.

Tom X No. 2 (1946)

Publishing History:
Tom X was originally serialized from late 1946 to September 1948 in 39 issues of its own, eponymous magazine, published by Éditions du Siècle. Bagage shared the artistic duties with artist Raoul Auger, who used the pseudonym of "Ariel." *Tom X* was never reprinted, nor was it collected in the graphic novel format.

Bibliography:
Issues drawn by Bagage are identified with a "B;" issues drawn by Auger with an "A." Three issues, Nos. 7, 9 and 18, did not feature any *Tom X* stories, and have therefore been omitted.
1. *Panique à Bikini* [*Panic at Bikini*] (1946) (B)
2. *La Vénus de Tarawa* [*The Venus of Tarawa*] (1946) (B)
3. *Le Boeuf Musqué* [*The Musk Ox*] (1946) (B)
4. *Le Tueur Étincelant* [*The Shining Killer*] (1946) (B)
5. *L'Ecran Diabolique* [*The Devil Screen*] (1946) (B)
6. *Le Piton Infernal* [*Hell Peak*] (1946) (B)
8. *Le Dragon Bleu* [*The Blue Dragon*] (1947) (B)
10. *Tom X contre les 13 Cagoules* [*Tom X vs. The 13 Hoods*] (1947) (B)
11. *Le Cavalier Miracle 1: L'Oiseau de Feu* [*The Miracle Rider 1: The Firebird*] (1947) (A)

12. *La Pagode Sanglante* [*The Pagoda of Blood*] (1947) (B)
13. *Le Cavalier Miracle 2: Le Chalet* [*The Miracle Rider 2: The Cabin*] (1947) (A)
14. *Les Ravisseurs des Mers Australes* [*The Kidnappers of the Southern Seas*] (1947) (B)
15. *Le Cavalier Miracle 3: La Fin du Tyran* [*The Miracle Rider 3: The End of a Tyrant*] (1947) (A)
16. *Sang et Ivoire* [*Blood and Ivory*] (1947) (B)
17. *Le Fantôme des Pyramides* [*The Ghost of the Pyramids*] (1947) (B)
19. *Le Zéro de la Mort* [*The Zero of Death*] (1947) (B)
20. *New York Va Sauter* [*New York Is Going To Be Destroyed*] (1947) (B)

Tom X No. 34 (1948)

21. *Le Cercle Rouge* [*The Red Circle*] (1947) (B)
22. *Le Secret de la Sierra* [*The Secret of the Sierra*] (1947) (B)
23. *L'Héritière du Soleil* [*The Heiress of the Sun*] (1947) (B)
24. *La Citadelle de l'Abime* [*The Citadel of the Abyss*] (1947) (B)
25. *La Terreur des Atlantes* [*The Terror of the Atlanteans*] (1947) (A)
26. *Les Gladiateurs de l'Océan* [*The Ocean Gladiators*] (1947) (A?)
27. *L'Enigme de Mysore* [*The Enigma of Mysore*] (1947) (B)

28. *Le Marécage des Morts-Vivants* [*The Swamp of the Living Dead*] (1947) (B)
29. *Document Secret* [*Secret Document*] (1947) (A?)
30. *Le Gang du Castor* [*The Beaver Gang*] (1947) (A)
31. *La Fusée des Neiges* [*The Snow Rocket*] (1948) (A)
32. *Le Masque de Soie* [*The Silk Mask*] (1948) (A)
33. *La Ronde Infernale* [*Hell Dance*](1948) (B)
34. *Panique sur la Banquise* [*Panic on the Ice Flow*] (1948) (B)
35. *Tom X contre Hitler* [*Tom X vs. Hitler*] (1948) (B)
36. *Victoire sur les SS* [*Victory against the SS*] (1948) (B)
37. *La Griffe du Vautour* [*The Claw of the Vulture*] (1948) (A)
38. *Le Cheik Rouge* [*The Red Sheik*] (1948) (A)
39. *Le Crabe des Neiges* [*The Snow Crab*] (1948) (A)

Tom X No. 37 (1948)

Website:
http://www.coolfrenchcomics.com/tomx.htm

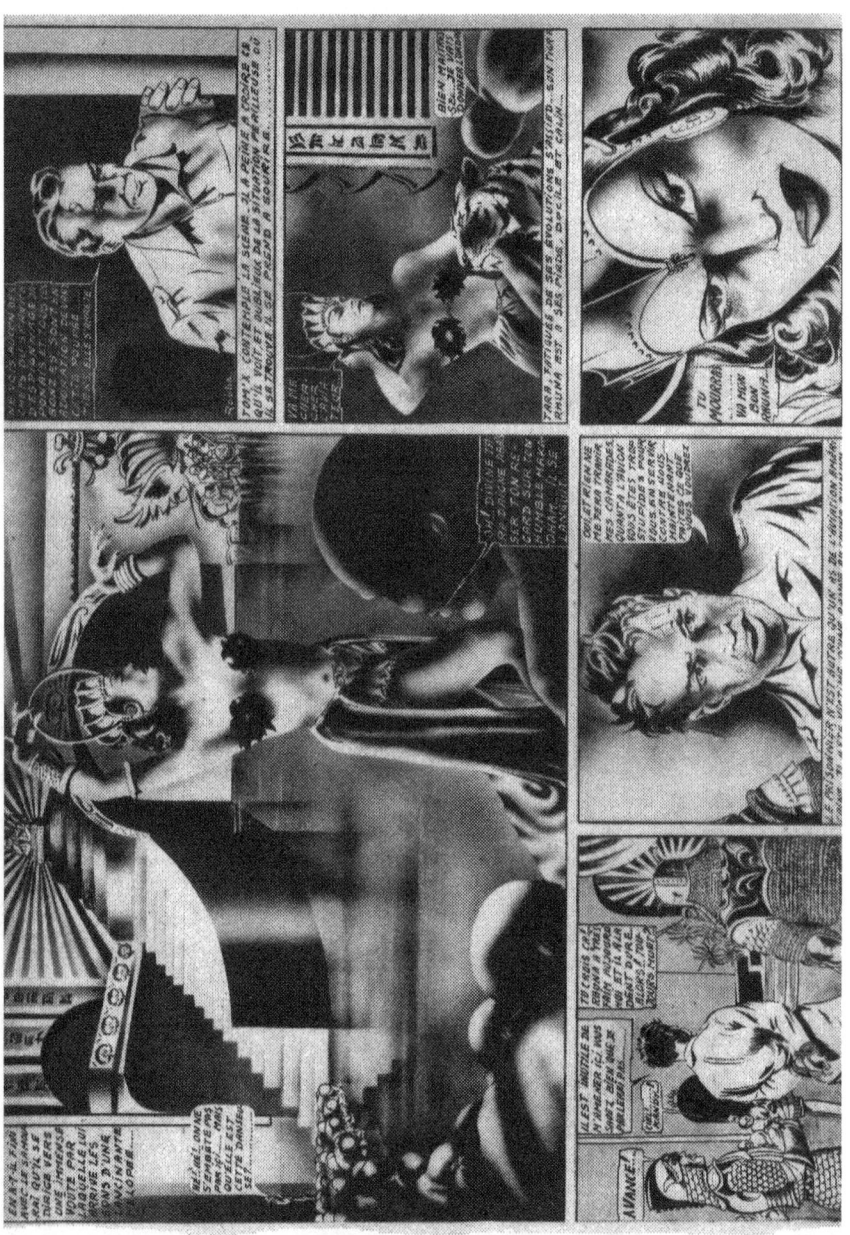

Tom X No. 2 (1946)

Salvator – Prifo reedition (1977)

Salvator (1947)

*"Forget the past. From now on, you shall be Salvator, my creation!
My son! And you shall fight for Good!"*
(Scientist Sirenus – *Salvator*)

Created by:
Writer-artist Auguste Liquois (see *Guerre à la Terre* entry).

Story:
The unknown man fated to become Salvator was shipwrecked on a mysterious island, inhabited by the equally mysterious Scientist Sirenus. Sirenus saved the man's life by bathing him in the rays of a machine he had invented that gave the stranger super-strength and super-speed, but not the power of flight or invulnerability.

Sirenus christened his creation Salvator, entrusted him with a wrist band that enabled the two to remain in telepathic contact and sent him into the world to fight for good. Sirenus also provided Salvator with an array of futuristic vehicles: a speedboat, a flying wing, etc.

The origins of Salvator (1947)

Salvator's first adventure pits him against Neptunas, the king of an undersea race who wants to rule the world. After the destruction of Neptunas' kingdom, Sirenus dispatches Salvator to an isolated island in New Guinea inhabited by prehistoric monsters. There, Salvator fights the dark-haired evil Queen of a scientific citadel bent on world domination.

Salvator and the Martians (1948)

Salvator then travels to Tibet to rescue the beautiful explorer Mary Morgan. He discovers the beachhead of a Martian invasion. He and Mary are taken to Mars, but they defeat the Martians by destroying their giant electronic brain.

Salvator's final adventure sees him and Mary save the friendly natives of Venus from an attack by remnants of the Japanese Imperial Army who have found refuge in outer space (a recurring theme in series of the times).

Publishing History:
Salvator was serialized in the magazine *Tarzan* in 1947 and 1948 (74 pages in total). It was reprinted in two volumes by Editions Prifo in 1977.

Website:
http://www.coolfrenchcomics.com/salvator.htm

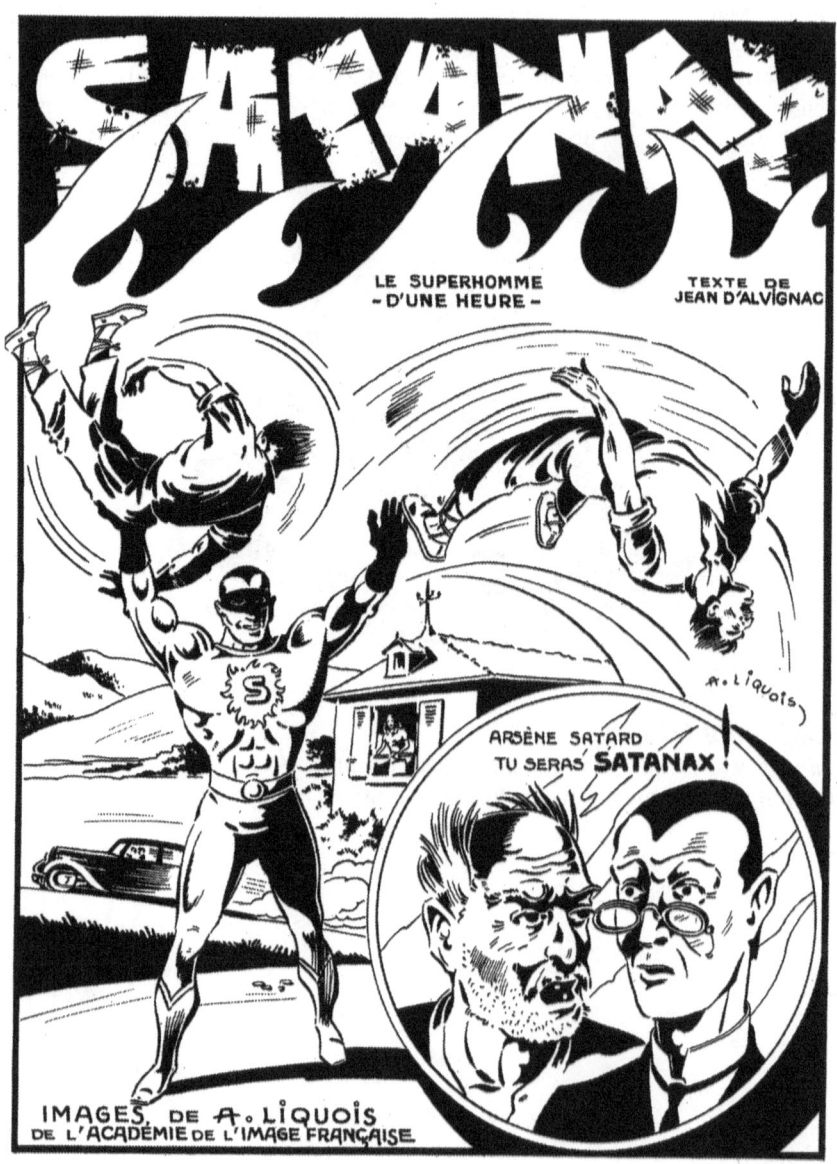

Satanax No. 1 (1948)

Satanax (1948)

"Your strength is that of a thousand men! You can fly into the air and probe the darkest depths! You will find and punish evil-doers and your name shall become synonymous with that of justice!"
(Athanase – *Satanax*)

Created by:
Writer Jean d'Alvignac and artist Auguste Liquois.

- Jean d'Alvignac's real name was Jean Bonert. *Satanax* seems to be his only known work.
- Auguste Liquois (see *Guerre à la Terre* entry).

Story:
Arsène Satard is a humble court recorder, married to the beautiful but shrewish Sylvia. While investigating a local murder, Satard meets Father Athanase, an old man living alone in the forest, who has the reputation of being a warlock. Athanase tests the honesty of the hapless Satard and, once satisfied that he is a virtuous man, makes him undergo a mystic ritual, at the end of which he orders the incredulous Satard to walk into a huge bonfire. Afraid, Satard does what Athanase wants, and emerges unscathed in the superhuman guise of Satanax.

Athanase explains to Satard that he is now endowed with super-strength and the power of flight, and that his task is to fight and punish criminals.

Satanax No. 6 (1948)

When Satard is brought in contact with fire, he will turn into Satanax, but can only remain in that form for an hour, and he is to reveal his secret to no one.

Athanase then walks into the fire and disappears in a puff of green smoke. (Athanase will occasionally reappears in Satanax's dreams to give him advice.)

Satanax goes on to fight a variety of mostly ordinary gangsters and criminals. His deadliest foe turns out to be the mad scientist Professor Zacharias, whom he meets during a stay in Africa. There, Satanax defeats a sect of Lion-Men and locates the legendary graveyard of elephants, acquiring vast wealth in the process. Sylvia, however, remains not only clueless about her husband's double-life–although many others suspect and accuse him of being Satanax–but continues to nag and put down poor Satard, who dearly wishes he could show her who he really is, but dares not disobey Athanase's orders.

Publishing History:

All 16 issues of *Satanax* were published by Editions Mondiales in 1948 and 1949, until the effects of the Law of July 1949 (see *Fantax* entry) forced the cancellation of the series. The series was partially reprinted in three volumes by Editions Prifo in 1977.

Bibliography:

1. *Satanax le Superhomme* [*Satanax the Superman*] (1948)
2. *Dans la Cheminée d'Enfer* [*Inside Hell's Chimney*] (1948)
3. *Lutte contre l'Inconnu* [*Fight against the Unknown*] (1948)
4. *Satanax contre les Hommes-Lions* [*Satanax vs. The Lion Men*] (1948)
5. *Le Défilé des Éléphants* [*The Canyon of the Elephants*] (1948)
6. *La Colère de Satanax* [*The Wrath of Satanax*] (1948)
7. *Zacharias contre Satanas* [*Zacharias vs. Satanax*] (1948)
8. *Satanax Joue et Gagne* [*Satanax Plays and Wins*] (1948)
9. *Bataille de Géants* [*Battle of Giants*] (1948)
10. *Contre ou Avec Satanax?* [*For or against Satanax?*] (1948)
11. *Guerre à la Guerre* [*War to War*] (1948)
12. *La Chute de l'Archange* [*The Fall of the Archangel*] (1949)
13. *Menace sur Vallorbe* [*Threat over Vallorbe*] (1949)
14. *Le Cauchemar est Terminé* [*The Nightmare Is Over*] (1949)
15. *Satanax et les Fantômes* [*Satanax and the Ghosts*] (1949)
16. *Satanax contre les Grands Maîtres* [*Satanax vs. The Grand Masters*] (1949)

Note: A 17th issue, *Terreur Verte* [*Green Terror*], was announced but was never published.

Satanax No. 3 (1948)

Website:
http://www.coolfrenchcomics.com/satanax.htm

Satanax No. 7 (1948)

Stany Beulé dans la Lune (1949)

Stany Beulé (1949)

"I think it is our solemn duty to help these little folks."
(Stany Beulé – *Stany Beulé dans la Lune*)

Created by:
Writer-artist Kline (see *Kaza le Martien* entry).

Story:
In the late 1950s, a team of French scientists, led by the spunky Jane Guérin, plans a rocket trip to the Moon. Once the journey begins, they discover a stowaway on board: *France-Matin* journalist Stany Beulé, who had previously interviewed (and tried to date) Jane.

The crew–Eric, Etienne, Jane and Stany–land on the Moon and discover that there is air inside some of its craters. They also come across signs of a technologically-advanced civilization. They meet Selenites, small humanoids with big heads, and are taken to a vast, underground city.

Stany Beulé dans la Lune (1949)

They then realize that the Selenites are slaves to a race of humanoid robots, who have made them their prisoners. They escape, rescue one of the Selenites who was about to be killed by the robots, and flee through the Lunar depths.

After a harrowing underground journey, Stany and his friends meet Keo, the leader of the rebels, who telepathically explains that his peaceful race was attacked and conquered by the robotic race from the Dark Side of the Moon. The humans agree to help the Selenites overthrow the robots, who are under the domination of the Great Selene and his warlords. During the course of the ensuing adventures, Jane is captured, then rescued. The humans meet the Free Robots, who assist them in infiltrating the capital city.

Eventually, the humans reclaim their rocket and use it to drop a harmless flare on the city, an act that nevertheless causes chaos and frightens the robots into surrendering. (The story parallels the surrender of Japan at the end of World War II.) Realizing their defeat, the Great Selene and his warlords commit ritual suicide. Peace again reigns on the Moon; Beulé and his friends return to Earth where they are greeted as heroes.

Publishing History:
Stany Beulé dans la Lune was serialized in the girl's comics magazine *Fillette* in 1949 (60 pages in total). Not surprisingly, it failed to capture the readership's interest, in spite of its nice romance between Stany and Jane, one of the first female rocket scientists (as opposed to the helpless Dale Arden archetype) in the history of comics. It was finally reprinted by Editions Apex in 1993.

Website:
http://www.coolfrenchcomics.com/stanybeule.htm

Le Monstre du Tonsberg – Glénat reedition (1978)

Arabelle, la Dernière Sirène (1950)

"My dear Arabelle, the whole world awaits you!"
(H.G.W. Bimbleton – *Arabelle, la Dernière Sirène*)

Created by:

Writer-artist Jean Ache. Jean Ache was the pseudonym of Jean Huet (1923-1985), who chose it as an homage to the famous illustrator Caran d'Ache. After working on numerous children's magazines during World War II, creating *Tonton Molécule* for *OK* and *Achille, Lastuce & Cremolet* for *Mon Journal*, Ache created *Arabelle the Mermaid* for the daily newspaper *France-Soir* in 1950. The mild eroticism and romance made the series very popular, including in Japan. Ache also created another sexy superheroine, *Coraline*, for *France-Dimanche*, and the long-running juvenile adventure series *Nic et Mino* for *Le Journal de Mickey* in 1958. He was also the author of a number of other popular series, such as *Archibald* for *Pilote*, and *Amanda*, a sexy female ghost, also for *France-Dimanche*. In 1973, Ache took over the art duties on the long-running detective series *Pat'apouf* published in the Catholic magazine *Le Pélerin* and stayed there until his death.

Arabelle's very first strip (1950)

Story:

Arabelle is (falsely, as it turned out) the last living mermaid. She is discovered by a rich American plastic surgeon, H.G.W. Bimbleton, on the island of Caprea near Sicily. Bimbleton operates on Arabelle and gives her a pair of very fetching human legs, but she retains her ability to breathe underwater.

At first, Arabelle falls in love with and becomes engaged to Bimbleton's son, John, but eventually leaves him behind to continue her adventurous life. Arabelle's regular sidekicks are a well-meaning but hapless reformed burglar nicknamed Fleur Bleue [*Blue Flower*, a term synonymous with a hopeless, naive romantic], and a pet monkey named Kouki.

Arabelle's surgery (1950)

The most fantastic of all of Arabelle's adventures, taking place virtually outside the continuity, involves a sequence published as Strips Nos. 340-408 (June-August 1951) in the *France-Soir* dailies. In it, Arabelle Fleur Bleue and Kouki travel to Venus, meet the amazons who live there and restore their queen, Vierge XXVII, to her rightful throne. Back on Earth, they then launch a plan to settle the planet with single men!

Arabelle and Fleur Bleue travel to Venus (1951)

At a later point in her life, Arabelle temporarily gains the ability to turn her legs back into fish tails. Most of her adventures, however, routinely revolved around ordinary villains, burglars, spies and saboteurs, with a few, occasional fantastic elements thrown in, such as a Sea Serpent in *The Tonsberg Monster* or the occasional mad scientist.

Arabelle and Fleur Bleue's relationship must have been rather frustrating for Fleur Bleue as it was clearly shown that they were just "good friends," notwithstanding Fleur Bleue's obvious pursuit of Arabelle and his jealousy when she kissed other men. Arabelle's romances were always romantic, and rather bittersweet as the Last Mermaid never really found true love.

When at Greg's suggestion, *Arabelle* returned in *Tintin Magazine* in 1972, Jean Ache revealed that she was, in fact, not the last Mermaid, and that other Mermaids lived secretly among men. Arabelle eventually became the leader of her people, a fitting conclusion for the series.

Publishing History/Bibliography:
A) The France-Soir Daily Strips:
Arabelle was first serialized in the form of daily strips in the newspaper *France-Soir* from May 3, 1950 to some time in 1962. In total, 3,350 strips were published. The stories were broken down into two series as follows:

1st Series:
The first series included Strips Nos. 1-1051, from May 3, 1950 to September 18, 1953, with narration under the panels. The episodes bore no individual titles, except *Arabelle, la Dernière Sirène* [*Arabelle, The Last Mermaid*]

2nd. Series:
The second series ran from Strips Nos. 1052-2550, renumbered Nos. 1-2499, from September 1953 to 1962, and featured word balloons. The episodes bore individual titles.
1. *Arabelle et le Prince* [*Arabelle & the Prince*] (Strips Nos. 1-166)
2. *Arabelle et l'Enfant-Sirène* [*Arabelle & The Merchild*] (Strips Nos. 167-318)
3. *Arabelle en Espagne* [*Arabelle in Spain*] (Strips Nos. 319-476)
4. *Arabelle et la Mer* [*Arabelle & The Sea*] (Strips Nos. 477-622)
5. *Arabelle contre Big Caugham* [*Arabelle vs. Big Caugham*] (Strips Nos. 623-740)
6. *Opération Cristobal / Rendez-vous avec l'Atome* [*Rendezvous with the Atom*] (Strips Nos. 741-1047)

7. *Arabelle et le Collier de Gengis Khan* [*Arabelle & Gengis Khan's Necklace*] (Strips No. 1048-1172)
8. *On A Volé Un Spoutnik!* [*They Stole a Sputnik!*] (Strips Nos. 1173-1345)

The Tonsberg Monster (1960)

9. *Arabelle et Bel Canto* [*Arabelle & Bel Canto*] (Strips Nos. 1346-1504)
10. *Kilt et Whisky* [*Kilt & Whisky*] (Strips Nos. 1505-1567)
11. *Paris by Night* (Strips Nos. 1658-1805)
12. *Arabelle et les Pénibles* [*Arabelle & The Difficult People*] (Strips Nos. 1806-1881)
13. *Arabelle en Norvège: Le Monstre du Tonsberg* [*Arabelle in Norway: The Tonsberg Monster*] (Strips Nos. 1882-2047)
14. *Arabelle du Côté d'Aden* [*Arabelle in Aden's Neighborhood*] (Strips Nos. 2048-2201)
15. *Arabelle et Lord Pennybox* [*Arabelle & Lord Pennybox*] (Strips Nos. 2202-2411)
16. *Arabelle et le Puchamoa* [*Arabelle & The Puchamoa*] (Strips Nos. 2412-2499)

B) Other Dailies:
1. *Arabelle, la Dernière Sirène* [*Arabelle, The Last Mermaid*] (53 weekly pages, *Le Journal du Dimanche*, 1957-1958)
2. *Grabuge sur l'Archipel* [*Battle on the Archipelago*] (16 pages, *L'Illustré du Dimanche* Nos. 18-24, 1967)

C) Reprints:
Paris by Night (Denoël, 1964)
Arabelle en Espagne [*Arabelle In Spain*] (Editions de Poche No. 1, 1967)
Arabelle et le Bel Canto [*Arabelle & Bel Canto*] (Editions de Poche No. 2, 1967)
Opération Cristobal (Editions de Poche No. 3, 1967)
Rendez-vous avec l'Atome [*Rendezvous with the Atom*] (Editions de Poche No. 4, 1968)
Le Monstre du Tonsberg [*The Tonsberg Monster*] (Glénat, 1978)

D) New Series:
1. *Les Sirènes Sont Parmi Nous* [*The Mermaids Are Among Us*] (*Tintin* Nos. 1218-1233, 1972)
2. *Méfiez-Vous des Sirènes!* [*Beware the Mermaids!*] (*Tintin* Nos. 1245-1257, 1972)
3. *Mission Spéciale pour un Dauphin* [*Special Mission for a Dolphin*] (*Tintin Sélection* No. 20, 1973)

Website:
http://www.coolfrenchcomics.com/arabelle.htm

Meteor No. 1 (1953)

Les Conquérants de l'Espace (1953)

"Having brought the benefits of civilization to the primitive people of Sylva, Doctor Spencer and his companions continue on their journey of exploration throughout the galaxy."
(*Space Girl*'s log – *La Guerre des Robots*)

Created by:
Writer R. Lortac and artists Raoul & Robert Giordan.

• R. Lortac (see *Fulguros* entry).

• Raoul Giordan (1926-) (right) and his brother Robert Giordan (1922-198?) began drawing comics for a variety of children's magazines in the late 1940s, but their major works were published by Artima (later Aredit) in the 1950s. Their most famous character was the French superhero *Vigor*. *Vigor* was originally an engineer named Max Vigor, created by writer-artist Pierre Duteurtre (see  *Guerre à la Terre* entry) in 1948; he was revamped merely as *Vigor* by writer-artist J.-A. Dupuich in 1952, and revamped again to become a superhero by the Giordans in 1954. The new *Vigor* was a *Captain America*-like super-soldier who fought for the United Nations. *Vigor* was written and drawn by the Giordans, with occasional help from writer R. Lortac, and ran without interruption in its own magazine from 1954 to 1962. In addition to *Les Conquérants de l'Espace*, the Giordans also wrote and drew *Les Francis*, the story of a *Space Family Robinson*, for *Meteor* and *Tom Tempest* for *Audax*. In the 1970s, they were assigned to illustrate comics adaptations of the science fiction novels of Editions Fleuve Noir for the magazines *Sidéral* and *Anticipation*. Raoul Giordan briefly returned to comics with *Space Gordon* in 1993.

Story:
The saga of the "Conquerors of Space" begins in an undefined near-future that very much resembles the present. As it continued, however, its universe became increasingly futuristic, reaching a *Star Trek: Enterprise*-like context of early space exploration.

When the series begins, Professor Spencer is asked to head the first interplanetary journey to the Moon in his new, prototype rocket. The rocket design will become slicker over the first dozen or so issues, but she was already named *Space Girl* in the first issue.

As his crew, Spencer recruits test pilot Sam Spade (obviously a descendent of the famed detective!) and mechanic Tex Brandley, nicknamed "Texas."

The first issue features a failed attempt by enemy agents to prevent the take-off of *Space Girl* and the construction of an orbital space station. The next three issues take our heroes to the Moon, the "silent planet."

Page 1 of Meteor No. 1 (1953)

Texas, Spade and Spencer

Then, having built a faster rocket (Model W-4), the Conquerors explore an heretofore unknown primitive world named Terra. How the planet could have remained hidden from Earth scientists is not explained; maybe it is a Counter-Earth. There, they meet the peaceful, advanced Venusians and become involved in an interplanetary rescue attempt to help the Martians leave their dying planet and relocate to Terra. As with *Star Trek*, the great majority of aliens in the series are humanoids with small facial differences from humans.

Thanks to the Venusiuans' help, the Conquerors now have an even faster and sleeker rocket, which can travel beyond the Solar System. They first visit the planet Titania where life has grown to be garguantuan and they are proportionately insect-sized. Then they help the Utopians in their conflict with neighboring Tyrannia. On Arbor, a forest world, they help reconcile two warring races, winged beings and troglodytes. Eventually, the series adopted a pattern where, in each episode, the Conquerors were able to help a beleaguered alien race. The emphasis was on exploration and making peaceful contact, very much like *Star Trek*, but without the Prime Directive.

Doctor Spencer was unfailingly wise but not all-knowing, Spade played the part of the daring, fearless action hero, and brash, often clueless Texas provided the comic relief. There was virtually no character development, the trio's respective personalities having been defined at the onset, and few female characters of note. In fact, there were virtually no other recurring characters in the series. Earth, while mentioned regularly, never played a major role.

Publishing History:

The Conquerors of Space was originally serialized in the comic magazine *Meteor* published by French publisher Artima, and later Aredit, from 1953 to 1964.

Artima was one of the earliest and most famous of the French small format publishers. Launched in 1946 by Emile Keirsbilk, Artima was headquartered in the industrial city of Roubaix in the North of France. Artima published numerous adventure titles with colorful names such as: *Audax* (1950-61; which carried *Fulguros*), *Dynamic* (1950-65), *Ardan* (1952-61), *Meteor* (1953-77), *Tarou* (1954-73), *Vigor* (1954-62), *Tempest* (1955-57), *Fulgor* (1955-58), *Hardy* (1955-58), *Ouragan* (1955-58), *Big Boy*, retitled *Big Boss* in 1960 (1956-62), *Cosmos* (1956-61), *Atome Kid*, a Spanish superhero (1956-59), *Spoutnik* (1957-60), *Mystic* (1957-59), *Eclair* (1957-58), *Vengeur* (1957-60), *Olympic* (1958-61), *Téméraire* (1958-62) and *Sidéral* (1958-62). A number of these magazines contained translations of early DC Comics science fiction series, such as *Martian Manhunter*, *Adam Strange* and *Space Ranger*.

In 1962, Keirsbilk sold Artima to the powerful French publishing corporation, Presses de la Cité, which renamed the company Aredit. Under Presses de la Cité's management, Aredit began to publish a slew of new black & white, pocket-sized magazines featuring translations of more DC Comics' series. These included *Etranges Aventures* (1966-83), *Aventures Fiction* (1966-87), *Spectre* (1967-68), *Brulant* (1967-81), *Eclipso* (1968-83), *Aquaman* (1970-74), *Spectral* (1974-77), *Demon* (1976-88), *L'Insolite* (1977-82), etc.

Simultaneously, Aredit also launched a series of titles devoted to comics adaptations of popular novels of espionage, science fiction and horror published by Presses de la Cité's paperback imprint, Fleuve Noir. These included titles such as *Flash Espionnage* (1966-83), *OSS 117* (1966-82), *Coplan FX-18* (1969-81), *Calone* (1974-78), *Le Commander* (1976-78), *Face d'Ange* (1974-83) and other espionage series, all launched with different degrees of success. Science fiction and horror titles included *Anticipation* (1975-81), *Atomos* (1968-77), *Hallucinations* (1969-89) and *Clameurs* (1976-81). Like their competition, Editions Lug, Aredit eventually concentrated on the publishing of American material, adding translations of Marvel Comics to their line with *L'Inattendu* (1975-80), *Conan* (1977-85), *Hulk* (1976-84), *Captain America* (1979-85), *Les Défenseurs* (1981-87), etc. Aredit went out of business in the early 1990s.

Reprints of *The Conquerors of Space* first appeared in *Cosmos* (1956-61). Episodes 1 to 23 were reprinted as four graphic novels by Belgian publisher Lefrancq–vols. 1 and 2 in 1990, vol. 3 in 1995, and vol. 4 in 1996.

Bibliography:
from Meteor Magazine

1. *Les Conquérants de l'Espace* [*The Conquerors of Space*] (1953)
2. *Vers la Lune* [*Towards the Moon*] (1953)
3. *La Planète du Silence* [*The Silent Planet*] (1953)
4. *Aventure dans la Lune* [*Adventure on the Moon*] (1953)
5. *Terra, Monde Nouveau* [*Terra, a New World*] (1953)
6. *Invasion Martienne* [*Martian Invasion*] (1953)
7. *Au Secours de Mars* [*To Mars' Rescue*]
8. *Croisière Sidérale* [*Star Cruise*] (1954)
9. *Titania* (1954)
10. *Guerre en Utopie* [*War in Utopia*] (1954)
11. *Menace sur Arbor* [*Threat to Arbor*] (1954)
12. *Aqua, Cité Sous-Marine* [*Aqua, the Underwater City*] (1954)
13. *Guerre aux Parasites* [*War against the Parasites*] (1954)
14. *Aventure en Kroscopie* [*Adventure in Kroscopia*] (1954)
15. *Mytho, Planète Fabuleuse* [*Mytho, the Fabulous Panet*] (1954)
16. *Invasion de Robots* [*Robot Invasion*] (1954)
17. *Alerte sur Pluton* [*Alert on Pluto*] (1954)
18. *Le Monde Parallèle* [*The Parallel World*] (1954)
19. *La Planète des Mirages* [*The Planet of Mirages*] (1954)
20. *Avatars sur la Planète "Sylva"* [*Trouble on Planet Sylva*] (1955)
21. *La Guerre des Robots* [*The War of the Robots*] (1955)
22. *Voleurs de Radium* [*Radium Thieves*] (1955)
23. *Grandes Chasses sur Orpito* [*Big Hunts on Orpito*] (1955)
24. *Le Robinson de l'Espace* [*Robinson of Space*] (1955)
25. *Cataclysme chez les Surhommes* [*Cataclysm amongst the Supermen*] (1955)
26. *Méfaits et Bienfaits du Bolide "Alpha"* [*Good and Bad Things about Rocket Alpha*] (1955)
27. *Nutricia, Planète Convoitée* [*Nutricia, the Coveted Planet*] (1955)
28. *Voyage dans le Passé* [*Journey into the Past*] (1955)
29. *La Planète du Sommeil* [*The Planet of Sleep*] (1955)
30. *La Planète des Amphibies* [*The Planet of Amphibians*] (1955)

31. *Menace pour la Terre* [*Menace to Earth*] (1955)
32. *Conspiration dans les Etoiles* [*Conspiracy amongst the Stars*] (1956)
33. *Les Pirates des Etoiles* [*The Star Pirates*] (1956)

Meteor No. 9 (1954)

34. *Les Ravisseurs de l'Espace* [*The Space Kidnappers*] (1956)
35. *Chercheurs d'Uranium* [*Uranium Seekers*] (1956)
36. *La Révolte des Animaux* [*The Revolt of the Animals*] (1956)
37. *Les Vampires de Pomena* [*The Vampires of Pomena*] (1956)
38. *Révolte sur Héraclos* [*Revolt on Heraklos*] (1956)
39. *En Route pour Mars* [*Destination Mars*] (1956)
40. *Les Naufragés de l'Espace* [*Shipwrecked in Space*] (1956)
41. *Le Rayon Lambda* [*The Lambda Ray*] (1956)
42. *Ugol le Conquérant* [*Ugol the Conqueror*] (1956)
43. *Aventure au Pays des Merveilles* [*Adventures in Wonderland*] (1956)
44. *Paradis sous Globe* [*The Domed Paradise*] (1956)
45. *Le Domino Volant* [*The Flying Domino*] (1957)
46. *À la Recherche du Domino Volant* [*Search for the Flying Domino*] (1957)
47. *L'Opération Déluge* [*Operation Flood*] (1957)
48. *La Planète Bagne 117* [*Penitentiary Planet 117*] (1957)
49. *La Planète Vagabonde* [*The Wandering Planet*] (1957)

50. *Deux Enfants dans l'Espace* [*Two Children in Space*] (1957)
No. Spécial (Annual). *Le Satellite en Détresse* [*Satellite in Distress*] - *Les Pirates du Chaos* [*The Pirates of Chaos*] (1957)
51. *Les Naufragés de l'infini* [*Shipwrecked in Infinity*] (1957)
52. *Au Pouvoir des Hommes Verts* [*In the Green Men's Power*] (1957)
53. *Les Evadés de Disciplina* [*Escape from Disciplina*] (1957)
54. *Terre Symétrique* [*Symmetrical Earth*] - *La Planète Lilliput* [*The Lilliputian Planet*] (1957)
55. *Ophénia, la Planète qui Meurt* [*Ophenia, the Dying Planet*] (1957)

56. *Planète Prohibée* [*Forbidden Planet*] (1957)
57. *La Comète Ecarlate* [*The Scarlet Comet*] (1958)
58. *Science sans Conscience* [*Soulless Science*] (1958)
59. *Au Pouvoir des Sorcières* [*In the Witches' Power*] (1958)
60. *Le Satellite V13 Ne Répond Plus* [*Satellite V13 Does Not Answer*] (1958)
61. *La Flore de l'Astre Eden* [*The Flora of the Eden Star*] (1958)
62. *La Planète des Fusées Perdues* [*The Planet of the Lost Rockets*] (1958)
63. *L'Ere du Prophète Electronique* [*The Era of the Electronic Prophet*] (1958)
64. *Les Curieux Hommes de Thorp* [*The Curious Men of Thorp*] (1958)
65. *Le Maître de Malva* [*The Master of Malva*] (1958)
66. *Les Surhommes de Kander* [*The Supermen of Kander*] (1958)
67. *La Ronde des Heures* [*The Dance of the Hours*] (1958)
68. *Les Raccourcis de l'Espace* [*The Shortcuts of Space*] (1958)
69. *Le Monstre des Sables* [*The Sand Monster*] (1959)
70. *Aventure Souterraine* [*Underground Adventure*] (1959)
71. *Les Derniers des Aroukans* [*The Last of the Arukans*] (1959)
72. *Les Pillards de la Cité Morte* [*The Looters of the Dead City*] (1959)
73. *Explorateurs des Temps Futurs* [*Explorers of the Future*] (1959)
74. *L'Etrange Robot* [*The Strange Robot*] (1959)
75. *Daphnis, Astre Convoité* [*Daphnis, the Coveted Star*] (1959)
76. *Mission Diplomatique* [*Diplomatic Mission*] (1959)
77. *Planètes Rivales* [*Rival Planets*] (1959)
78. *Guerre Climatique* [*Weather War*] (1959)
79. *Croisière de Luxe* [*Luxury Cruise*] (1959)
80. *Vers la Terre Promise* [*Towards the Promised Land*] (1959)
81. *Une Planète s'est évadée* [*A Planet Has Escaped*] (1960)
82. *Les Cercueils d'Or* [*The Gold Coffins*] (1960)
83. *Les Naufragés de Zamora* [*Shipwrecked on Zamora*] (1960)
84. *Etranges Empreintes* [*Strange Trails*] (1960)
85. *La Chasse aux Satellites* [*The Satellite Hunt*] (1960)

Meteor No. 15 (1954)

Meteor No. 16 (1954)

86. *Bonheur à Perpétuité* [*Happiness for Life*] - *Le Mal des Espaces* [*The Space Sickness*] (1960)
87. *Les Profs des Etoiles* [*The Star Teachers*] (1960)
88. *La Reine du Cosmos* [*The Cosmic Queen*] (1960)

89. *La Fin des invisibles* [*The End of the Invisibles*] - *L'Astre des Immortels* [*The Star of the Immortals*] (1960)
90. *La Terre est Folle* [*Earth Goes Mad*] - *Plus Vite que la Lumière* [*Faster than Light*] (1960)
91. *Cités Volantes* [*Flying Cities*] - *Les Derniers Géants* [*The Last Giants*] (1960)
92. *La Révolte des Nyctalopes* [*The Revolt of the Nyctalopes*] - *Le Paradou* [*The Paradoo*] (1960)
93. *Au Pouvoir des Chmoks* [*In the Chmoks' Power*] - *Chez les Hommes-Méduses* [*Amongst the Medusa Men*] (1961)
94. *Les Hommes-Gymnotes du Fulgura* [*The Gymnote-Men of the Fulgura*] - *La Boue Vivante d'Eldorado* [*The Living Mud of Eldorado*] (1961)
95. *Les Diamants de l'Astre Thesaurus* [*The Diamonds from the Star Thesaurus*] - *Les Esclavagistes de l'Espace* [*The Space Slavers*] (1961)
96. *L'Astre des Bien Portants* [*The Star of the Healthy*] - *Séjour chez les Métamorphes* [*Staying amongst the Metamorphs*] (1961)
97. *Le Congrès ne s'amuse pas* [*Congress Is Not Amused*] - *Les Hommes de Pierre de Gwaldin* [*The Stone Men of Gwaldin*] (1961)
98. *La Planète des Cyclones* [*The Hurricane Planet*] - *Le Robot qui Voulut Être Roi* [*The Robot Who Would Be King*] (1961)
99. *La Chose* [*The Thing*] - *L'Arme Absolue* [*The Absolute Weapon*] (1961)
100. *Océania, Planète sans Terre* [*Oceania, the Landless Planet*] - *Traître à la Paix* [*Traitor to Peace*] (1961)
101. *Planète sans nom* [*Nameless Planet*] (1961)
102. *L'Astre des Naufrageurs* [*The Star of the Ship Wreckers*] (1961)
103. *Survivants sous les Ruines* [*Survivors in the Ruins*] (1961)
104. *Le Grain de Sable* [*The Grain of Sand*] (1961)
105. *La Déesse Aveugle* [*The Blind Goddess*] (1962)
106. *On a volé le RZ.000* [*They Stole The RZ.000*] (1962)
107. *La Croix du Mal* [*The Evil Cross*] (1962)
108. *La Planète Blessée* [*The Wounded Planet*] (1962)
109. *Chute dans l'infini* [*Fall into Infinity*] (1962)
110. *Planète sans Equilibre* [*Planet Without Balance*] (1962)
111. *Robots Humains* [*Human Robots*] (1962)

Meteor No. 111 (1962)

Meteor No. 20 (1955)

112. *Le Voleur d'Etoiles* [*The Star Thief*] (1962)
113. *Trahison à Mulcina* [*Betrayal in Mulcina*] (1962)
114. *Erreur de Tir* [*Stray Shooting*] (1962)
115. *Les Hommes sont toujours des Hommes* [*Men Are Always Men*] (1962)

116. *Les Diamants de Ramira* [*The Diamonds of Ramira*] (1963)
117. *Experimenta, Planète Curieuse* [*Experimenta, the Curious Planet*] (1963)
118. *Le Bagne de l'Espace* [*The Space Penitentiary*] (1963)
119. *Rendez-vous dans l'Espace* [*Rendez-vous in Space*] (1963)
120. *Révole sur Ténigra* [*Revolt on Tenigra*] (1963)
121. *Planète intoxiquée* [*Intoxicated Planet*] (1963)
122. *Le Voleur d'Orage* [*The Storm Thief*] (1963)
123. [no story]
124. *Un Homme Perdu... Lequel?* [*A Man Is Lost... But Which One?*] (1963)
125. *Le Virus Timeo* [*The Timeo Virus*] (1963)
126. *Devant le Nuclerama* [*Before the Nuclerama*] (1963)
127. *Panique sur le Monde* [*World Panic*] (1963)
128. *Le Mystère des ondes Perdues* [*The Mystery of the Lost Waves*] (1964)
129. *Les Valises Infernales* [*The Suitcases from Hell*] (1964)
130. *Le Monde a Faim* [*The World is Hungry*] - *Alerte sur la Terre!* [*Alert on Earth*] (1964)
131. *Voyage sans Retour* [*Journey of No-Return*] (1964)
132. *Le Maître du Silence* [*The Master of Silence*] (1964)
133. *Voleur de Satellite* [*The Satellite Thief*] (1964)
134. *La Planète du Silence* [*The Silent Planet*] (1964) (not the same story as No.3)
135. *Le Secret des Montagnes Ennemies* [*The Secret of the Enemy Mountains*] (1964)
136. *Satellite Pirate* [*Pirate Satellite*] (1964)
137. *La Planète Sans Nom* [*The Nameless Planet*] (1964) (not the same story as No.101)

Website:
http://www.coolfrenchcomics.com/meteor.htm

Monsieur Choc (Tif & Tondu) (1955)

"Monsieur Choc is at his deadliest when you think he has lost."
(Gina – *Choc 235*)

Created by:
Writer Maurice Rosy and artist Will.

• Maurice Rosy (1927-) joined the editorial team of *Spirou* in the early 1950s. In 1955, he took over the writing on the popular humor-detective series *Tif & Tondu* (originally created by Fernand Dineur in 1938) and created the villainous *Monsieur Choc*. Rosy continued writing *Tif & Tondu* until 1968, when he handed the task to Maurice Tillieux. In 1967, also for *Spirou*, Rosy and artist Derib co-created the character of *Attila*, a bio-engineered dog with human-like intelligence and the power of speech. Rosy's most popular creation was the cartoony convict, *Bobo*, with Paul Deliège. Rosy retired from comics in the late 1960s to go into advertising and children's book illustration.

• Will, a pseudonym of Willy Maltaite (1927-2000), was one of the first artists along with André Franquin, Joseph Gillain (Jijé), Pierre Culliford (Peyo) and Maurice de Bevere (Morris), to join the editorial team of *Spirou* after World War II. He took *Tif & Tondu* over from Dineur in 1949, and worked on it regularly until his retirement in 1990. Will also assisted Peyo on *Benoît Brisefer* and Franquin on *Spirou*. His other creation was the whimsical fantasy, *Isabelle*, with Franquin, Yvan Delporte and Raymond Macherot.

Story:
Tif (a colloquial word for hair) is a bald–and bold–adventurer who, early in his career (No. 5 of *Spirou*), met a stranded captain named Tondu (a colloquial word for shaven) on a desert island. For comic effect, Tondu sports luxurious hair, mustache and beard. He is the thinker and planner of the team. The adventures of *Tif & Tondu* did not rise above the level of other, ordinary, *Tintin*-like juvenile series of the times, and were in fact beginning to flounder when Maurice Rosy took over writing the series and, in his first episode, introduced the charismatic character of Monsieur Choc, who soon became Tif & Tondu's arch-nemesis.

Monsieur Choc is striking because of his unique visual design: a tall, lanky man, often portrayed with a cigarette-holder in his hand, dressed in a tuxedo and hiding his features behind a medieval helmet. The design of the helmet was modified between the first and second episodes. Choc, a master of disguise, is also known to use facial masks *à la Mission: Impossible* to look like other people.

Traitement de Choc (1984)

First appearance of M. Choc in Tif et Tondu contre la Main Blanche (1955)

Monsieur Choc is the leader of a world-spanning criminal empire called the *Main Blanche* [*White Hand*] and often signs his crime with a card bearing the dreaded symbol of the organization. We later find that the White Hand is affiliated with the Mafia, the Chinese Tongs and the Russian Mafia.

In the first adventure, Tif & Tondu meet Choc, and dismantle the White Hand's drug trafficking network that ranges from the Far East to America. In the second adventure, they help millionaire Count Del Marco thwart Choc's attempt to take over his private island and steal a new prototype hydrofoil. At the end of the story, Choc is captured, unmasked and revealed to be Del Marco's private secretary. However, in the third installment of the saga, Choc escapes from jail, leaving behind him a latex mask in the likeness of said secretary, so his true face remains unknown. In that episode, he uses a gravity-attractor to commit daring robberies.

M. Choc unmasked in Le Retour de Choc *(1956)*

The next story was a lackluster adventure involving a transamerican car race. In 1958, Will and Rosy took a well-deserved six-year break from *Tif & Tondu*, but returned in top form in 1964 with *Choc au Louvre*, in which Choc masterminds a daring burglary of the famous Parisian museum. The series' popularity soared. A number of flamboyant exploits pitting the resourceful Tif & Tondu against Choc followed.

In *La Villa du Long-Cri* [*The Villa of the Long Howl*] (1964), Choc used robotic twins of Tif & Tondu to commit a burglary. In *Les Flèches de Nulle Part* [*The Arrows from Nowhere*] (1965), he kidnapped scientists and took over a secret, abandoned Nazi base to find long-forgotten weapons of mass destruction. In *Le Réveil de Toar* [*Toar Awakens*] (1966), one of the most memorable books in the series, Choc discovered a giant, medieval robot buried beneath a small village in Britanny and brought it back to life in order to find a hidden treasure.

Finally, in *Le Grand Combat* [*The Great Clash*] (1967), a fitting title for what was to be the heroes' greatest confrontation with their arch-foe, Choc used mystic secrets stolen from Tibetan lamas to enter the world of dreams and blackmail heads of state into surrendering to the White Hand by plaguing them with deadlly nightmares. The lamas sent one of their own to assist Tif & Tondu, who also gained the ability to enter the dreamworld. Ultimately, Choc was believed to have been buried in the destruction of his headquarters.

Le Grand Combat (1969)

Le Grand Combat (1969)

That was to be Monsieur Choc's last appearance until 1984 when new writer Stephen Desberg asked, and received, the permission of Maurice Rosy to bring Choc back in a series of new adventures.

By then, *Tif & Tondu*, while still drawn by Will in his characteristic cartoony style, had become more adult. Tif was depicted as an inveterate womanizer, and the stories did not shrink from depicting various acts of violence and mayhem. In *Traitement de Choc* [*Shock Treatment*] (1984), Choc exploits a drug that confers super-speed to commit spectacular burglaries all over London. In a traditional James Bondian fashion, he is ably assisted by the beautiful and deadly martial arts expert, Fleur-de-Jade.

The last two stories see Tif & Tondu meet the stunning Gina Felicita who plays a deadly game of betrayal between them and Choc. The stakes have been raised as Choc plots to use stolen uranium to become master of the world, challenging his old allies–the Mafia, the Tongs, etc.

Choc 235 (1985)

Publishing History:
Tif & Tondu was originally created by Fernand Dineur for the weekly comic magazine *Spirou* in 1938. The series was taken over by Will in 1949. Writer Maurice Rosy came on board in 1955 and left in 1968, passing the baton to Maurice Tillieux, who went on to write it until his death in 1977. *Tif & Tondu* was then taken over by Stephen Desberg. Will finally retired in 1990. The series continued until 1996 written by Denis Lapière and drawn by Alain Sikorski.

Bibliography:
(Episodes featuring Monsieur Choc only.)
Writer: Maurice Rosy.
Artist: Will.
Tif et Tondu contre la Main Blanche [*Tif & Tondu vs. The White Hand*] (*Spirou* Nos. 873-894, 1955; graphic novel No. 4, 1956)
Le Retour de Choc [*The Return of Choc*] (*Spirou* Nos. 913-933, 1956; graphic novel #5, 1958)
Passez Muscade [*Hot Potatoes*] (*Spirou* Nos. 942-963, 1956; graphic novel #6, 1958)
Plein Gaz [*Full Throttle*] (*Spirou* Nos. 988-1029, 1956; graphic novel #7, 1959)
Choc au Louvre [*Choc at the Louvre*] (*Spirou* Nos. 1350-1370, 1964; graphic novel #8, 1966)
La Villa du Long-Cri [*The Villa of the Long Howl*] (*Spirou* Nos. 1373-1393, 1964; graphic novel #9, 1966)
Les Flèches de Nulle Part [*The Arrows from Nowhere*] (*Spirou* Nos. 1399-1420, 1965; graphic novel #10, 1967)
Le Réveil de Toar [*Toar Awakens*] (*Spirou* Nos. 1474-1495, 1966; graphic novel #12, 1968)
Le Grand Combat [*The Great Clash*] (*Spirou* Nos. 1501-1521, 1967; graphic novel #13, 1968)

Writer: Stephen Desberg.
Artist: Will.
Traitement de Choc [*Shock Treatment*] (*Spirou* Nos. 2400-2403, 1984; graphic novel #32, 1984)
Choc 235 (*Spirou* Nos. 2448-2451, 1985; graphic novel #33, 1985)

Dans les Griffes de la Main Blanche [*In the Clutches of the White Hand*] (*Spirou* Nos. 2501-2501, 1986; graphic novel #35, 1986)

Website:
http://www.coolfrenchcomics.com/choc.htm

Bibi Fricotin et les Soucoupes Volantes (1955)

Bibi Fricotin et les Martiens (1955)

"Funny-looking planet. It looks nothing like Paris."
(Bibi Fricotin – *Bibi Fricotin et les Soucoupes Volantes*)

Created by:
Writer R. Lortac and artist Pierre Lacroix.
- R. Lortac (see *Fulguros* entry).
- Pierre Lacroix (1912-1994) learned his skills by becoming Louis Forton's assistant at age 17. (Forton was the original creator of both *Bibi Fricotin* and *Les Pieds Nickelés*.) After a stint in advertising following World War II, Lacroix returned to comics in 1947 to take over *Bibi Fricotin*, which he continued drawing until his retirement in 1988. He also occasionally substituted for Pellos on *Les Pieds Nickelés* in 1953-54. In 1974, he took over the girl's comics series *Aggie* from Gérard Alexandre. Lacroix died in 1994.

Story:
We are concerned here with only a brief period of *Bibi Fricotin*, during which the series flirted with science fiction themes, departing from the more traditional, mundane adventures for which it was usually known.

Bibi Fricotin is a typically clever Parisian streetwise kid. In his origin story, he is shown working as a lad on a racetrack. Bibi Fricotin is far more roguish and insolent, and far less law-abiding, than *Tintin*. Bibi is a cross between the early *Mickey Mouse* and Charlie Chaplin's *Little Tramp*.

His sidekick is an African youth named Razibus Zouzou, who is no less smart and agile than Bibi. Unlike other black sidekicks, Razibus (a slang nickname evoking his bald head) is not a comic relief or a bumbler, but an equal, a Huey to Bibi's Dewey.

Supporting characters include the kindly scientist and brilliant inventor Professor Radar, a Gyro Gearloose in human form, whose role is particularly important in the adventures reviewed here. Another supporting character is the Clouseau-like Inspector Martin, who often tries to arrest Bibi.

In *Bibi Fricotin et les Soucoupes Volantes* [*Bibi Fricotin & The Flying Saucers*] (1955), Bibi, Razibus and two tennis players are abducted via tractor beam by a Martian flying saucer during the French Open. The Martians turn out to be a green humanoids with trunks and super-stretching abilities. They have intelligent robots.

After an eventful journey, Bibi and Razibus land on Mars, escape their captors, and meet up with Professor Radar, who has arrived there on his own rocket. Recaptured, they are locked in a zoo, but then freed by Zig Bi, one of the Martian leaders favorable to peace with Earth. However his rival, Frack, seeks war. Thanks to Bibi's efforts, Frack is neutralized.

Bibi Fricotin et les Soucoupes Volantes (1955)

Bibi and his friends return to Earth with Zig Bi, who wants to discover life on his neighboring world, in tow. Even though his head is covered with bandages, the Martian attracts the attention of two gangsters who steal his paralyzing ray gun and use it to commit crimes. The story ends with the signing of a peace treaty between Earth and Mars and the opening of interplanetary tourism.

As the next book, *Bibi Fricotin et les Martiens* [*Bibi Fricotin & The Martians*] (1955), opens, Bibi and Razibus are becoming very rich managing organized tours of Mars. Radar, who is back on Mars, summons them for a demonstration of a new destructive weapon, the "Super-Martium." However, the communication has been intercepted by enemy agents from the warlike nation of Pataponia, who wish to steal the deadly gadget. The rest of the book is devoted to Bibi and Razibus' efforts, this time assisted (or handicapped) by Inspector Martin, to reclaim the weapon stolen by the Pataponians.

The next science fiction saga was comprised of *Bibi Fricotin et la Fantastique Machine KBX Z2* [*Bibi Fricotin & The Fantastic Machine KBX Z2*] and *Bibi Fricotin en l'An 3000* [*Bibi Fricotin in the Year 3000*], both published in 1963. In it, Professor Radar invents a time machine, coveted by his arch-rival, the aptly-named, glory-grabbing Professor Trublion. When Bibi and his friends reach the year 3000, they discover a technologically-advanced society suffering from overreliance on robots, that has lost touch with nature. They teach it to rediscover the merits of labor and organic food.

The last installment of this series-within-a-series was *Bibi Fricotin Découvre l'Atlantide* [*Bibi Fricotin Discovers Atlantis*], in which Bibi frees a captured man-fish who turns out to be an Atlantean. Atlantis is a peaceful underwater city located off of the Canary Islands. Unfortunately, its wealth is coveted by an unscrupulous salvage captain. Seeking peace and isolation, the Atlanteans decide to relocate to another, unknown location and destroy their city.

Publishing History:

Bibi Fricotin was created in 1924 for the magazine *Le Petit Illustré* by Louis Forton, the author of the equally famous *Pieds Nickelés*. In 1936, after Forton's death, the character was taken over by Gaston Callaud. In 1947, it was entrusted to Pierre Lacroix. After the War, the series was published in *L'Epatant*, then starting in 1955, in *Jeunesse Joyeuse* which was renamed *Le Journal de Bibi Fricotin* in 1964. Numerous writers worked with Lacroix, including R. Lortac who penned the science fiction stories featured in this chapter.

Bibliography:

Bibi Fricotin et les Soucoupes Volantes [*Bibi Fricotin & The Flying Saucers*] (*Bibi Fricotin* No. 45, 1955)
Bibi Fricotin et les Martiens [*Bibi Fricotin & The Martians*] (*Bibi Fricotin* No. 46, 1955)
Bibi Fricotin et la Fantastique Machine KBX Z2 [*Bibi Fricotin & the Fantastic Machine KBX Z2*] (*Bibi Fricotin* No. 60, 1963)
Bibi Fricotin en l'An 3000 [*Bibi Fricotin in the Year 3000*] (*Bibi Fricotin* No. 62, 1963)
Bibi Fricotin Découvre l'Atlantide [*Bibi Fricotin Discovers Atlantis*] (*Bibi Fricotin* No. 63, 1963)

Website:
http://www.coolfrenchcomics.com/bibifricotin.htm

Bibi Fricotin en l'An 3000 (1963)

Jacques Flash – Jeunesses & Vacances reedition (1977)

Jacques Flash (1957)

"Invisibility is not invulnerability."
(Jacques Flash – *Les Esclaves de la Forêt*)

Created by:

Artist Pierre Le Guen. The very first writer of *Jacques Flash* was uncredited; however it was most likely one of *Vaillant*'s editorial team, Jean Ollivier, Roger Lecureux or Georges Rieux.

• Pierre Le Guen (1929-) joined the editorial team of *Vaillant* in 1950 after drawing *Tangor* for *OK* from 1947 to 1949. He also drew *Nasdine Hodja*. After working for various children's magazines in the 1970s, he helped establish the Five Stars Studio, where he worked on comics adaptations of Japanese animation series such as *Albator* and *Captain Fulgur*.

• Jean Ollivier (1925-) (right) was one of the major writers of *Vaillant* starting in 1947 and its editor-in-chief until 1958. In addition to *Jacques Flash*, Ollivier co-created *Yves Le Loup* (1947-66) with René Bastard, *Ragnar le Viking* with E.T. Coelho, *Davy Crockett* with Kline, *Docteur Justice* with Raphael Marcello and many other historical and adventure heroes.  Starting in 1978, he wrote historical comics for collections like *L'Histoire de France en Bandes Dessinées* [French History Through Comics] and *La Découverte du Monde en Bandes Dessinées* [Discovery of the World Through Comics]. In the 1980s, Ollivier penned several new series such as *Gavroche*, drawn by André Chéret, *Croc Blanc* [White Fang], drawn by Pham Minh Son, *La Mémoire des Celtes* [Celtic Memory] drawn by Coelho, *Fils du Dragon* [Son of the Dragon], drawn by Pierre Dupuis, and *La Nuit Barbare* [Barbarian Night], drawn by Marcello. In 1991, Ollivier succeeded Jean-Michel Charlier on *Barbe-Rouge*, drawn by Christian Gaty.

• Roger Lecureux (see *Les Pionniers de l'Espérance* entry).

• Georges Rieux (right) – no information available. Rieux wrote some prose stories featuring *Jacques Flash* for *Vaillant*.

Other creators who took over the *Jacques Flash* series include writer Pierre Castex, and artists Gerald Forton, René Deynis, Max Lenvers and Pierre Legoff.

• Pierre Castex (1924-1991) wrote *Jean & Jeanette*, drawn by Souriau, and *P'tit Joc*, drawn by André Joy, for *Vaillant*. He also created the series *Nic Reporter* in 1958 with Lina Buffolente. Castex contributed to *Le Journal de Mickey* and to *L'Histoire de France en Bandes Dessinées*.

- Gerald Forton (1931-) is the grandson of Louis Forton, creator *of Les Pieds Nickelés*. Forton started working in comics in the early 1950s, working for *Spirou* on science fiction series such as *Alain Cardan* written by Delporte and *Kim Devil* written by Charlier, and to *Vaillant* with *Jacques Flash* and the popular Western *Teddy Ted*. In the 1960s, he took over the popular *Bob Morane* series for *Pilote*. In 1976, he co-created the fantasy series *Yvain de Kanheric*, while drawing a number of comic adaptations of television series, such as *The Wild Wild West*, *Spider-Man*, etc. Forton emigrated to the United States in the early 1980s, where he has worked on a number of comic book series such as *Jonah Hex*, *Arak* (with Jean-Marc & Randy Lofficier), as well as animated television series such as *Masters of the Universe*, *BraveStarr* and others.

- René Deynis (1929-1994) joined the editorial team of *Vaillant* in 1959 and worked on *Jean & Jeanette* and *Jacques Flash*. He drew *Oscar Mittoman* for *Tintin Magazine* in 1975. In the 1980s, he joined Le Guen's Five Stars Studio.

- Max Lenvers (1933-) also began his career in *Vaillant* with *Louk Chien Loup* [*Louk Wolf Dog*] During the late 1960s and 1970s, in addition to taking over *Jacques Flash*, he also worked as an artist-reporter for *France-Soir*. In the 1980s, he joined Le Guen's Five Stars studio, while continuing a prolific career as a commercial artist.

- Pierre Legoff began his comics career in the 1960s by illustrating short stories for *Zorro*, *Hurrah* and *L'Intrépide*, also using the pen-name of Pierre Brisson. Under the pseudonym of Pol Greffiere, he drew the comics adaptation of French espionage thriller hero *Coplan FX-18* (over 3,000 strips) for the Opera Mundi syndicate. He has also worked for *Mickey*, *Vaillant* and *Tele-Junior*.

Story:

With the semi-mythological impact of characters like *Tintin* and Gaston Leroux's *Rouletabille*, the newspaper reporter became a common template for the comics heroes of the 1950s and 1960s. Journalists who fought crime, unmasked villains and protected widows and orphans included *Marc Dacier* in *Spirou*, *Guy Lebleu* in *Pilote*, *Ric Hochet* and *Guy Lefranc* in *Tintin*–and *Jacques Flash* in *Vaillant*. Jacques Flash is a French journalist working for *Les Dernières*, a newspaper edited by the bombastic but soft-hearted Gros Léon. Flash is the model investigative reporter, fearless, handsome in his trenchcoat, always ready to travel to the ends of the Earth to investigate a new mystery.

Jacques Flash drawn by Le Guen (1957)

In his first recorded adventure, Flash, with the help of bumbling police Inspector Pipard, investigates crimes seemingly committed by an invisible man. Eventually, the journalist discovers that this is the unfortunate consequence of the discovery of an invisibility drug by Professor Folven. Flash befriends the scientist and obtains a supply of invisibility pills which enable him to become a very effective crime-fighter.

The effects of Folven's invisibility drug last only for a limited amount of time, so the hero is always racing against the clock. They also do not render clothes invisible, so Flash must fight crime naked, which as one might guess, is not as easy at it seems. The hero's body outline is generally drawn by the artist to indicate his presence.

Jacques Flash's adventures involve the usual assortment of criminals, saboteurs, spies and mad scientists.

Publishing History:

Jacques Flash was originally serialized in the weekly comic magazine *Vaillant* (which became *Pif* in 1969) from 1956 to 1973. In spite of its popularity, only the first four episodes were collected in the graphic novel format by the publishers of *Vaillant*, respectively in 1960 and 1961 in their *Les Grandes Aventures [Great Adventures]* imprint. A short-lived *Jacques Flash* magazine (six issues only) was published by Jeunesses & Vacances in 1977.

Bibliography:

Except where otherwise mentioned, the *Jacques Flash* stories were usually 12-pages long, switching to 20 pages from episode 42 onward, and self-contained.
Writer: ?
Artist: Pierre Le Guen.
1. *Jacques Flash* (17 p.) (*Vaillant* Nos. 567-583, 1957)
2. *Jacques Flash contre l'Homme Invisible* [*Jacques Flash vs. The Invisible Man*] (50 p.) (*Vaillant* Nos. 584-633, 1957)
3. *Jeux de Mains, Jeux de Vilains* [*Hand Games, Evil Games*] (27 p.) (*Vaillant* Nos. 678-702, 1958) **(written by Georges Rieux)**
4. *Le Retour de l'Homme Invisible* [*The Return of the Invisible Man*] (29 p.) (*Vaillant* Nos. 710-740, 1959)

Writer: ?
Artist: Gerald Forton.
5. *Jacques Flash contre Cyrano de Bergerac* [*Jacques Flash vs. Cyrano de Bergerac*] (16 p.) (*Vaillant* Nos. 751-766, 1959-60)
6. [untitled] (10 p.) (*Vaillant* Nos. 767-776, 1960)

7. *Bagarres en Birmanie* [*Battle in Burma*] (22 p.) (*Vaillant* Nos. 777-798, 1960)
8. *Matricule 9929 FK 75* [*License Plate 9929 FK 75*] (43 p.) (*Vaillant* Nos. 799-841, 1960-61)

Writer: Pierre Castex.
Artist: René Deynis (except where otherwise indicated).
9. *Le Trésor de l'Homme Invisible* [*The Invisible Man's Treasure*] (11 p.) (*Vaillant* Nos. 878-888, 1962)
10. *Jacques Flash contre les Hommes Invisibles* [*Jacques Flash vs. the Invisible Men*] (26 p.) (*Vaillant* Nos. 910-922, 1962)
11. *Invisiblement Votre* [*Invisibly Yours*] (30 p.) (*Vaillant* Nos. 925-942, 1963)
12. *La Fiancée de l'Homme Invisible* [*The Invisible Man's Fiancée*] (32 p.) (*Vaillant* Nos. 944-960, 1963)
13. *Faites Chauffer la Colle* [*Heat Up The Glue*] (34 p.) (*Vaillant* Nos. 961-977, 1964)
14. *L'Homme Invisible Joue et Gagne* [*The Invisible Man Plays to Win*] (10 p.) (*Vaillant* No. 997, 1964)
15. *L'Homme Invisible fait des siennes* [*The Invisible Man Plays Tricks*] (63 p.) (*Vaillant* Nos. 1001-1033, 1964-65)
16. *Le Fantôme de l'Homme Invisible* [*The Ghost of the Invisible Man*] (*Vaillant* No. 1041, 1965)
17. *Jacques Flash contre 3.1416* [*Flash vs. Pi*] (*Vaillant* No. 1051, 1965)
18. *Cache-Cache Catcheur* [*Hide and Seek with a Wrestler*] (*Vaillant* No. 1046, 1965)
19. *Le Grand Chantage* [*The Big Blackmail*] (*Vaillant* No. 1061, 1965)
20. *Enlevez, c'est Pesé* [*Take It Away, It's Been Weighed*] (*Vaillant* No. 1071, 1965)
21. *Les Pirates de l'Air* [*The Air Pirates*] (*Vaillant* No. 1076, 1965)
22. *Teuf-Teuf Polka* [*Jalopy Polka*] (*Vaillant* No. 1081, 1966)
23. *Les Hercules d'Acier* [*The Steel Hercules*] (*Vaillant* No. 1090, 1966)
24. *Ballet Ballon* [*Balloon Ballet*] (*Vaillant* No. 1096, 1966)
25. *Le Gang des Tracteurs* [*The Tractor Gang*] (*Vaillant* No. 1102, 1966)
26. *Scandale chez les As* [*Scandal amongst the Aces*] (*Vaillant* No. 1118, 1966)
27. *Branle-bas chez les Radios Pirates* [*Alert amongst the Radio Pirates*] (*Vaillant* No. 1124, 1966)

Jacques Flash drawn by Deynis (1964)

28. *Les Pères Noël de l'Épouvante* [*The Terrifying Santa Clauses*] (8 p.) (*Vaillant* No. 1126, 1966)
29. *Avez-vous vu Mirza?* [*Have You Seen Mirza?*] (*Vaillant* No. 1134, 1967)

30. *Les Voyageurs du Futur* [*The Travellers from the Future*] (*Vaillant* No. 1141, 1967)
31. *Méfiez-vous des Fantômes* [*Don't Trust the Ghosts*] (*Vaillant* No. 1147, 1967)

Jacques Flash drawn by Deynis (1969)

32. *Le Grand Maître de Bornéo* [*The Master of Borneo*] (*Vaillant* No. 1153, 1967)
33. *Le Commando Libellule* [*The Dragonfly Commando*] (*Vaillant* No. 1173, 1967)
34. *Les Abominables Petits Hommes Verts* [*The Abominable Little Green Men*] (*Vaillant* No. 1179, 1967)
35. *La Marée Noire* [*The Black Tide*] (Vaillant No. 1187, 1968)
36. *Le Jour où les Dauphins* [*The Day when the Dolphins*] (*Vaillant* No. 1195, 1968)
37. *L'Etrange Safari* [*The Strange Safari*] (*Vaillant* No. 1211, 1968)
38. *Rapt en Plein Ciel* [*Skyjacking*] (*Vaillant* No. 1222, 1968)
39. *Alerte au X43* [*Alert X43*] (*Vaillant* No. 1226, 1968)
40. *Le Fantôme du Zoo* [*The Ghost of the Zoo*] (*Vaillant* No. 1230, 1968) **(drawn by Max Lenvers or Pierre Legoff?)**
41. *Les Chevaliers de l'Hélibulle* [*The Knights of the Helibubble*] (*Vaillant* No. 1237, 1969)
42. *Les Esclaves de la Forêt* [*The Slaves of the Forest*] (*Pif* No. 5, 1969)

Writer: Pierre Castex.
Artist: Max Lenvers (except where otherwise indicated).
43. *La Nuit des Vampires* [*The Night of the Vampires*] (*Pif* No. 11, 1969)
44. *La Folie des Diamants* [*The Diamond Madness*] (*Pif* No. 18, 1969)
45. *Terreur sur la Manche* [*Terror over the Channel*] (*Pif* No. 24, 1969)
46. *Aller sans Retour* [*One-Way Ticket*] (*Pif* No.31, 1969)
47. *Miracle à Colombes* [*Miracle in Colombes*] (*Pif* No. 38, 1969)
48. *Furie sur l'Or Noir* [*Black Gold Fury*] (*Pif* No. 44, 1969)
49. *La Cadena de Uro* (*Pif* No. 50, 1970)
50. *Les Disparus d'Alcatraz* [*Disappearances in Alcatraz*] (*Pif* No. 55, 1970)
51. *Le Mur des 9000 Soleils* [*The Wall of 9000 Suns*] (*Pif* No. 63, 1970)
52. *24 Heures dans l'Autre Monde* [*24 Hours in the World Beyond*] (*Pif* No. 68, 1970) **(drawn by René Deynis)**
53. *Le Mammouth du Ciel* [*The Sky Mastodon*] (*Pif* No. 73, 1970)
54. *Bien Joué, Fillette!* [*Well Played, Little Girl!*] (*Pif* No. 100, 1971)
55. *Safari à l'Héritage* [*Inheritance Safari*] (*Pif* No. 132, 1971)
56. *Nuages sur Nouakcholt* [*Clouds over Nouakcholt*] (*Pif* No. 237, 1973) **(drawn by Pierre Legoff)**

Website:
http://www.coolfrenchcomics.com/jacquesflash.htm

Super Boy (1958)

"The only man we have to fear is Super Boy!"
(Ségor – *Terre II*)

Created by:

The authors of *Super Boy* were not credited in the magazine. It is generally agreed that the first issue was written by the first wife of writer-artist Robert Bagage (see *Tom X* entry) *née* Schwarz, and drawn by artist Félix Molinari. Both Bagage and Molinari contributed stories to the series.

Felix Molinari (1931-) began his career as a comics artist with *L'Aigle des Mers* [*The Sea Eagle*] in the late 1940s, before creating the popular World War II adventure series, *Garry* in 1948. He then worked on *Super Boy* until 1970, before going into advertising and illustration. Molinari recently returned to comics to work on *Les Héritiers d'Orphée* [*Orpheus' Heirs*] in 1992 and *Les Tigres Volants* [*The Flying Tigers*] in 1994.

Super Boy (1959)

Super Boy No. 123 (1959)

Story:

The French Super Boy (two words) owes nothing to DC Comics' adventures of *Superman* as a boy. Instead, he is the son of a scientist who protects Earth against supervillains and various extraterrestrial threats. The world in which he lives is a vaguely futuristic Earth, but not so advanced as to be too strange or too alien to the reader.

Super Boy is a resourceful, highly intelligent young man who uses super-science to solve the mysteries he encounters, or defeat the aliens who invariably threaten the planet. He has no specific superpowers and his exploits are reminiscent of those of the DC character *Adam Strange*, a comparison bolstered by his helmet (sporting an antenna instead of a fin) and the two belt rockets enabling him to fly.

Most of Super Boy's gadgetry appears to have been designed by his uncle Matt, a bearded scientist who lives at Peak House and resembles the Chief of *The Doom Patrol*. Super Boy has a younger sister, Rochelle, who lives with Uncle Matt, but plays little part in his adventures.

Unlike the elaborate universes of characters and concepts assembled in American comics, Super Boy's world is relatively simple and unsophisticated. The ever-present threat of censorship prevented the creation of a rogues' gallery worthy of fighting the hero. The stories are almost always self-contained. The villains (The Harlequin, Mister Cat, Delta, Earth-II) rarely, if ever, return. There are virtually no developed cast of supporting characters, and no evolution of any kind. The plots are often clever, but more like what one would expect from *The Twilight Zone* or *The Outer Limits*.

Super Boy wore two different chest logos: first, a yellow "SB" inside a triangle; then the SB in white against a black circle. No explanations were given for that change.

Publishing History:

One of the longest-lasting French superhero series was *Super Boy*, published as a digest-sized, black & white comic magazine by Imperia. Curiously, Imperia launched a magazine entitled *Super Boy* in October 1949, without a feature entitled *Super Boy* in it. The eponymous character only made his first appearance in No. 112 published in December 1958.

New stories drawn mostly by Molinari, appeared without any interruption until No. 247 in 1970. From that point onward, the magazine began to publish a mix of reprints and new

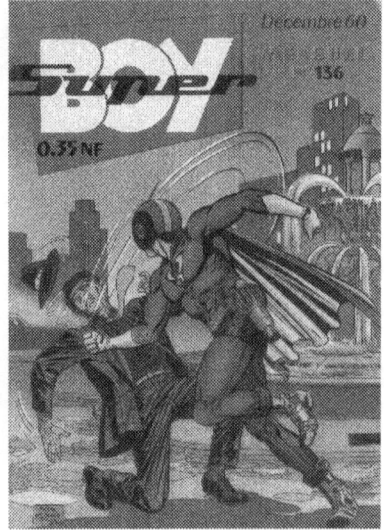

stories, drawn by Spanish artists Rafael Mendez, José Maria Ortiz and Jaime Forns. The magazine was eventually discontinued with No. 402 in May 1986, when Bagage retired and shut Imperia down.

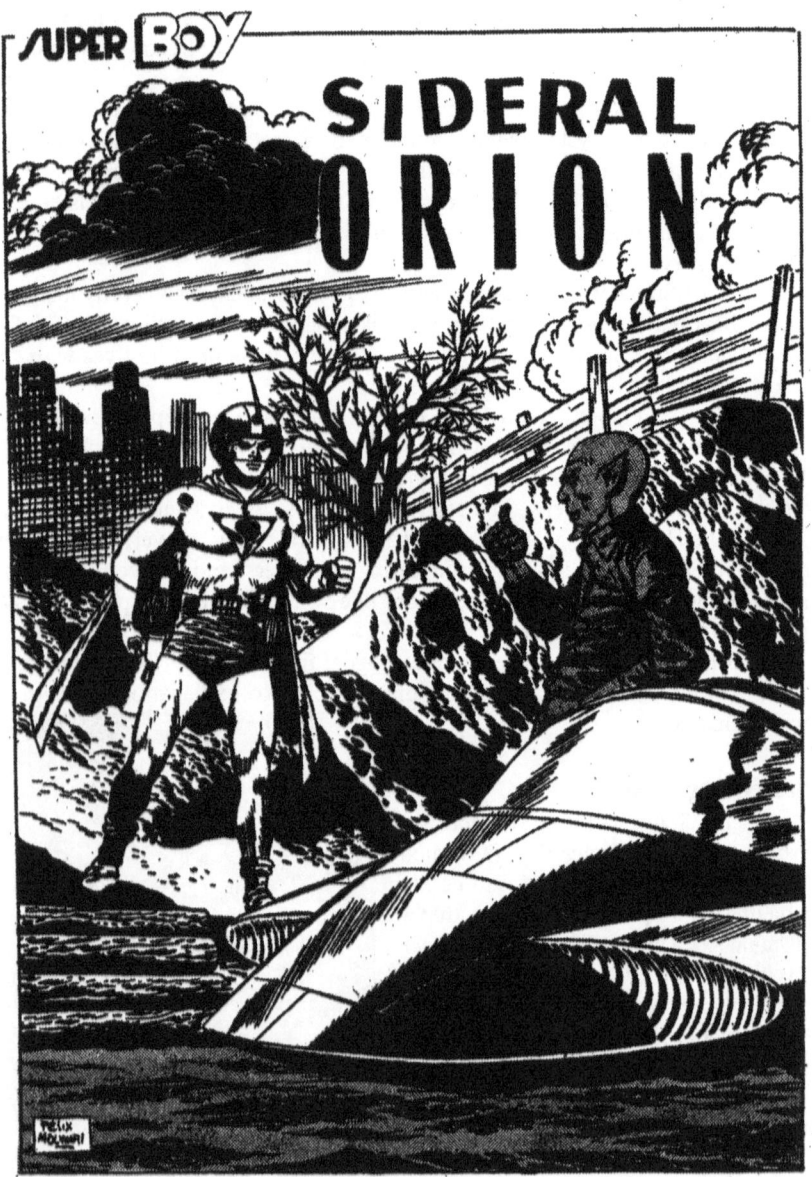

Super Boy No. 136 (1960)

Bibliography:

112. *Contre 100.000 Dollars* [*For $100,000*] (1958)
113-114. *Panique à Death Valley* [*Panic in Death Valley*] (1959)
115. *Prisonniers de l'Izalco* [*Prisoners of the Izalco*] (1959)
116. *La Voix sans Visage* [*The Voice Without A Face*] (1959)
117. *Le Chiffonnier de Candle Street* [*The Ragman of Candle St.*] (1959)
118. *Les Inconnus du Désert Rouge* [*The Unknown Men of the Red Desert*] (1959)
119. *Station Rapace ne répond plus!* [*Station Hawk Doesn't Answer!*] (1959)
120. *La Fin du Nouka Kéa* [*The End of Nouka Kea*] (1959)
121. *Ce Sympathique Mr. Morroway* [*That Nice Mr. Morroway*] (1959)
122. *Passage pour Karachi* [*Passage for Karachi*] (1959)
123. *Le Tombeau sous la Mer* [*The Underwater Tomb*] (1959)
124-125. *Un Oeil dans le Ciel* [*An Eye in the Sky*] (1959)
126. *Victime de l'Espace* [*Victim of Space*] (1960)
127. *Manoeuvres en Haute-Mer* [*High Seas Maneuvers*] (1960)
128 & 129. ?
130. *Menace sur la Terre* [*Menace on Earth*] (1960)
131. *Menaces sur l'Alaska* [*Menace in Alaska*] (1960)
132. *Les Chemins du Ciel* [*The Pathways of Space*] (1960)
133. *Pêche aux Diamants* [*Fishing for Diamonds*] (1960)
134-135. *Contact Terre* [*Contact Earth*] (1960)
136. *Sidéral Orion* [*Sideral Orion*] (1960)
137-138. *Un Missile a Disparu* [*A Missile Has Vanished*] (1961)
139. *Brouillard sur Sandsfield Forest* [*Fog Over Sandsfield Forest*] (1961)
140. *Les Zantas* [*The Zantas*] (1961)
141. *Distance 4,3 Années Lumière* [*Distance 4.3 Light Years*] (1961)
142. *Bas les Masques* [*Masks Off*] (1961)
143. *Le Bal de l'Araignée* [*The Spider's Ball*] (1961)
144. *L'Homme aux Ballons Rouges* [*The Man With the Red Balloons*] (1961)
145. *Opération Argos* [*Operation Argos*] (1961)
146. *Les Survivants* [*The Survivors*] (1961)
147. *Le Domaine des Ombres* [*The Domain of Shadows*] (1961)
148. *Les Explorateurs du Temps* [*The Time Explorers*] (1961)
149. *Le Frisson des Abimes* [*The Shiver of the Abyss*] (1962)

Super Boy No. 136 (1960)

150. *Danger... Virus!* [*Danger... Virus!*] (1962)

151. *Attractions Dangereuses* [*Dangerous Attractions*] (1962)
152. *L'Apprenti-Sorcier* [*The Sorcerer's Apprentice*] (1962)
153. *Fortune en Bouteille* [*Fortune in a Bottle*] (1962)
154. *Complot dans l'Ombre* [*Conspiracy in the Shadows*] (1962)
155. *D'Origine Inconnue* [*Of Unknown Origin*] (1962)
156. *Les Monstres des Abimes* [*The Monsters of the Abyss*] (1962)
157. *Témoin Gênant* [*Embarrassing Witness*] (1962)
158. *Chasse aux Requins* [*Shark Hunt*] (1962)
159. *Tel est pris...* [*Backfire*] (1962)
160. *Le Sérum de Vérité* [*The Truth Serum*] (1962)
161. *Les Pirates de l'Espace* [*The Space Pirates*] (1963)
162. *Les Fils du Soleil* [*The Sons of the Sun*] (1963)
163. *Le Mur de Cristal* [*The Crystal Wall*] (1963)
164. *Piège dans les Algues* [*The Algae Trap*] (1963)
165. *Le Génie Destructeur* [*The Destroyer Genius*] (1963)
166. *Poupées Vivantes* [*Living Dolls*] (1963)
167. *Un Vol Audacieux* [*A Daring Robbery*] (1963)
168. *Les Faux et les Vrais* [*The False and the True*] (1963)
169. *Super Boy, Chirurgien de la Mécanique* [*Super Boy, Machine Surgeon*] (1963)
170-171. *La Lettre* [*The Letter*] (1963)
172. *Affaire Classée* [*Closed Case*] (1963)
173. *Le Laser* [*The Laser*] (1964)
174. *Menace sur la Ville* [*Menace in the City*] (1964)
175. *Une Invention Diabolique* [*A Diabolical Invention*] (1964)
176. *Le Météore de la Nuit* [*The Night Meteor*] (1964)
177. *Une Incroyable Histoire* [*An Incredible Story*] (1964)
178. *Le Miroir de l'Espace* [*The Space Mirror*] (1964)
179. *Un Certain Mr. Gardner* [*A Certain Mr. Gardner*] (1964)
180. *La Souricière* [*The Mousetrap*] (1964)
181. *Prisonniers de l'Enfer Vert* [*Prisoners of the Green Hell*] (1964)
182. *Le Monstre des Ténèbres* [*The Monster of Darkness*] (1964)
183. *L'Edelweiss* [*The Edelweiss*] (1964)
184. *Le Trésor des Abimes* [*The Treasure of the Abyss*] (1964)

Super Boy's Uncle Matt and sister Rochelle (1967)

185. *Les Statues de Glace* [*The Ice Statues*] (1965)
186. *Le Rayon Diabolique* [*The Diabolical Ray*] (1965)

187. *Arme Absolue* [*Absolute Weapon*] (1965)
188. *Les Pélerins de l'Espace* [*The Space Pilgrims*] (1965)
189. *Les Hommes des Neiges* [*The Snow-Men*] (1965)
190. *Station ATAFU ne répond plus* [*Station ATAFU Doesn't Answer*] (1965)
191. *Le Secret sous les Sables* [*The Secret Beneath the Sands*] (1965)
192. *Super Boy, je vous arrête!* [*Super Boy, You're Under Arrest!*] (1965)
193. *Menace sur New York* [*Menace in New York*] (1965)
194. *Super Boy, Assurance Évasion* [*Super Boy, Escape Insurance*] (1965)
195. *Le Retour d'Arlequin* [*The Harlequin Returns*] (1965)
196. *L'Homme Invisible* [*The Invisible Man*] (1965)
197. *Super Boy contre Delta* [*Super Boy vs. Delta*] (1966)
198. *La Barrière Invisible* [*The Invisible Barrier*] (1966)
199. *Ultrasons* [*Ultrasounds*] (1966)
200. *Panique dans la Pègre* [*Panic in the Underworld*] (1966)
201. *Mister Cat* (1966)
202. *L'ACX-20* (1966)
203. *Recrutements* [*Recruiting*] (1966)
204. *Attentat contre le Président* [*Attack on the President*] (1966)
205-206. *Le Dernier Inca* [*The Last Inca*] (1966)
207. ?
208. *Encore le Cachalot!* [*The Sperm Whale Again!*] (1966)

Super Boy No. 218 (1967)

209. ?
210. Rapt à l'O.N.U. [Kidnapping at the U.N.] (1967)
211. Super Boy contre le Commando Vert [Super Boy vs. the Green Commando] (1967)
212. Chasse aux Spectres [Spectral Hunt] (1967)
213 & 214. ?
215. Le Bateau Fantôme [The Ghost Ship] (1967)
216 & 217. ?
218. Terre II [Earth II] (1967)
219. Coup Dur au Nevada [Hard Luck in Nevada] (1967)
220. Du Travail en Série [Serial Tasks] (1967)
221. Le Secret du V-37 [The Secret of the V-37] (1968)
222. Un Projet Presque Oublié [An Almost Forgotten Project] (1968)
223. Le Cobra [The Cobra] (1968)
224. Attentats à Los Angeles [Attacks in Los Angeles] (1968)
225. Le Brouillard du Sommeil [The Fog of Slumber] (1968)
226-228. ?
229. Mystère dans le Pacifique [Mystery in the Pacific] (1968)
230-232. ?
233. La Grotte Infernale [The Infernal Cavern] (1969)
234. ?
235. Le Bouc Émissaire [The Scapegoat] (1969)
236. Le Libérateur Mental [The Mental Liberator] (1969)
237. Les Pillards [The Looters] (1969)
238. La Doublure du Champion [The Champion's Stand-In] (1969)
239. La Vérité [The Truth] (1969)
240 & 241. ?
242. L'Etranger [The Stranger] (1969)
243. Le Mauvais Côté [The Bad Side] (1969)
244. Black contre Black [Black vs. Black] (1969)
245. Les Micro-Radars [The Micro-Radar] (1970)
246. Cataclysme [Cataclysm] (1970)
247. Au Risque de sa Vie [At His Life's Peril] (1970)

Note: From this point onward, *Super Boy* began to mix reprints with new stories drawn by Spanish artists. We have identified new titles (which may be reprints of previous, unidentified issues?) whenever possible.

248. *L'Homme qui Voulait Noyer la Terre* [*The Man Who Wanted to Drown the Earth*] (1970)
249. *Boomerang* (1970)
250. *Les Amphibies* [*The Amphibians*] (1970)
251. *Opération Haut Rayon* [*Operation High Ray*] (1970)
252. *Touriste d'Honneur* [*Tourist of Honor*] (1970)
253. *Le Grand Chantage* [*The Big Blackmail*] (1970)
254. *Pirates de l'Air* [*The Air Pirates*] (1970)
255. *Le Collier Royal* [*The Royal Necklace*] (1970)
256. *Un Monde Fantastique* [*A Fantastic World*] (1970)

257. *Le Grand Tourbillon* [*The Great Maelstrom*] (1971)
258. *Le Vol des Robots* [*Flight of the Robots*] (1971)
259. *Le Gladiator* (1971)
260. *Vent Divin* [*Divine Wind*] (1971)
261. *Au Coeur du Volcan* [*At the Heart of the Volcano*] (1971)
262-268. Reprints
269. *Les Fantômes de l'Espace* [*The Space Ghosts*] (1972)

270. *Le Clown Fantôme* [*The Phantom Clown*] (1972)
271. *Rebellion* (1972)
272. *La Terre des Géants* [*The Land of Giants*] (1972)
273. *La Planète Bleue* [*The Blue Planet*] (1972)
274. *Moloch et les 7 Nains* [*Moloch & the 7 Dwarves*] (1972)
275. *Les Gorilles Noirs* [*The Black Gorillas*] (1972)
276. *Les Inférieurs* [*The Inferiors*] (1972)
277. *Désert Fou* [*Mad Desert*] (1972)
278. *Le Génie du Mal* [*The Evil Genius*] (1972)
279. *Méprise* [*Misunderstanding*] (1972)
280. Reprint
281. *Une Partie Dangereuse* [*A Dangerous Game*] (1973)
282. *Le Froid du Délire* [*The Coldness of Delirium*] (1973)
283 & 284. Reprints
285. *Base 1* (1973)
286. *Un Enfant et un Ballon* [*The Child and his Balloon*] (1973)
287-299. Reprints
300. *Onda Star* (1974)
301-303. Reprints
304. *Le Maître du Temps* [*The Time Master*] (1974)
305. Reprint
306. *Les Hommes Verts* [*The Green Men*] (1975)

307-315. Reprints
316. *Accusés au Nom de l'Humanité* [*Accused in the Name of Mankind*] (1975)
317. *L'Homme à Abattre* [*The Man to Kill*] (1976)
318-323. Reprints
324. *Le Gorille* [*The Gorilla*] (1976)
325. *Le Tyuni* [*The Tyuni*] (1976)
326. *Le Requin* [*The Shark*] (1976)
327-344. Reprints
344. *Orphée Vert* [*Green Orpheus*] (1978)
345-347. Reprints
348. *Les Vampires d'Acier* [*The Steel Vampires*] (1978)
349-351. Reprints
352. *Race de Géants* [*The Race of Giants*) (1979)

353-362. Reprints
363. *Question d'Honneur* [*A Question of Honour*] (1979)
364-371. Reprints
372. *Hors du Temps* [*Beyond Time*] (1980)
373-379. Reprints
380. *Le Nuage Écarlate* [*The Scarlet Cloud*] (1981)
381. Reprint
382. *L'Ile du Fou* [*Madman's Island*] (1981)
383-393. Reprints
394. *W-3 Répondez* [*W-3 Answer*] (1984)
395. *Des Jouets Étranges* [*Strange Toys*] (1985)
396. Reprints
397. *Jakson Wong* (1985)
398. *Les Chasseurs de la Kill-Co* [*The Hunters from Kill-Co*] (1985)
399. *Le Piège Okéïdo* [*The Okeido Trap*] (1985)
400. *Services Spéciaux* [*Special Services*] (1986)
401. *Tanaka, Ville Morte* [*Tanaka, Dead City*] (1986)
402. *Xurus 1* (1986)

Website:
http://www.coolfrenchcomics.com/superboy.htm

Le Semble-Lune (1977)

Barbarella (1962)

"An Angel has no memory."
(Pygar to Barbarella – *Barbarella*)

Created by:

Writer-artist Jean-Claude Forest. Jean-Claude Forest (1930-1998) was one of France's most talented comic book artists, as well as a distinguished writer and editor. Born in a Parisian suburb in 1930, Forest graduated from the Paris School of Design, and began working as an illustrator in the early 1950s. His first comic strip, *Flèche Noire* [*Black Arrow*], was drawn while in art school. He went on to publish *Le Vaisseau Hanté* [*The Haunted Ship*] and contribute covers to many French newspapers and magazines, including *France-Soir*, *Les Nouvelles Littéraires* and *Fiction*, the French edition of *F & SF*. During that period, Forest became the premier cover artist of the then-leading French science-fiction paperback imprint, *Le Rayon Fantastique*, illustrating novels by Catherine L. Moore, A.E. Van Vogt, Jack Williamson, William Sloane and others. He also drew several issues of the popular *Charlot* comic book series, loosely based on Charlie Chaplin's *Little Tramp*.

Forest became world-famous when he created the character of *Barbarella* in 1962. *Barbarella* was an immediate runaway bestseller and was soon translated in a dozen countries. Not long after, it was adapted into a major motion picture. Forest's comic book career also included several other colorful comic book series: *Bébé Cyanure* [*Baby Cyanide*] (1964), the Jules Verne-inspired *Mystérieuse Matin, Midi et Soir* (1971), and the madcap adventures of a younger version of Barbarella, *Hypocrite* (1971) as well as more serious works, such as *La Jonque Fantôme Vue de l'Orchestre* [*The Phantom Junk As Seen From The Orchestra*] (1981) and *Enfants, C'est l'Hydragon qui Passe* [*Children, Watch The Hydragon Go By*] (1984).

Forest wrote scripts for several of France's most gifted comic artists: *Les Naufragés du Temps* [*Castaways in Time*] for Paul Gillon (1964), *Ici Même* [*Same Here*] for Jacques Tardi (1979), *Le Roman de Renart* [*The Novel of Renart*] for Max Cabanes (1985), *Leonid Beaudragon* for Didier Savard (1986) and *Il Faut y Croire pour le Voir* [*You Must Believe It To See It*] for Alain Bignon (1996). Forest also penned a 1983 juvenile fantasy novel, *Lilia entre l'Air et l'Eau* [*Lilia Between Air and Water*], and a number of scripts for French television. In recognition of his talent, he was awarded the Grand Prize at the 1984 Angoulême Comics Festival, and in 1986 in Sierre (Switzerland). He was honored with a French postage stamp in 1989.

Prior to creating Barbarella, Forest illustrated Catherine L. Moore's Shambleau in 1955 for V-Magazine.

The science fiction art of Jean-Claude Forest

First appearance of Barbarella (1962)

Story:

The first saga of Barbarella is comprised of eight episodes. The young heroine is introduced as a space wanderer in a solar system far from Earth. Crash-landing on planet Lythion, she becomes involved in a war between the Crystallians, who inhabit a giant greenhouse, and the barbaric Orhomrs, who live in the frozen wasteland outside. With a little bit of love, she prompts them to make peace with each other. While attempting to leave Lythion, Barbarella is hijacked by a race of undersea people led by Medusa, who steals Barbarella's likeness.

From that point, her adventures take her through the den of Strickno, the sadistic hunter, and the icy region of Yesteryear, which has patterned its civilization after Earth's 19th century. Traveling via underground mechanical mole, Barbarella eventually reaches the realm of Sogo, ruled by the sadistic Black Queen. The last four episodes are entirely devoted to Barbarella's battle against the Queen, and her final victory over Sogo's evil.

In *Les Colères du Mange-Minutes* [*The Wrath of the Minute-Eater*] (a nickname for Time), Barbarella is now in charge of the Galactic Delirium Circus, which journeys from planet to planet in the spaceship Big Bug. Having fallen in love with her latest acquisition, a handsome merman named Narval, Barbarella takes him to the planet Spectra, which exists in a time zone slower than the rest of the universe. There, she discovers that Narval has deceived her, and intends to conquer Spectra for his own people.

Barbarella encounters a princess whose fate is linked to a pack of magic Tarot cards, pirates who travel on flying kites, green-haired amazons, arctic people living inside giant chickens, a beautiful female android and the Black Queen of Sogo in a time-traveling Eiffel Tower!

Barbarella (1962)

Les Colères du Mange-Minutes (1968)

In *Le Semble-Lune* [*The False Moon*], Barbarella explores a dream dimension and marries a planetary master-architect named Browningwell (who resembles Forest). She has a baby–Little Fox. Barbarella also serves as the model for a giant space-sculpture.

The final volume, *Le Miroir aux Tempêtes* [*The Storm Mirror*] is a complex time-travel adventure in which a man-fish, who lives 360,000 years in the future, observes events from the past in order to amuse himself.

In a spin-off graphic novel entitled *Mystérieuse, Matin, Midi et Soir* [*Mysterious, Morning, Noon and Evening*], patterned after Jules Verne's *Mysterious Island*, Professor Alizarine and his friends find themselves shipwrecked on a question mark-shaped island on an alien planet. As in the Verne novel, the heroes are always aided by a mysterious unseen figure. At the book's end, the reader discovers that this Captain Nemo-like presence is an older Barbarella!

The characters eventually reappeared in another of the adventures of *Hypocrite*, thus helping to form the tapestry of a vast, intertwined Forest universe.

Publishing History:

Forest created the character of *Barbarella* for *V-Magazine* in 1962. Two years later, French publisher Eric Losfeld, who specialized in fantasy and erotic literature, offered to collect the stories in book form. Published in 1964, the graphic album was a phenomenal success. It quickly sold more than 200,000 copies, despite the censors' ruling that the book could not be publicly displayed. For the sequel, *Les Colères du Mange-Minutes* [*The Wrath of the Minute-Eater*], since Forest didn't want to be typecast as an erotic artist, he emphasized elements of science fiction and poetry, but that shift in style was a mistake from a commercial standpoint.

Mystérieuse was first serialized in *Pif* in 1971; *Barbarella* then returned in 1977. For the last book, *Le Miroir aux Tempêtes* [*The Storm Mirror*], published in 1982, Forest entrusted the art to Daniel Billon.

Jean-Claude Forest on the creation of Barbarella

George H. Gallet, the editor of the science-fiction imprint *Le Rayon Fantastique* for which I was drawing covers, was also in charge of a quarterly adult publication called *V-Magazine*. One day, he asked me if I wanted to do a strip for him—no holds barred! We were then living in a time of complete censorship in the comics. In fact, that's why I was doing mostly illustrations and book covers. Everything was forbidden, and in particular, the female form. Fantasy was also frowned upon, because it was felt that it would corrupt the morals of children.

Gallet had asked me to do a kind of female *Tarzan*, *Tarzella*, but that idea didn't particularly interest me. It led me to come up with *Barbarella*. For the next two years, at the rate of eight pages every three months, I told her adventures, going with the flow of inspiration, without any pre-planning.
(Starlog No. 92, March 1985, Randy & J.-M. Lofficier)

Bibliography:
Writer-artist: Jean-Claude Forest.
Barbarella (*V-Magazine*, 1962; rep. Eric Losfeld, 1964)
Les Colères du Mange-Minutes [*The Wrath of the Minute-Eater*] (drawn 1968; pub. Kesselring, 1974)
Mystérieuse, Matin, Midi et Soir [*Mysterious, Morning, Noon and Evening*] (*Pif*, 1971; rep. Serg, 1972)
Le Semble-Lune [*The False Moon*] (Horay, 1977)

Writer: Jean-Claude Forest.
Artist: Daniel Billon.
Le Miroir aux Tempêtes [*The Storm Mirror*] (Albin Michel, 1982)

Barbarella, Husband and Son from Le Miroir aux Tempêtes (1982)

Film:
Barbarella (color, 98 min., 1967)
Dir: Roger Vadim; *Wri*: Terry Southern, Jean-Claude Forest, Roger Vadim, Vittorio Bonicelli, Brian Degas, Claude Brule, Tudor Gates, Clement Biddle Wood; based on the graphic novel by Jean-Claude Forest.
Cast: Jane Fonda (Barbarella), John Philip Law (Pygar), Anita Pallenberg (Black Queen), Milo O'Shea, Marcel Marceau, Ugo Tognazzi, David Hemmings, Claude Dauphin.

Jean-Claude Forest on the Barbarella motion picture

One of producer Dino De Laurentiis' agents happened to be in France. It was a woman who had read and liked the book, then proposed it to De Laurentiis. He bought the rights and offered the role to Jane Fonda. According to what her then-husband, director Roger Vadim, told me, her first reaction was to throw it in the garbage can, saying that this kind of thing wasn't for her! Vadim corrected her, saying that, on the contrary, it was extremely interesting, and that something original and exciting could be done with the subject. Vadim was interested himself. I believe that, even today, notwithstanding the audience response, Vadim still defends *Barbarella*. He says that it's one of the films that he found the most interesting to shoot.

The fact is: When I was on the set, Vadim was always there. Everybody kept telling me that this was incredible. Apparently, he rarely involves himself with the day-to-day production. With Barbarella, he was always there on time, and he was the one saying, "Action!" Therefore, I believe that it did interest him.

I worked eight months on the picture. I was completely involved in the set design. At that time, I didn't care about my strip, what really interested me was the movie business. The Italian artists were incredible; they could build anything in an extremely short time. I saw all the daily rushes, an incredible amount of film. The choices that were made for the final cut from those images were not the ones I would have liked, but I was not the director. It wasn't my affair.
(Starlog No. 92, March 1985, Randy & J.-M. Lofficier)

Barbarella motion picture (1967)

Websites:
http://www.hollywoodcomics.com/forest.html
http://membres.lycos.fr/angel/Barbarella/

Alain Landier (1962)

"Was it a dream? Or did I really travel up there? But where?"
(Alain Landier – *Les Inconnus*)

Created by:

Writer-artist Albert Weinberg. Albert Weinberg (1922-) began his comics career by working as an assistant to artist Victor Hubinon (*Buck Danny*) on *Tarawa*, a book devoted to the War in the Pacific. He also assisted Joseph Gillain (Jijé) on *Blondin & Cirage*. From 1949 to 1956, Weinberg wrote and drew two series for *Heroic-Albums*: *Luc Condor* and the science fiction hero *Roc Meteor*. Weinberg joined the editorial team of *Tintin* in 1950, for which he created two series, *Dan Cooper* (1954), the story of a test pilot in  the Canadian Air Force, and *Alain Landier* (1952). Another character Weinberg created for *Tintin* was blonde tour guide *Vicky* in 1970. (Dan Cooper later met Vicky in the story *L'Affaire Minos*.) In the early stories, Cooper became involved in futuristic attempts at space exploration, and led the first space mission to reach the satellites of Mars. Later stories became more grounded in present-day events, but occasional episodes would pit Cooper against mysterious blue-skinned humanoids observing Earth from space.

Story:

Alain Landier is first introduced as a world-famous surgeon. The first ten episodes form a complete story in which he is abducted by mysterious, pale-skinned aliens to perform delicate brain surgery on one of their own. The aliens leave Landier with a chunk of space rock that leads him to join an expedition organized by his geologist friend, Marc, deep inside Earth's crust. After his adventures beneath the surface of the Earth, Landier is recontacted by the aliens and taken aboard a flying saucer to Phebea, a hollow, artificial world where the survivors of a long-destroyed planet now reside. Some of the Phebeans would like to relocate to Earth, but Landier discovers that they could not survive in our non-sterile environment. A handful of Phebeans nevertheless land in the Amazon, but die as Landier had predicted.

Upon his return from Phebea, Landier grew a beard. The rest of the series was comprised of self-contained stories in which Landier, now behaving more like a polymath and an archeologist than a brain surgeon, and his friend Marc, compiled an *X-Files*-like record of strange encounters around the globe: a prehistoric monster, strange light creatures from a returning Venus probe, ancient astronauts, an Inca mummy coming back to life, etc.

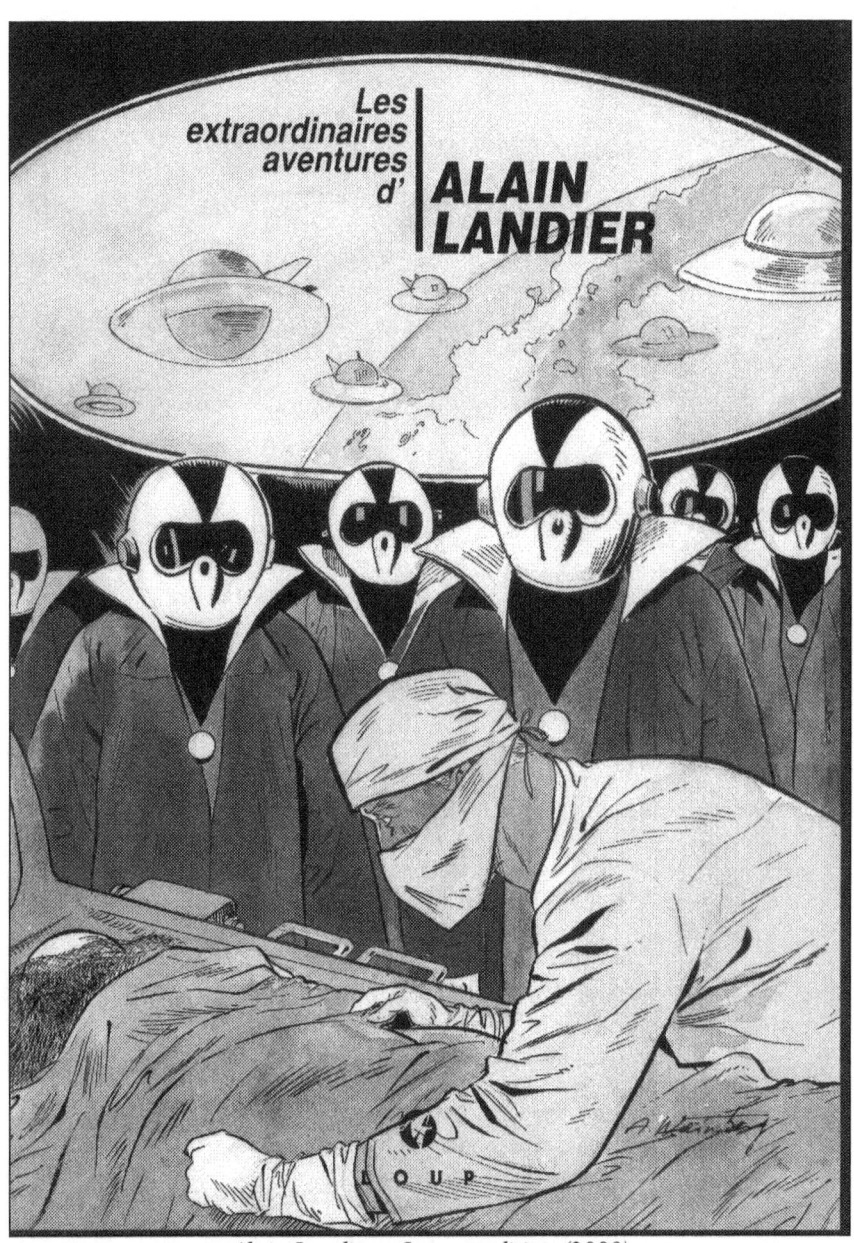

Alain Landier – Loup reedition (2000)

Publishing History:

Alain Landier was published as a series of short stories (8 to 12 pages-long) in the weekly *Tintin* magazine from 1962 to 1970. The stories were collected in two graphic novels by Belgian publisher Loup in 2000 and 2001.

Bibliography:
1. *Les Inconnus* [The Unknown Men] (*Tintin* No. 701, 1962)
2. *L'Algue Mystérieuse* [The Mysterious Algae] (*Tintin* No. 710, 1962)
3. *Exploration Fantastique* [Fantastic Exploration] (*Tintin* No. 711, 1962)
4. *Les Naufragés des Ténèbres* [The Castaways in Darkness] (*Tintin* No. 715, 1962)
5. *Le Messager d'un Autre Monde* [The Messenger From Another World] (*Tintin* No. 719, 1962)
6. *Les Naufragés de l'Espace* [The Castaways in Space] (*Tintin* No. 726, 1962)
7. *La Planète Insolite* [The Strange Planet] (*Tintin* No. 732, 1962)
8. *Les Emigrants du Cosmos* [The Immigrants of the Cosmos] (*Tintin* No. 738, 1962)
9. *Les Cobayes* [The Guinea Pigs] (*Tintin* No. 744, 1963)
10. *Danger en Amazonie* [Danger in Amazonia] (*Tintin* No. 751, 1963)
11. *Le Dinosaure* [The Dinosaur] (*Tintin* No. 765, 1963)
12. *Les Champignons* [The Mushrooms] (*Tintin* No. 770, 1963)
13. *Le Calendrier de Pierre* [The Stone Calendar] (*Tintin* No. 776, 1963)
14. *Le Voyageur de l'Espace* [The Space Traveller] (*Tintin* No. 783, 1963)
15. *Les Pierres de Lune* [The Moon Stones] (*Tintin* No. 790, 1963)
16. *Cauchemar* [Nightmare] (*Tintin* No. 803, 1964)
17. *Le Primate* (*Tintin* No. 810, 1964)
18. *L'Homme Volant* [The Flying Man] (*Tintin* No. 817, 1964)
19. *La Momie* [The Mummy] (*Tintin* No. 995, 1967)
20. *Les Lumières de Vénus* [The Lights of Venus] (*Tintin* No. 1022, 1968)
21. *Le Monstre* [The Monster] (*Tintin* No. 1108, 1970)

Websites:
http://www.coolfrenchcomics.com/alainlandier.htm
http://www.coolfrenchcomics.com/dancooper.htm

La Momie (1967)

Zembla No. 1 (1963)

Zembla (1963)

"Zembla does not kill; he saves"
(Zembla – *La Loi de la Jungle*)

Created by:

Zembla was created in 1963 at the initiative of Marcel Navarro (see *Fantax* entry), publisher and editor-in-chief of Editions Lug, to compete with the highly successful pseudo-*Tarzan*, *Akim*, published by his competitor, Editions Aventures & Voyages. *Akim* had been created in 1950 by writer Robert Renzi and artist Augusto Pedrazza for the Italian magazine *Albo Gioiello* and was published in France in an eponymous small format title which started in 1958.

The writer of the very first episode of *Zembla* is unknown, but most of the Italian writers working for Lug at the time wrote episodes of the series. That list includes Cesare Solini, Attilio Mazzanti and Maurizio Torelli.

The first episode of *Zembla* was drawn by *Akim* artist Augusto Pedrazza, but not being able to juggle the workload of two popular series, Pedrazza had to bow out and the task was delegated to artists Franco and Fausto Oneta, who from that point on, remained the main artists and creators of *Zembla*, with a few, occasional fill-in artists.

• Augusto Pedrazza (1923-1994) began his career in comics in 1943. Among his early creations were *Jean Bolide* and *La Dama di Picche* [*The Queen of Spades*]. In 1948, he began working for publisher Marino Tomasina, for whom he co-created numerous series including: *Pierino* (1948), *Kid Meteora* (1949), *Scugnizzo* (1949), *Piccolo Corsaro* (1950), *Akim* (1950), *Il Principe Nero* (1950), *Lazo Jim* (1951), *Fulgor* (1952), *Virgola* (1953), *Tabor* (1954), *Tony Comet* (1954), *Dinamite Kid* (1957) and *Guingla Bill* (1958).

• Franco Oneta (1934-) is an Italian artist who began his comics career in 1949 at Giurleo with *Trottolino*. He then worked for Messagero dei Ragazzi for which he co-created *Anacleto*, *Spiritello*, *Robin Poot* and *Pallino*, before working for Lug on *Zembla* and a number of other series, including *Galaor*, *Ozark* and *Motoman*. More recently, Oneta worked for *Il Giornalino* for which he drew comic adaptations of animated series such as *Snorky*, *Scooby-Doo* and *Yogi Bear*. His brother, Fausto, also worked for Lug on series such as *Akewa* and *Yatan*.

Story:

Zembla is virtually identical to *Akim*, except for his long hair, and is one of the numerous *Tarzan* "clones" created in the 1940s and 1950s to cash in on the popularity of Edgar Rice Burroughs' creation.

In the first episode, we are introduced to Zembla, a powerfully-built jungle lord who has the ability to communicate with the various beasts of the jungle. Zembla speaks pidgin of the "me Tarzan you Jane" variety, a stylistic approach that eventually was allowed to disappear. His pet is a white lion named Bwana. During the course of his first adventures, Zembla defeats a would-be rival gorilla, Grinka, and acquires a boy sidekick, Kenny, stranded in the jungle.

Zembla and Kenny – Art by Pedrazza (1963)

Kenny soon disappears and is replaced by two far more colorful sidekicks. The first is a grouchy and inept *Mandrake*-like circus magician named Rasmus, whom Zembla rescues in the first episode of his own title. The other is a young, somewhat reckless African teenager nicknamed Yeye, who wears an MP helmet. On the animal front, Bwana the lion is supplemented by Petoulet the kangaroo (don't ask) and Satanas, an irritable, wild cat-like beast of unknown origins. A recurring character is the beautiful African Queen Takuba who might see Zembla as more than a mere friend. This cast of characters remains unchanged over the life of the series.

Zembla's adventures pit him not only against ordinary villains but also a host of mad scientists, would-be world conquerors, super-powered adversaries, intelligent gorillas and lost races. His origins were finally revealed in 1972. It turned out that Zembla's real name is Pierre Marais. He is the only child of Paul

Marais, a French adventurer seeking his fortune in Africa. Paul was forced to flee into the jungle to escape the police after a tragic barroom brawl. Injured, he was rescued by a secretive tribe. Paul then fell in love with Ula, the tribal princess. Unfortunately, Ula's father, King Naghar, wanted his daughter to marry Prince Thudor, so Ula and Paul had no choice but escape. Eventually, their son, Zembla, was born.

Paul Marais and Ula – Art by Oneta (1972)

However, an enraged Thudor, bent by jealous rage, managed to find the two lovers, and killed them both. Thudor would have also murdered their baby boy, if a lioness whose cub he had previously killed for fun, had not lept to his throat. Once Thudor was dead, his men ran back to the village. The baby was then raised by the Lions and became known as Zem-Bla, meaning the Lion-Child in the language of the lions. Raised amongst the Lions, young Zem-Bla (soon known as Zembla) eventually saved the life of a young white lion, who became his faithful companion, Bwana.

Baby Zembla raised by the Lions – Art by Oneta (1972)

Zembla has the ability to speak the languages of all the animals in the jungle, and is stronger, taller and more powerful than the average man. He knows many of the secrets of the jungle, especially that of an herb called *wascian* that has the power to heal injuries.

In a new series of adventures written in 2000, Zembla was modernized. He was shown to care deeply for his native land, now dubbed the African republic of Karunda. He is concerned about the constant encroachement of the modern world: poachers, trafficants of all kinds, slavers, guerillas from neighboring states and oil drillers. In particular, since Karunda is home to the mystical Mount Damuin, which contains untold mineral wealth as well as a strange, mystical gateway to other dimensions. (Some of these concepts were taken from two of the other jungle series published by Lug, *Tanka* and *Yatan*.)

The new Zembla uses his considerable wealth to fund a Greenpeace-like ecological taskforce under United Nations control, which monitors, investigates and, if necessary, takes action to protect the world's ecological balance.

First page of Zembla No. 1 (1963)

Publishing History:
Zembla's adventures began in *Special-Kiwi* No. 15 in June 1963, before moving into its own monthly title the following month. A year later, a companion title, *Special-Zembla*, was launched. Until No. 200, *Zembla* published only new sto-

ries. Then, from No. 200 to about No. 300, it alternated between the occasional new story and reprints. The last new story appeared in No. 297. The magazine was eventually cancelled with No. 479 in 1994.

Special-Zembla published mostly original stories in Nos. 1-85, then switched to reprints only. A new series of adventures began in No. 152 in 2000. The title was cancelled with No. 175 in 2003.

Introduction of Rasmus in Zembla No. 1 – Art by Pedrazza (1963)

Bibliography:
All stories are drawn by Franco or Fausto Oneta unless otherwise indicated.

Special-Kiwi No. 15 (1963):
Zembla (**drawn by Pedrazza**)
La Loi de la Jungle [*The Law of the Jungle*] (**drawn by Augusto Pedrazza**)

Zembla:
1. *Seul contre Tous* [*Alone Against Everyone*] (**drawn by Pedrazza**) (1963)
2. *Représailles* [*Reprisal*] (**drawn by Pedrazza**) (1963)

3. *Le Diable du Lac* [*The Devil in the Lake*] (**drawn by Pietro Gamba**) (1963)
4. *Zembla contre Zembla* [*Zembla vs. Zembla*] (**drawn by Pedrazza**) (1963)
5. *Au Pays des Bo* [*In the Land of Bo*] (**drawn by Gamba**) (1963)
6. *Document Secret* [*Secret Document*] (**drawn by Pedrazza**) (1963)
7. *La Terreur Vient de la Mer* [*Terror From the Sea*] (1964)
8. *L'Ile Maudite* [*The Cursed Island*] (1964)
9. *Enfer Vert* [*Green Hell*] (1964)
10. *La Petite Sue* [*Little Sue*] (1964)
11. *L'Epée de Samasur* [*The Sword of Samasur*] (1964)
12. *Dernier Espoir* [*Last Hope*] (1964)
13. *Une Reine en Péril* [*A Queen in Peril*] (1964)
14. *Les Guerriers de la Cité Secrète* [*Warriors of the Secret City*] (1964)
15. *En Danger de Mort* [*Danger of Death*] (1964)
16. *Les Naufrageurs* [*The Wreckers*] (1964)
17. *La Tour du Sorcier Blanc* [*The Tower of the White Wizard*] (**drawn by Gamba**) (1964)
18. *Le Justicier* [*The Avenger*] (1964)
19. *Le Chat Noir* [*The Black Cat*] (1965)
20. *La Lagune des Géants* [*Lagoon of the Giants*] (1965)
21. *Le Champion Pétoulet* [*Petoulet Champion*] (1965)
22. *La Cohorte des Damnés* [*Army of the Damned*] (1965)
23. *La Prisonnière du Désert* [*Prisoner of the Desert*] (1965)
24. *Un Vieil Ami* [*An Old Friend*] (**drawn by Gamba**) (1965)
25. *La Charge des Mastodontes* [*Charge of the Mastodons*] (1965)
26. *La Montagne Invisible* [*The Invisible Mountain*] (1965)
27. *Les Chasseurs d'Ivoire* [*The Ivory Hunters*] (1965)
28. *La Panthère Blanche* [*The White Panther*] (1965)
29. *Zembla contre l'Homme Invisible* [*Zembla vs. the Invisible Man*] (1965)
30. *Croc de Tigre* [*Tiger's Fang*] (1965)
31. *Le Trône de Jade* [*The Jade Throne*] (1966)
32. *La Révolte des Esclaves* [*The Slave Revolt*] (1966)
33. *La Grande Soif* [*The Great Thirst*] (1966)
34. *L'Héritière* [*The Heiress*] (1966)
35. *La Montagne Maudite* [*The Cursed Mountain*] (1966)
36. *La Princesse des Urelan* [*The Urelan Princess*] (1966)
37. *Une Aventure de la Taupe* [*The Mole's Adventure*] (1966)
38. *Les Sables Brûlants* [*The Burning Sands*] (1966)
39. *La Flèche d'Or* [*The Golden Arrow*] (1966)
40. *La Cité de Pierre* [*The Stone City*] (1966)
41. *Terreur dans la Savane* [*Terror in the Savanna*] (1966)
42. *L'Homme des Abimes* [*The Man from the Abyss*] (1966)
43. *S.O.S. du Désert* [*SOS from the Desert*] (1967)
44. *Le Grand Match* [*The Great Match*] (1967)

45. *Les Plumes d'Or* [*The Golden Feathers*] (1967)
46. *Le Grand Cobra* [*The Great Cobra*] (1967)
47. *La Statue Vivante* [*The Living Statue*] (1967)
48. *Trahison* [*Betrayal*] (1967)
49. *Le Singe Tatoué* [*The Tattooed Ape*] (1967)
50. *La Ligne Blanche* [*The White Line*] (1967)
51. *Une Guerre Mystérieuse* [*A Mysterious War*] (1967)
52. *Le Cargo des Désespérés* [*Cargo of Despair*] (1967)
53. *Le Cri du Corbeau* [*The Shout of the Crow*] (1967)
54. *Il y a Trois Mille Ans* [*3000 Years Ago*] (1967)
55. *Le Secret d'Elly Corbett* [*Elly Corbett's Secret*] (1968)
56. *Une Corde pour Zembla* [*A Rope for Zembla*] (1968)
57. *Le Petit Roi* [*The Little King*] (1968)
58. *L'Ile aux Serpents* [*Serpents' Isle*] (1968)
59. *Drame sur le Kilimandjaro* [*Drama at Kilimanjaro*] (1968)
60. *Wazilla* (1968)
61. *Les Diamants de Cap Funeste* [*The Diamonds of Cape Doom*] (1968)
62. *La Loi du Mahdi* [*The Mahdi's Law*] (1968)
63. *Une Femme à Abattre* [*A Woman to Kill*] (1968)
64. *La Plantation des Brumes* [*The Plantation in the Mist*] (1968)
65. *La Forteresse de Pamore* [*The Fortress of Pamore*] (1968)
66. *La Patrouille de la Mort* [*Death Patrol*] (1968)
67. *Yankar, l'Esprit du Mal* [*Yankar, the Evil Spirit*] (1968)
68. *La Race des Damnés* [*The Cursed Race*] (1968)

69. *Les Deux Idoles* [*The Twin Idols*] (1968)
70. *L'Araignée* [*The Spider*] (1968)
71. *La Jeune Fille à la Valise* [*The Girl with a Suitcase*] (1968)
72. *Le Mystère du Train Bleu* [*The Mystery of the Blue Train*] (1968)
73. *Le Désert de Kalar* [*The Desert of Kalar*] (1968)
74. *Terreur à Mawango* [*Terror in Mawango*] (1969)
75. *Le Colonel Husswald* [*Colonel Husswald*] (1969)
76. *Tête de Serpent* [*Snake Head*] (1969)
77. *Le Trésor des Ikanous* [*The Treasure of the Ikanus*] (1969)
78. *Mort d'un Empereur* [*Death of an Emperor*] (1969)

Zembla and friends – Art by Oneta (1970)

79. *L'Homme de Pierre* [*The Stone Man*] (1969)
80. *Le Fils des Chacals* [*The Son of the Jackals*] (1969)
81. *La Proie Humaine* [*The Human Prey*] (1969)
82. *La Fleur Ecarlate* [*The Scarlet Flower*] (1969)
83. *Rendez-vous avec la Mort* [*Rendezvous with Death*] (1969)
84. *Les Croix de Zarban* [*The Crosses of Zarban*] (1969)
85. *Tempête sur Madagascar* [*Storm over Madagascar*] (1969)
86. *La Porte de l'Enfer* [*The Gate of Hell*] (1969)
87. *Le Fantôme de la Baie Noire* [*The Ghost of Black Bay*] (1969)
88. *Les Envahisseurs* [*The Invaders*] (1969)
89. *Tuez Zembla!* [*Kill Zembla!*] (1969)
90. *Haine Implacable* [*Merciless Hatred*] (1969)
91. *Jeu Dangereux* [*Dangerous Game*] (1969)
92. *Les Fleurs du Mal* [*The Flowers of Evil*] (1969)
93. *Les Clés d'Or* [*The Golden Keys*] (1969)
94. *La Terrible Prophétie* [*The Dreadful Prophecy*] (1969)
95. *La Soif du Pouvoir* [*The Thirst for Power*] (1969)
96. *Ignoble Trafic* [*Awful Traffic*] (1969)
97. *Le Crâne Sacré* [*The Sacred Skull*] (1969)
98. *Le Lion Blanc* [*The White Lion*] (1970)
99. *La Fille de la Lune* [*The Moon Girl*] (1970)

100. *Les Hommes Simba* [*The Simba Men*] (1970)
101. *S.O.S pour les Gombars* [*SOS for the Gombars*] (1970)
102. *Les Perles du Samantha* [*The Pearls of the Samantha*] (1970)
103. *Lutte pour l'Oasis* [*Battle for the Oasis*] (1970)
104. *Ultimatum à Zembla* [*Ultimatum for Zembla*] (1970)
105. *Le Mort qui Ressuscite* [*The Resurrected Dead*] (1970)
106. *Une Visite Inattendue* [*An Unexpected Visit*] (1970)
107. *Le Grand Ra-Smus* [*The Great Ra-Smus*] (1970)
108. *Une Fille à Sauver* [*A Girl to Rescue*] (1970)
109. *Pétoulet, le Dieu Vivant* [*Petoulet, the Living God*] (1970)
110. *Chasse aux Contrebandiers* [*Hunting Poachers*] (1970)
111. *Takuba va mourir!* [*Takuba Will Die!*] (1970)
112. *Expérience sur un Condamné* [*Experiment on a Prisoner*] (1970)
113. *Le Terroriste* [*The Terrorist*] (1970)
114. *Le Diable Jaune* [*The Yellow Devil*] (1970)
115. *Rencontre Secrète* [*Secret Meeting*] (1970)

Rasmus, Yeye and Petoulet – Art by Oneta (1970)

116. *La Sagaie d'Or* [*The Golden Lance*] (1970)
117. *Poga-Pongo, Terre de Salut* [*Poga-Pongo, Safe Land*] (1970)
118. *Le Labyrinthe de la Mort* [*The Maze of Death*] (1970)
119. *Une Reine pour les Looks* [*A Queen for the Looks*] (1970)
120. *Rédemption* [*Redemption*] (1970)
121. *Requiem pour un Traître* [*Requiem for a Traitor*] (1970)
122. *Les Diables de l'Oasis* [*The Oasis Devils*] (1970)
123. *La Guerre des Lions* [*The War of the Lions*] (1970)
124. *La Forêt des Horreurs* [*The Forest of Horrors*] (1970)
125. *Le Médaillon* [*The Medallion*] (1970)
126. *Zembla sur le Ring* [*Zembla in the Ring*] (1971)
127. *La Révolte de Boor* [*Boor's Revolt*] (1971)
128. *Les Gorilles d'Anthar* [*The Gorillas of Anthar*] (1971)
129. *Le Trésor des Gombars* [*The Treasure of the Gombars*] (1971)
130. *Mission Dangereuse* [*Dangerous Mission*] (1971)
131. *L'Esprit Maléfique* [*The Evil Spirit*] (1971)
132. *Les Monstres du Marais* [*The Swamp Monsters*] (1971)
133. *La Prêtresse des Amazones* [*The Amazon Priestess*] (1971)
134. *Le Courage de Rasmus* [*The Courage of Rasmus*] (1971)
135. *Le Cercle Magique* [*The Magic Circle*] (1971)
136. *Silence, on tourne!* [*Silence! Action!*] (1971)
137. *Jafeth, l'Arabe* [*Jafeth the Arab*] (1971)
138. *A la Recherche des Diamants* [*Searching for Diamonds*] (1971)
139. *Spectacle de Variétés* [*Variety Show*] (1971)
140. *La Terreur des Anyotos* [*The Terror of the Anyotos*] (1971)
141. *La Volonté du Grand Nyanga* [*The Will of the Great Nyanga*] (1971)
142. *Les Exterminateurs d'Aigles* [*The Eagle Exterminators*] (1971)
143. *Le Siège des Bukavus* [*The Siege of the Bukavus*] (1971)
144. *Le Faux Zembla* [*The Fake Zembla*] (1971)
145. *Les Femmes-Singes* [*The She-Apes*] (1971)
146. *Le Monstre du Lac Céleste* [*The Monster of Heavenly Lake*] (1972)
147. Reprint
148. *La Forêt Enchantée* [*The Enchanted Forest*] (1972)
149. *La Révolte de Hargen* [*Hargen's Revolt*] (1972)

150. *L'Antilope Sacrée* [*The Sacred Antelope*] (1972)
151. *La Légende d'Ahrumi* [*The Legend of Ahrumi*] (1972)
152. *La Fille de la Jungle* [*The Jungle Girl*] (1972)
153. *Dans la Nuit* [*Into the Night*] (1972)
154. *La Fontaine de Jouvence* [*The Fountain of Youth*] (1972)
155. *Le Trésor des Kavaghs* [*The Treasure of the Kavaghs*] (1972)
156. *L'Homme-Loup* [*The Man-Wolf*] (1972)
157. *Les Evadés de Fort Bwanga* [*Escape from Fort Bwanga*] (1972)
158. *Les Adorateurs du Feu* [*The Fire Worshippers*] (1972)
159. *Le Signe du Serpent* [*The Sign of the Serpent*] (1972)
160. *Le Seigneur de la Forêt* [*The Lord of the Forest*] (1972)
161. *La Bande des Cent* [*The Gang of 100*] (1972)
162. *La Reine des Amazones* [*The Queen of the Amazons*] (1972)
163. *La Plante Hallucinogène* [*The Hallucinogenic Plant*] (1972)
164. *Les Singes du Ciel* [*The Celestial Apes*] (1972)
165. *Les Prisonniers de Kamanjdur* [*The Prisoners of Kamanjdur*] (1972)
166. *La Terreur vient du Ciel* [*Terror from the Sky*] (1972)
167. *La Forteresse des Otages* [*Fortress of Hostages*] (1972)
168. *Une Brume Maléfique* [*The Evil Mist*] (1972)
169. *Les Insignes du Commandement* [*The Symbols of Command*] (1972)
170. *Le Monstre des Mers* [*The Sea Monster*] (1973)
171. *Le Tyran de Cabinda* [*The Tyrant of Cabinda*] (1973)
172. *Défi au Roi* [*Challenge to the King*] (1973)
173. *Le Cauchemar* [*The Nightmare*] (1973)
174. *L'Epouse du Fleuve* [*The River Bride*] (1973)
175. *Les Mutants* [*The Mutants*] (1973)
176. *Terre de Conquête* [*Conquered Land*] (1973)
177. *Panique dans la Forêt* [*Panic in the Forest*] (1973)
178. *Le Sentier des Hommes Perdus* [*The Path of the Lost Men*] (1973)
179. *Les Serpents d'Or* [*The Golden Snakes*] (1973)
180. *La Perle de Katombo* [*The Pearl of Katombo*] (1973)
181. *Le Chemin de l'Espérance* [*The Path of Hope*] (1973)
182. *Un Raid Périlleux* [*A Perilous Raid*] (1973)
183. *Un Océan d'Herbes* [*An Ocean of Grass*] (1973)

Queen Takuba – Art by Oneta (1973)

184. *La Colline Sacrée* [*The Sacred Hill*] (1973)
185. *Les Frères Blake* [*The Brothers Blake*] (1973)
186. *La Folie de Takuba* [*Takuba's Madness*] (1973)
187. *L'Ombre de la Mort* [*The Shadow of Death*] (1973)
188. *Les Crimes de Rasmus* [*Rasmus' Crimes*] (1973)
189. *La Voix de Mephis* [*The Voice of Mephis*] (1973)
190. *Le Mystère des Geladas* [*The Mystery of the Geladas*] (1973)
191. *Un Périlleux Voyage* [*A Perilous Journey*] (1973)
192. *Le Trésor des Kassars* [*The Treasure of the Kassars*] (1973)
193. *Le Voyage de Takuba* [*Takuba's Journey*] (1973)
194. *Le Dernier Tombeau* [*The Last Grave*] (1974)
195. *Les Fils d'Hororo* [*The Sons of Hororo*] (1974)
196. *Les Yeux sans Sourire* [*Eyes Without a Smile*] (1974)
197. *L'Enfer de Togaramba* [*The Hell of Togaramba*] (1974)
198. *La Digue de Tanaraz* [*The Dam of Tanaraz*] (1974)
199. Reprint (From that point onward, all odd-numbered issues are reprints except where otherwise indicated.)

200. *Le Fantôme du Rayon de Lune* [*The Ghost of the Moonbeam*] (1974)
202. *Le Chien de Pierre* [*The Stone Dog*] (1974)
204. *Ibish le Fauve* [*Wild Ibish*] (1974)
206. *Cérémonie Secrète* [*Secret Ceremony*] (1974)
208. *Le Renard* [*The Fox*] (1974)
210. *Prise de Guerre* [*Spoils of War*] (1974)
212. *Le Fils de Princess Ma* [*The Son of Princess Ma*] (1974)
214. *Nuit de Terreur* [*Night of Terror*] (1974)
216. *Le Vol de la Mouette* [*The Flight of the Seagull*] (1974)
218. *La Déesse des Moraks* [*The Goddess of the Moraks*] (1975)
220. *Une Chasse Impitoyable* [*A Merciless Pursuit*] (1975)
222. *La Cité Cachée* [*The Hidden City*] (1975)
224. *L'Insaisissable Tituk* [*The Elusive Tituk*] (1975)
226. *Le Lion Noir* [*The Black Lion*] (1975)
228. *La Saga des Kanimbos* [*The Saga of the Kanimbos*] (1975)
230. ? (1975)
232. *La Révolte des Chombos* [*The Revolt of the Chombos*] (1975)

Zembla to Takuba's rescue – Art by Oneta (1974)

234. *Le Tourbillon* [*The Maelstrom*] (1975)
236. *Mystère à Sagoville* [*Mystery in Sagoville*] (1975)
238. *Odieux Chantage* [*Odious Blackmail*] (1975)
240. *Un Safari Mouvementé* [*An Eventful Safari*] (1975)
242. *Le Fleuve Noir* [*The Black River*] (1976)
244. *Le Drame de Korongo* [*The Tragedy at Korongo*] (1976)
246. *La Fin d'un Lâche* [*The End of a Coward*] (1976)
248. *La Prisonnière des Mercenaires* [*The Prisoner of the Mercenaries*] (1976)
250. *La Montagne Ensorcelée* [*The Spellbound Mountain*] (1976)
252. *Le Chien Noir* [*The Black Dog*] (1976)
254. *Le Prisonnier de Satanik* [*Prisoner of Satanik*] (1976)
256. *Le Fort du Déshonneur* [*The Fort of Dishonor*] (1976)
258. *La Sonde Spatiale* [*The Space Probe*] (1976)
260. *Le Secret de l'Empereur* [*The Emperor's Secret*] (1976)
262. *La Mouette Bleue* [*The Blue Seagull*] (1976)
263. *L'Idole des Cent Lunes* [*The Idol of 100 Moons*] (1976)
264. *La Bataille de Gambèze* [*The Battle of Gambeze*] (1977)
265. *Où est passé Clifford?* [*Where Is Clifford?*] (1977)
266. *L'Oeil de Jade* [*The Jade Eye*] (1977)
267. *Zoltar* (1977)
268. *Le Royaume du Diable* [*The Devil's Kingdom*] (1977)
269. *Le Prisonnier de la Vallée des Serpents* [*The Prisoner of Snake Valley*] (1977)
270. *Fin d'un Tyran* [*End of a Tyrant*] (1977)
271. *Le Royaume de Hyr* [*The Kingdom of Hyr*] (1977)
272. *Le Bateau Fantôme* [*The Ghost Ship*] (1977)
273. Reprint
274. *La Longue Nuit des Chacals* [*The Long Night of the Jackals*] (1977)
275. *Ciel en Feu* [*Fire in the Sky*] (1977)
276. *La Vallée de la Mort* [*The Valley of Death*] (1978)
277. *Un Trésor Disputé* [*A Disputed Treasure*] (1978)
278. *Le Tigre Noir* [*The Black Tiger*] (1978)
279. *La Pierre de Karanaganda* [*The Stone of Karanaganda*] (1978)
280. *Le Secret de Rasmus* [*Rasmus' Secret*] (1978)
281. *Le Retour de Laur* [*Laur's Return*] (1978)
282. *Tono* (1978)
283. *Les Pillards du Katugan* [*The Looters of Katugan*] (1978)
284. *Fièvre Noire* [*Black Fever*] (1978)
285. *Le Tyran de Kapur* [*The Tyrant of Kapur*] (1978)
286. *L'Histoire de Han* [*The Story of Han*] (1978)
287. *Le Tombeau de Komoth* [*The Tomb of Komoth*] (1978)
288. *Le Massacre des Antilopes* [*The Slaughter of the Antelopes*] (1979)

Zembla by Pedrazza (1963)

289. *Le Vampire Rouge* [*The Red Vampire*] (1979)
290. *Le Nouveau Nautilus* [*The New Nautilus*] (1979)
291. *Magie* [*Magic*] (1979)
292. *Le Soldat Rasmus* [*Rasmus the Soldier*] (1979)

293. *La Malédiction de Guk* [*Guk's Curse*] (1979)
294. *Une Croisière Mouvementée* [*An Eventful Cruise*] (1979)
295. *Le Cauchemar de Takuba* [*Takuba's Nightmare*] (1979)
296. *La Rome Africaine* [*The African Rome*] (1979)
297. *La Fosse du Diable* [*The Devil's Pit*] (1979)
298-479. Reprints (1980-94)

Spécial-Zembla:
1. *Ennemis Mortels* [*Mortal Foes*] (1964)
2. *Alerte dans la Jungle* [*Alert in the Jungle*] (**drawn by Pedrazza**) (1964)
3. *Le Safari Tragique* [*Tragic Safari*] (**drawn by Pedrazza**) (1964)
4. *Le Chasseur de Papillons* [*The Butterfly Hunter*] (**drawn by Pedrazza**) (1965)
5. *Le Trésor des Kyassas* [*The Treasure of the Kyassas*] (**drawn by Pedrazza**) (1965)
6. *L'Attaque du Train* [*The Train Attack*] (1965)
7. *La Folie de Zembla* [*Zembla's Madness*] (**drawn by Gamba**) (1965)
8. *Deux contre Tous* [*Two Against All*] (**drawn by Alessandro Biffignandi**) (1966)

9. *Le Colosse de Singa Binda* [*The Colossus of Singa Binda*] (**drawn by Gamba**) (1966)
10. *Le Roi de Richmond Park* [*The King of Richmond Park*] (**drawn by Gamba**) (1966)
11. *Rasmus et les Sept Nains* [*Rasmus & the Seven Dwarves*] (**drawn by Gamba**) (1966)
12. *La Horde* [*The Horde*] (1967)
13. *Les Frères de la Jungle* [*Brothers of the Jungle*] (**drawn by Gamba**) (1967)
14. *Un Royaume Mystérieux* [*A Mysterious Kingdom*] (1967)
15. *Condamnation à Mort* [*Death Sentence*] (1967)
16. *Deux Cents Samourais* [*200 Samurais*] (**drawn by Bertrand Charlas**) (1968)
17. *L'Homme qui Volait les Consciences* [*The Man Who Stole Consciences*] (**drawn by Charlas**) (1968)
18. *La Mission de Tragar* [*Tragar's Mission*] (**drawn by Charlas**) (1968)
19. *La Statue Animée* [*The Animated Statue*] (1968)
20. *S.O.S. sur le Fleuve Bleu* [*SOS on the Blue River*] (**drawn by Charlas**) (1969)

21. *La Cité des Gorilles* [*The City of Gorillas*] (**drawn by Charlas**) (1969)
22. *L'Hirondelle de la Mort* [*The Skylark of Death*] (**drawn by Charlas**) (1969)
23. *Opération Spatiale* [*Operation Space*] (**drawn by Charlas**) (1969)
24. *Les Damnés de Fort Mallon* [*The Damned of Fort Mallon*] (**drawn by Charlas**) (1970)
25. *L'Arbre du Mal* [*The Tree of Evil*] (**drawn by Charlas**) (1970)
26. *Les Noces de Zembla* [*Zembla's Wedding*] (1970)
27. *La Soif du Pétrole* [*The Thirst for Oil*] (**drawn by Charlas**) (1970)
28. *Je Tuerai Zembla* [*I Will Kill Zembla*] (**drawn by Charlas**) (1971)
29. *Le Spectre de la Bombe* [*The Spectre of the Bomb*] (1971)
30. *Tragique Enigme* [*Tragic Enigma*] (**drawn by Charlas**) (1971)
31. *Le Trésor Caché* [*The Hidden Treasure*] (**drawn by Charlas**) (1971)
32. *Le Fantôme des Marais* [*The Swamp Ghost*] (**drawn by Charlas**) (1972)
33. *La Vallée des Romains* [*Valley of the Romans*] (**drawn by Charlas**) (1972)
33B. *L'Enfance de Zembla* [*Zembla's Childhood*] (1972)
34. *Le Diable Noir* [*The Black Devil*] (1972)
35. *Rasmus en Danger!* [*Rasmus in Danger!*] (**drawn by Charlas**) (1972)
36. *La Fosse de la Mort* [*The Pit of Death*] (**drawn by Charlas**) (1973)
37. *La Reine des Neiges* [*The Snow Queen*] (**drawn by Charlas**) (1973)
38. *La Jeunesse de Zembla* [*Young Zembla*] (1973)
39. *Le Secret des Hommes Mambas* [*The Secret of the Mamba Men*] (**drawn by Charlas**) (1973)
40. *Le Retour des Mangbetous* [*The Return of the Mangbetous*] (1974)
41. *Le Soldat Jump* [*Soldier Jump*] (**drawn by Charlas**) (1974)
42. *Les Otages de Dogotombo* [*The Hostages of Dogotombo*] (**drawn by Charlas**) (1974)
43. *La Forêt de Midor* [*The Forest of Midor*] (1974)
44. *Coup d'Etat* (**drawn by Charlas**) (1975)
45. *Les Vendeurs d'Armes* [*The Gun Merchants*] (**drawn by Charlas**) (1975)
46. *Le Massacre des Gorilles* [*The Slaughter of the Gorillas*] (**drawn by Charlas**) (1975)
47. Reprint

48. *Une Poursuite Acharnée* [*A Fierce Pursuit*] (1976)
49. *La Grande Razzia* [*The Great Plunder*] (1976)
50. *Le Pur-Sang* [*The Pure Blood*] (1976)
51. *Le Grand Chef* [*The Great Chief*] (1976)
52. *Requiem pour Zembla* [*Requiem for Zembla*] (1977)
53. *L'Héritage de Malinda* [*Malinda's Inheritance*] (1977)
54. *Le Milliardaire* [*The Billionaire*] (1977)
55. *La Félonie d'Asciaida* [*Asciaida's Betrayal*] (1977)
56. *La Proie de Nayem* [*Nayem's Prey*] (1978)
57. Reprint
58. *Le Sorcier des Rogs* [*The Wizard of the Rogs*] (1978)
59. *Le Prisonnier de Fort Kaiser* [*The Prisoner of Fort Kaiser*] (1978)
60. *La Déesse Kali* [*The Goddess Kali*] (1979)
61. *Le Jour du Scorpion* [*The Day of the Scorpion*] (1979)
62. *Où sont passés les Gombars?* [*Where Have the Gombars Gone?*] (1979)
63. *Les Invincibles* [*The Invincibles*] (1979)
64. *Le Roi Rasmus* [*King Rasmus*] (1980)
65. *La Mission de Kapolango* [*Kapolango's Mission*] (1980)
66. *Les Cinq Sépulcres* [*The Five Tombs*] (1980)
67. *La Capture de Zembla* [*The Capture of Zembla*] (1980)
68. *Marakoun* (1981)
69. *Le Dernier des Bazankis* [*The Last of the Bazankis*] (1981)
70-71. Reprints
72. *L'Ouragan* [*The Storm*] (1982)
73-82. Reprints
83. *Au Voleur!* [*Thief!*] (1984)
84. *Chasse à l'Evadé* [*Hunt for an Escaped Prisoner*] (1985)
85-175. Reprints (1985-2003)

New Stories:

152-153. *Le Roi des Magiciens* [*The King of the Magicians*] (**Wri**: Thierry Mornet & Christophe Malgrain; **Art**: Malgrain) (2000)

154. *À la Recherche d'Ozark* [*Searching for Ozark*] (guest-starring Ozark) (**Wri**: Mornet & "Jefferson Martin London" (Jean-Marc Lainé); **Art**: Lainé) (2000)

155. *Il Faut Sauver Mustang* [*We Must Save Mustang*] (guest-starring Ozark) (**Wri**: Mornet & Lainé; **Art**: Lainé) (2000)

156. *Le Kalutah* (**Wri-Art**: Cyril Bouquet) (2000)

158-160. *Le Chasseur* [*The Hunter*] (**Wri**: Eduardo Alpuente & Mornet; **Art**: Alpuente & Moron) (2001)

161-162. *L'Orchidée Magique* [*The Magic Orchid*] (guest-starring Mozam) (**Wri**: Lainé; **Art**: Manuel Garcia) (2001)

163. *Les Montagnes du Karunda* [*The Mountains of Karunda*] (**Wri**: Jean-Marc Lofficier & Lainé; **Art**: Jean-Jacques Dzialowski) (*left*) (2001)

164. *La Chair du Temps* [*The Flesh of Time*] (guest-starring Kabur) (**Wri**: Lofficier & Mornet; **Art**: Mike Ratera) (2002)

165. *Le Destin de Zembla* [*Zembla's Destiny*] (guest-starring Kabur) (**Wri**: Lofficier & Mornet; **Art**: Ratera) (2002)

165-166. *Secrets* (**Wri-Art**: Willy & Jonathan Hudic) (2002)

167-168. *Le Secret des Monts de la Lune* [*The Secret of the Moon Mountains*] (**Wri**: François Corteggiani; **Art**: Dominique Cebe) (2002)

169-171. *La Trahison de Radak* [*Radak's Betrayal*] (**Wri-Art**: Thierry Olivier) (2003)

171. *L'Héritage des Marais* [*The Marais Inheritance*] (**Wri**: Lainé; **Art**: Malgrain & Jean-Marie Minguez) (2003)

172. *Un Poison Nommé Silure* [*A Poison Named Silure*] (**Wri-Art**: Reed Man) (2003)

173. *La Fondation Marais* [*The Marais Foundation*] (**Wri**: Lainé; **Art**: Malgrain & Minguez) (2003)

173. *Le Bon Sauvage* [*The Good Savage*] (**Wri**: Thomas Barrichella & Jim Dandy; **Art**: Jim Dandy) (2004)

175. *La Jeunesse de Zembla* [*Young Zembla*] (**Wri**: Dandy; **Art**: Oneta)

previous page: cover by Gil Formosa (bottom right).

Website:
http://www.coolfrenchcomics.com/zembla.htm

Zembla faces Kabur – Art by Mike Ratera (2002)

Ténébrax (1963)

Ténébrax (1963)

"With a mere gesture, I can cause collisions, create panic. The Métro is mine!"
(Ténébrax – Ténébrax)

Created by:
Writer Lob and artist Georges Pichard.

• Lob, a pseudonym of Jacques Loeb (1932-1990), began his career in the 1950s as a science fiction cartoonist, contributing to magazines such as *Planète*, *Fiction* and *Hara-Kiri*. In the 1960s, he teamed up with Georges Pichard to create *Submerman* for *Pilote*, *Ténébrax* for the short-lived *Chouchou*, *Ulysse* for *Linus* and the adult *Blanche-Epiphanie* for *V-Magazine*. In the 1970s, Lob wrote *Delirius*, a chapter in the *Lone Sloane* saga, for Philippe Druillet, *Les Mange-Bitume* [*The Tar Eaters*] for José Bielsa and *Dossiers Soucoupes Volantes* [*The UFO Files*] for Robert Gigi. In 1972, Lob and Marcel Gotlib teamed to create the hugely popular superhero parody, *Super Dupont*. In the 1980s, Lob penned the remarkable science fiction saga *Le Transperceneige* [*The Snow-Plow Train*] with Rochette for *A Suivre*. Lob also wrote and drew his own parodies of science fiction and superheroes with *Roger Fringant*, *Batmax* and *L'Homme au Landau* [*The Man in the Pram*].

• Georges Pichard (1920-2003) began his comics career in the 1960s after a successful stint as a commercial artist and illustrator. He first teamed up with Lob on a number of fantasy series such as *Submerman*, *Ténébrax*, *Ulysse* and *Blanche-Epiphanie*. Pichard then embarked on the creation of a number of remarkable erotic comics, as well as *Bornéo Jo* written by Danie Dubos, and *Ceux-Là* [*These People*] written by noted science fiction author Jean-Pierre Andrevon. He also produced a free adaptation of the classic Greek tragedy, *Les Sorcières de Thessalie* [*The Witches of Thessalia*].

Story:
Edgar Dunor, a writer of detective novels, and his faithful assistant Doum, thwart the plans of mad scientist Ténébrax, who lives in a huge underground metropolis secretly connected to the Paris Subway, and controls an army of giant, intelligent rats. Ténébrax plots to take over Paris by placing candy laced with "hilarine," a laughing drug, in the subway's vending machines. Ténébrax's beautiful daughter, Princesse, helps Dunor and Doum escape and they return in force with the police. They use the waters of the river Seine to drown Ténébrax's rodent armies.

Ténébrax (1963)

Ténébrax is a wonderful satire of the megalomaniacal villains of pulp literature. The mephistophelean-looking arch-villain travels in his personal railcar, served by his giant rats, listening to the music of Wagner, while exposing his grandiose plans to become master of the Paris subway. The opening scene in which a hapless commuter is taken prisoner by Ténébrax's rats is a classic. The depiction of an underworld with giant mushroom plantations, secret subway lines and even a mysterious "Phantom of the Métro" is archetypal pulp. Pichard's undeniable talent for sexy comics were in evidence for the first time in *Ténébrax* with the ingenue character of Princesse, who ends up falling in love with the honest, practical and unimaginative Doum.

Publishing History:
Ténébrax was originally serialized in *Chouchou* in 1963, but was left uncompleted when the magazine folded. The end of the story was published the following year in the Italian magazine *Linus*. *Ténébrax* was eventually collected in the graphic novel format by S.E.R.G. in 1966.

Website:
http://www.coolfrenchcomics.com/tenebrax.htm

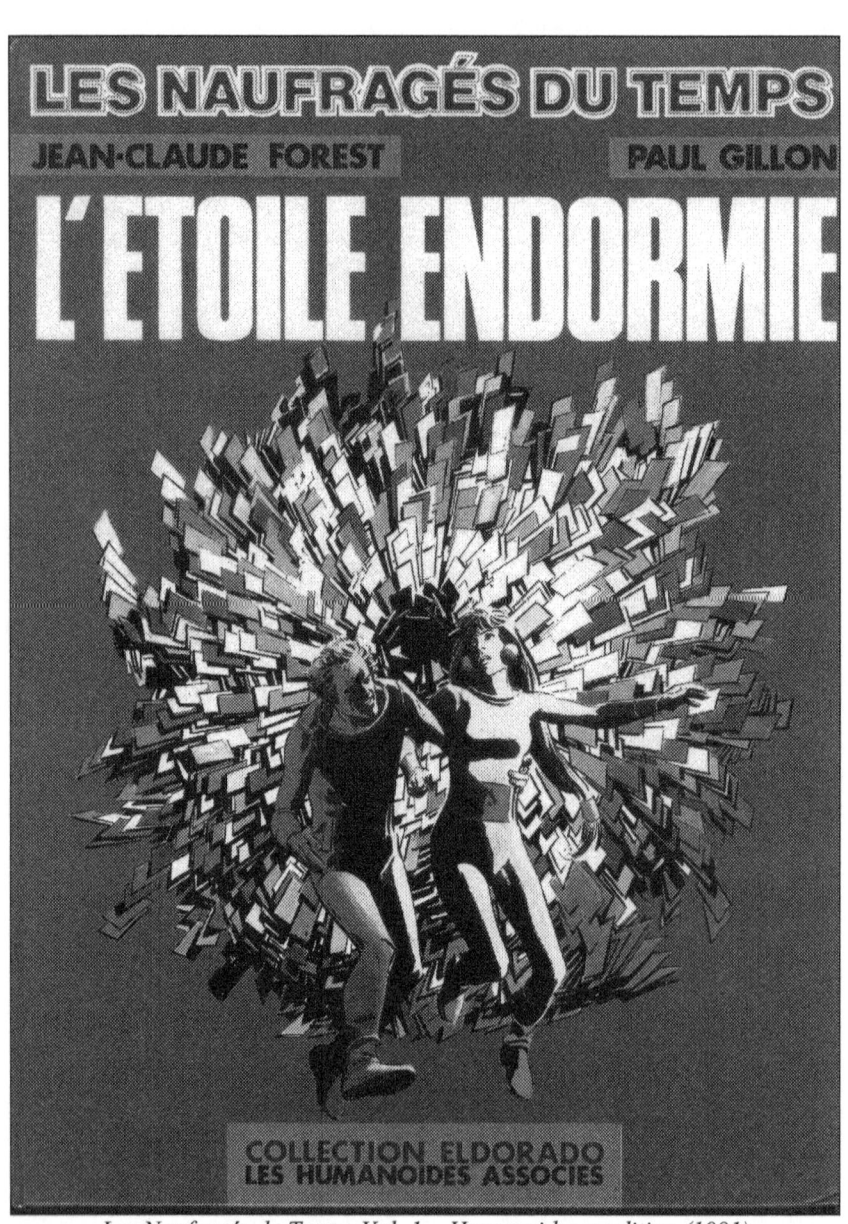

Les Naufragés du Temps Vol. 1 – Humanoides reedition (1981)

Les Naufragés du Temps (1964)

"Our destiny is not ours. We are not ours. We belong to the future."
(Christopher to Valerie – *Le Cryptomère*)

Created by:
Writer Jean-Claude Forest and artist Paul Gillon.
- Jean-Claude Forest (see *Barbarella* entry).
- Paul Gillon (1926-) joined the editorial team of *Vaillant* in 1947, illustrating numerous adventure stories such as *Lynx Blanc* [*White Lynx*], *Fils de Chine* [*Son of China*], *Le Cormoran* [*The Cormorant*] and its popular spin-off, *Jeremie*. In 1959, he began drawing the famous daily romance strip *13, Rue de l'Espoir* [*13 Hope St.*], a French *Heart of Juliet Jones* written by Gall for *France-Soir*. His science fiction series include *Les Naufragés du Temps*, co-created with Jean-Claude Forest for *Chouchou*, and *La Survivante* [*The Survivor*] for *L'Echo des Savanes* in 1985. Other works include the spy thriller *Les Léviathans* (1978), and two collections of shorter stories, *Processus de Survie* [*Survival Process*] (1984) and *La Dernière des Salles Obscures* [*The Last of the Dark Rooms*] (1998).

Story:
Les Naufragés du Temps, a title that could be translated as *Shipwrecked in Time*, *Castaways in Time* or merely *Lost in Time*, is based on the premise that, in 1990, as Mankind is under attack by a mysterious plague, two people, Christopher Cavallieri and Valerie Haurele, are placed into individual hibernation capsules and sent into space. A thousand years later, Chris is brought back to life and helps the Solar System to fight the Trasses, a collective intelligence comprised of alien, winged rats. In the process, Chris finds Valerie's capsule and reanimates her. However, during their thousand-year sleep, the two voyagers have kept idealized images of each other. They soon discover that their love cannot withstand the ravages of reality...

Volume 3 introduces two new villains: one is a fantastic creature called the Tapir, who is the crimelord of the Solar System. The other is a mad scientist, Leobart. Both are trying to take over a mysterious world that lies within a gargantuan, worm-like space-roaming creature. Their schemes are thwarted by Chris and a group of friends, including the beautiful Mara–Valerie's rival for Chris' love–Major Lisdal (a cyborg) and other colorful characters.

In Books 5 and 6, Chris discovers that the real Valerie was kidnapped by the Tapir and sent through space to his home planet, where she is the prisoner of giant slug-like creatures with the power to materialize dreams.

L'Etoile Endormie – First Version (Chouchou) (1964)

L'Etoile Endornie (Second Version) – Hachette (1974)

To free Valerie, Chris allies himself with the Tapir's race, and once again defeats his old enemies, the Trasses. Then, Chris and his friends are taken to Orkand, a planetary system used as a prison. There, the heroes battle the fanatical cultists of Beselek, who hold the system under their domination. In order to defeat their foes, they have to secure the alliance of the Ortho-Mentas, a guild of scientists who live in orbit, in the wreck of a giant spaceship.

In the final two books in the series, Chris and Valerie are taken back to the Solar System, where the High Council is determined to wipe out the plague which has infested Earth since the beginning of the series, as well as the mutated monsters which it created. But Valerie betrays the Council and flees to the planet's surface. On Terra, she and Chris at last discover the truth: the plague is the original native lifeform of Earth, and the race of men were invaders from space. Mankind then surrenders Earth willingly, in exchange for a galactic destiny.

Chris and Valerie leave Earth at last in Le Cryptomère (1989)

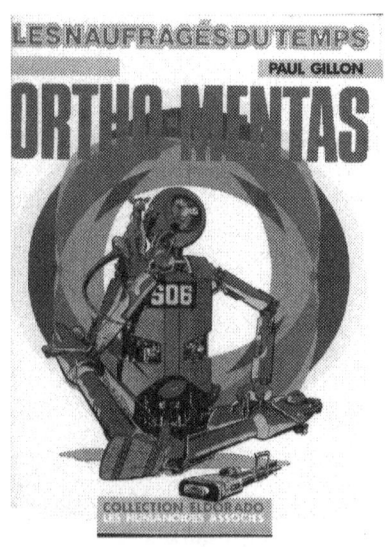

Publishing History:

Les Naufragés du Temps premiered in 1964 in the short-lived French comic magazine *Chouchou*, but was left uncompleted when the magazine folded. In its original version, the story was drawn without word balloons. The complete story was eventually partially redrawn by Gillon; word balloons were added, and it was serialized in the daily newspaper *France-Soir* in 1974. Publisher Hachette then compiled it as two, bichromic graphic novels released in 1974 and 1975. Two more volumes, in color, were then released, also by Hachette, in 1976.

The entire saga was then serialized in the magazine *Métal Hurlant* in 1977. This time, *Métal*'s publisher, Les Humanoides Associés, had Gillon recolor the earlier two volumes, and released all four volumes in handsome, new editions. At that point, Gillon expressed the desire to continue the series alone, and took over the writing from Forest. *Les Naufragés du Temps* continued to be published by Les Humanoides until its end, in 1989.

Bibliography:

Writer: Jean-Claude Forest.
Artist: Paul Gillon.
1. *L'Etoile Endormie* [*The Sleeping Star*] (*Chouchou*, 1964; rep. b&w Hachette, 1974; rep. color Humanoides, 1981)
2. *La Mort Sinueuse* [*The Creeping Death*] (b&w Hachette, 1975; rep. color Humanoides, 1981)
3. *Labyrinthes* [*Labyrinths*] (Hachette, 1976; rep. Humanoides, 1979, 1981)
4. *L'Univers Cannibale* [*The Cannibal Universe*] (Hachette, 1976; rep. Humanoides, 1979, 1980)

Writer-artist: Paul Gillon.
5. *Tendre Chimère* [*Tender Chimera*] (Humanoides, 1977, 1980)
6. *Les Maîtres Rêveurs* [*The Master Dreamers*] (Humanoides, 1978, 1980)
7. *Le Sceau de Beselek* [*The Seal of Beselek*] (Humanoides, 1979)
8. *Ortho-Mentas* (Humanoides, 1981)
9. *Terra* (Humanoides, 1984)
10. *Le Cryptomère* (Humanoides, 1989)

Website:
http://www.coolfrenchcomics.com/naufragesdutemps.htm

L'Etoile Endormie (1974)

Titan (1963)

Titan (1963)

"They call you the Titan. You might have to live up to that nickname."
(Texier to Villeroy – *Titan*)

Created by:

Writer-artist Pierre Dupuis. Pierre Dupuis (1931-) was a prolific artist who studied with Paul Gillon, then went on to work for *Vaillant* in 1949, and then for *Spirou*. Dupuis produced numerous historical and adventure series for a variety of magazines published by S.F.P.I., including *Anton Marcus* and *Alan Bruce* for *Zorro*, *Mac Gallan* for *Cap 7*, *Aigle d'Or* for *Arc-en-Ciel*, *Bison Noir* for *Special-Zorro* and the eponymous heroes of *Olac le Gladiateur* and *Erik le Viking*, originally created by Don Lawrence. His science fiction series include *Titan*, *Les Pirates de l'Infini* [*Pirates of Infinity*], published in *Zorro*, and *Kronos* (1980). Dupuis is better known for his biographies and a detailed history of World War II in comics form.

Story:

Commandant Titan is the nickname of French astronaut Michel Villeroy. He and his teammate Lucien Texier, a.k.a. Tex, are sent to the Moon in the rocket Diamant IX. There, they meet aliens from the planet Lux, whom they rescue. They then travel to Lux where they help their new alien friends defeat the threat of the Sharks, inhuman cosmic machines who seek to destroy all life in the universe. Titan and Tex eventually return to Earth, where they use their newly-gained alien technology to bring peace to the world.

Peace on Earth (1963)

Le Dernier Quart d'Heure (1963)

Publishing History:

Titan was originally serialized in an eponymous black & white digest-sized magazine published by the Société Française de Presse Illustrée (S.F.P.I.) in 1963. The magazine lasted only 16 issues. *Titan* was first reprinted in two volumes, *Titan* and *Le Retour de Titan* (*Titan's Return*) by publisher Glénat in 1977 and then again in a huge 480-page omnibus volume in 1981.

Bibliography:

Titan magazine (1963):
1. *Titan*
2-4. *Diamant IX ne répond plus* [*Diamond IX Doesn't Answer*]
5. *Bombik Menace Zukor* [*Bombik Threatens Zukor*]
6. *F = E x mm'/ d2*
7. *Terminus Lux*
8. *L'Attaque* [*The Attack*]
9. *Transmitor 7.207*
10. [Untitled]
11. [Untitled]
12. *Toute l'Eau du Ciel...* [*All the Water in the Sky...*]
13. *Cryptolegnia*
14. *Le Dernier Quart d'Heure* [*The Last Fifteen Minutes*]
15. *Titan et l'Anti-Monde* [*Titan & the Anti-World*]
16. *Paix sur la Terre* [*Peace on Earth*]

Website:
http://www.coolfrenchcomics.com/titan.htm

Les Iles du Vents Sauvage in Pilote (1970)

Lone Sloane (1966)

"I do not ask whence you came. Nor why your presence on that rock. Your very eyes mark you as a tool of the gods."
(Shonga to Lone Sloane – *Les Iles du Vent Sauvage*)

Created by:

Writer-artist Philippe Druillet. Philippe Druillet (1944-) burst onto the French comics scene with his first *Lone Sloane* graphic novel published by Losfeld in 1966. At that time, he also became a science fiction illustrator for Editions Opta, illustrating hardcover editions of Michael Moorcock's *Elric* and Fritz Leiber's *Fafhrd & the Gray Mouser* novels. In 1970, after aborted attempts at drawing a second *Lone Sloane* graphic novel for Losfeld, and a comics adaptation of *Elric*, he began serializing six new *Lone Sloane* stories in *Pilote*. In 1974, with Moebius and J.-P. Dionnet, Druillet was one of the four founding fathers of the ground-breaking magazine *Métal Hurlant*.

Druillet continued to be one of comics' most radical ground-breakers throughout the 1970s with stories such as *La Nuit* [*The Night*] (1975), inspired by the death of his first wife, the *Elric*-influenced *Yragaël* (1974) and its sequel *Urm le Fou* [*Urm the Mad*] (1975), both written by science fiction writer Michel Demuth, and the underground *Vuzz* (1974), which he later connected to the *Lone Sloane* saga. Also of note is *Nosferatu* (1978), a baroque, futurisic tale.

From 1978 to 1983, Druillet collaborated on Rolf Liebermann's *Wagner Space Opera*. He founded Space Art Creation in 1984 and made his first sculptures. He was also involved with the renovation and the architecture of the Porte de la Villette subway station in Paris, and illustrated *Manuel, L'Enfant-Rêve* [*Manuel, the Dream-Child*] written by Jacques Attali in 1994. He drew the film posters for Jean-Jacques Annaud's *Quest for Fire* and *The Name of the Rose*. Druillet was awarded the Grand Prix of Angoulême in 1988. He returned to comics, and *Lone Sloane*, in 2000 with *Chaos*, his latest graphic novel.

Story:

The prototype for Lone Sloane, a cosmic freebooter and rebel who has truckings with dark gods and Lovecraftian beings, is Catherine L. Moore's Northwest Smith. The saga of Lone Sloane takes place in the Year 800 of the "New Era," an unfathomable future when Earth is the seat of an oppressive galactic empire ruled by the mysterious and evil Shaan.

The first graphic novel introduces Lone Sloane, a roguish adventurer haunting the red light district of New Chicago, and his friend Yearl the Martian. Sloane is duped by a mysterious priest into gathering three bloodstones, but ultimately, that turns out to be only a test to determine if he is worthy of becoming the mate of a cosmic goddess. Sloane frees the goddess, who had been trapped by an evil cult of serpent-priests, by making love to her.

A few pages of an uncompleted sequel in which Sloane and Yearl were taken prisoners by the worshippers of a dark god on the planet Nahab remain.

Uncompleted Lone Sloane story (1967)

In 1970, Druillet totally revamped the story, which became *The Throne of the Black God*, published in *Pilote*. We are now in the Year 804, and Sloane alone is captured by the Dark Priests. However, when they try to reincarnate their Black God inside his body, he is able to use a word of power given to him by the God-Kings to banish the evil entity. Sloane remains marked by the gods, and his eyes now burn with a supernatural red fire.

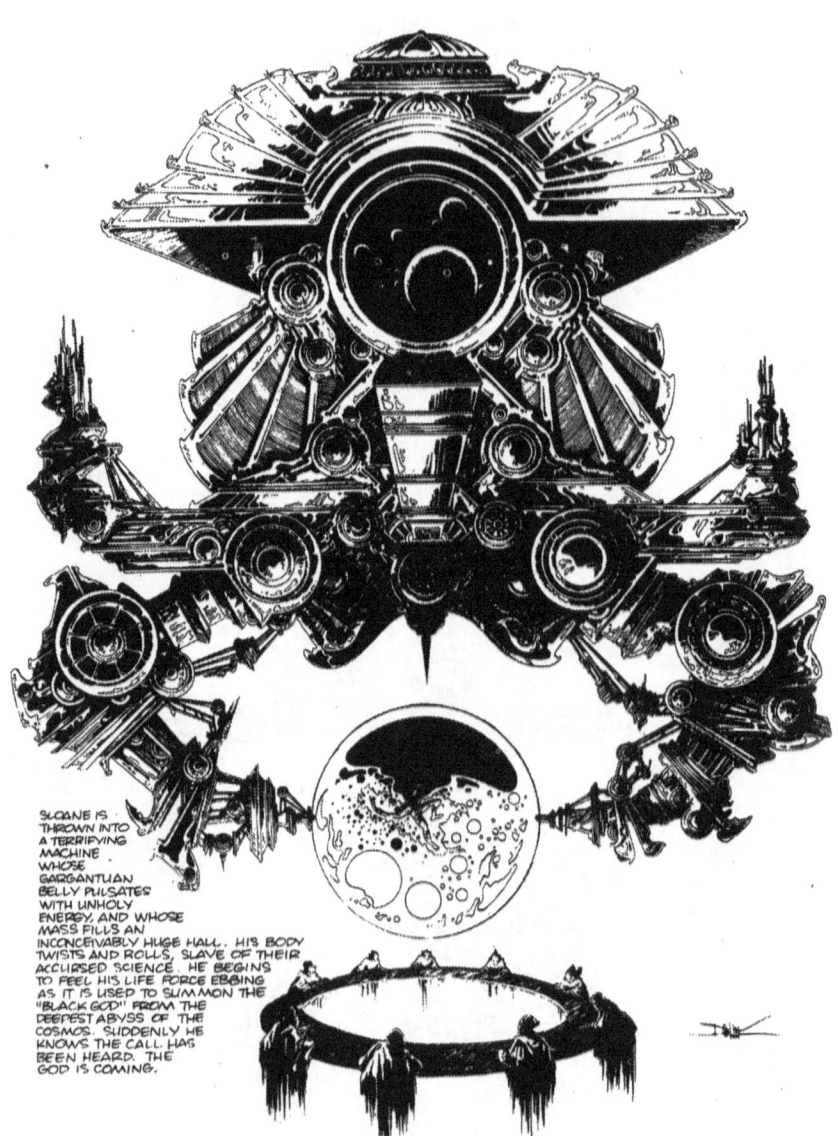

Le Trône du Dieu Noir (1970)

In the next story, *Les Iles du Vent Sauvage* [*The Isle of the Doom Wind*], Sloane is found by a pirate named Shonga who hopes the Earthman will lead him to the treasure of the gods. But Sloane dupes Shonga and trades his soul for those of Shonga and his men.

Terra (1970)

After a brief interlude involving an old man stranded in a graveyard of spaceships, and an encounter with Torquedara Varenkor, master of the Starbridge, Sloane returns to his ship, the powerful *O Sidarta*, captained in his absence by Yearl and the mysterious Kurt Kurtsteiner, named after a French science fiction author.

The final episode of this saga has Sloane and his men locate Original Earth which, in this version of events, is a long-lost world taken by the gods who use it as their refuge. The God of Earth is Wul, also named after a French science fiction writer, Stefan Wul.

The next installment in Sloane's saga is *Delirius*, a novel-length story written by Jacques Lob (see *Ténébrax* entry). In it, Sloane and Yearl are again manipulated by sinister priests to rob Delirius, a planet-wide casino and den of vices, heavily guarded and ruled by the corrupt Kadenborg. Various doublecrosses ensue and Delirius falls into chaos. This is the novel which introduces the character of Shaan the Imperator.

The next book, *Gail*, was started by Druillet when *Métal Hurlant* was launched in 1974, then interrupted when his wife Nicole died, and restarted only in late 1977. In it, Sloane has been captured by the forces of Shaan, except that they do not know the identity of their prisoner. He is taken to a cosmic penitentiary. One man, however, has recognized him: Irian Merennen the Mad, a servant of the Dark Gods, who plots to use him in a bid to overthrow the Imperator. But Sloane is no man's pawn, and he escapes after causing Merennen's destruction.

The next three volumes are an oddity: Druillet decided to loosely adapt Gustave Flaubert's classic 1858 novel *Salammbo*, and retrofit Lone Sloane into it. With *Salammbo*, French novelist Gus-

tave Flaubert (1821-1880) produced what may very well be the first work of modern heroic fantasy in the French language. It is a brash, colorful and exotic novel about ancient Carthage, the North-African city-state which challenged Roman domination during the Punic Wars in the 2nd century BC, and was loosely based on an incident reported by Roman historian Polybius. Flaubert created the fictional character of Salammbo, the daughter of Carthagenian general Hamilcar, and told of her doomed love story with Matho, the leader of the rebel mercenaries who were besieging Carthage. While the supernatural was, at best, understated, Salammbo was a worthy precursor to the opulent, colorful, savage fantasies of Robert E. Howard, and Matho was a true proto-Conan.

When Druillet's adaptation begins, Shaan's empire is in ruins, replaced by a republic, although the villainous Imperator dreams of regaining power. Sloane is searching for Yearl and *O Sidarta* aboard the *Silver Claw*, a ship he stole from Shaan when suddenly he catches a vision of Salammbo. Sloane alone plunges into the past and finds himself transported back to Carthage, where he assumes the identity of Matho. Eventually, after Hamilcar's victory, Matho (Sloane) is put to death but is rescued by Yearl who has at last found him.

The latest book, *Chaos*, picks up the story ten years later, when Sloane's body has been slowly regenerating in a golden sarcophagus-like machine. He is finally returned to life by a beautiful blue-skinned girl called Légende to face his arch-enemy Shaan. Sloane teams up with Vuzz, another of Druillet's characters, and finally confronts Shaan who turns out to be an amalgalm of his darkest future 300 years from now. Sloane banishes Shaan and is finally reunited with Yearl.

Publishing History:

Lone Sloane was first published in 1966 by Eric Losfeld, the publisher of *Barbarella* and *Jodelle*. After the aborted start of a second graphic novel, it migrated to the pages of *Pilote* in 1970 in the form of six short stories, and one full-length graphic novel, *Delirius*, written by Jacques Lob.

The fourth episode, *Gail*, was serialized in *Métal Hurlant* in 1974, but completed only in 1978. Then, Druillet embarked on a retelling of Gustave Flaubert's *Salammbo* with Sloane retroactively implanted in the story, published in three volumes between 1981 and 1986. After a long absence, Lone Sloane returned in 2000 in a graphic novel, *Chaos*, based on a treatment written by Druillet with Benjamin Legrand, Xavier Gelin and Denis Chateau for a 1987 3D animated production called *Kazhann* that was never completed.

Bibliography:

1. *Le Mystère des Abîmes* [*The Mystery of the Abyss*] (Losfeld, 1966; rep. as *Lone Sloane 66*, Humanoides, 1977, also including *Nova*, a short *Lone Sloane* story originally published in *Pilote Mensuel* No. 1, 1974)
2. *Les Six Voyages de Lone Sloane* [*The Six Voyages of Lone Sloane*] (Dargaud, 1972) collecting:
    a. *Le Trône du Dieu Noir* [*The Throne of the Black God*] (*Pilote* No. 538, 1970)
    b. *Les Iles du Vent Sauvage* [*The Isle of the Doom Wind*] (*Pilote* No. 553, 1970)
    c. *Rose* (*Pilote* No. 562, 1970)
    d. *Torquedara Varenkor: Le Pont sur les Etoiles* [*The Bridge over the Stars*] (*Pilote* No. 569, 1970)
    e. *O Sidarta* (*Pilote* No. 578, 1970)

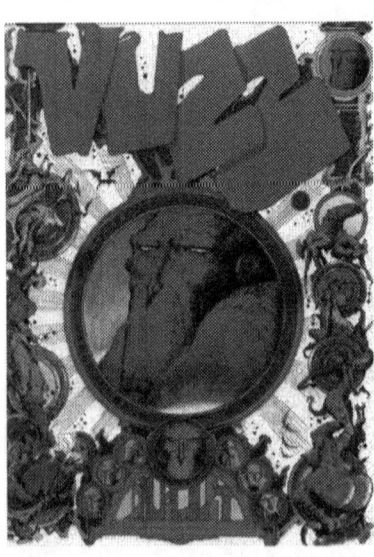

    f. *Terra* (*Pilote* No. 598, 1971)
3. *Delirius* (**written by Jacques Lob**) (*Pilote* Nos. 651-666, 1972; rep. Dargaud, 1973)
4. *Gail* (*Métal Hurlant* Nos.18-27, 1977-78; rep. Humanoides, 1978)
5. *Salammbo* (*Métal Hurlant* Nos. 48-54, 1980; rep. Dargaud, 1981)
6. *Salammbo 2: Carthago* (Dargaud, 1982)
7. *Salammbo 3: Matho* (Dargaud, 1986)
8. *Chaos* (Albin Michel, 2000)

Vuzz:
Vuzz (Phénix, 1973; rep. b&w Dargaud, 1974; col. Humanoides, 1981)
Là-Bas [*Out There*] (b&w Humanoides, 1978; col. 1982)

Website:
http://www.coolfrenchcomics.com/lonesloane.html

Right page:
  (top) Michael Moorcock's *Elric*; Fritz Leiber's *Fafhrd & the Gray Mouser*.

The science fiction art of Philippe Druillet

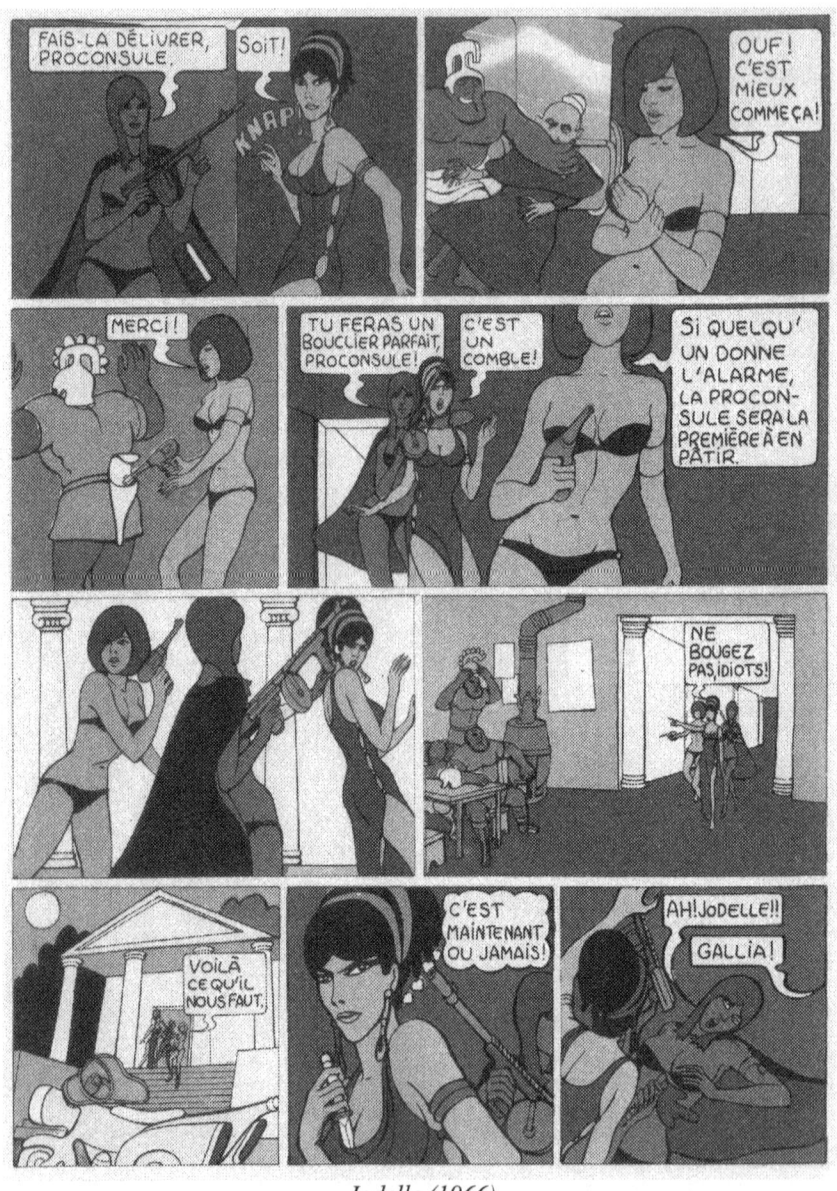

Jodelle (1966)

Jodelle (1966)
"Vanitas!"
(The Druid – *Jodelle*)

Created by:
Writer-artist Guy Pellaert with writing assistance from Pierre Bartier. Guy Pellaert (1934-) was born in Brussels and studied at the Beaux-Arts. After working in advertising, he drew *Jodelle* in 1966, followed by *Pravda la Survireuse*, serialized in *Hara-Kiri* in 1967 and collected as a graphic novel the following year. In 1968, Pellaert produced a series of pop art-inspired photo-comics for *Hara-Kiri*: *The Game, She and the Greenhairs*, written by Roger Wolfs. He also produced a more traditional comic book series, *Karachi!* Pellaert then left comics to work in theater and television. In 1973, he produced *Rock Dreams*, a book collecting a series of paintings featuring pop music artists. He drew the covers for David Bowie's *Diamond Dogs* and the Rolling Stones' *It's only rock n' roll*.

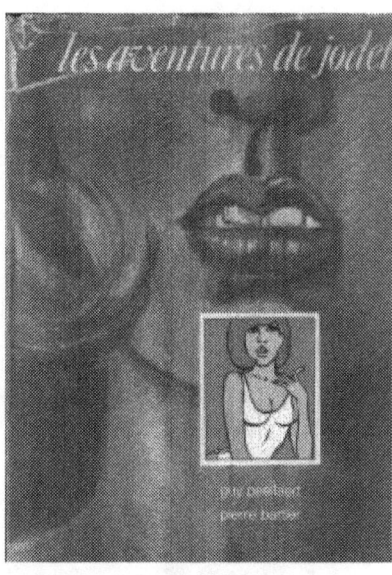

Story:
Jodelle (who bears a strong resemblance to French pop singer Sylvie Vartan) is a sexually liberated heroine whose exploits take place in a pseudo-futuristic Roman Empire. There, television, juke-boxes, souped-up motorbikes and modern weapons cohabit with druids, centurions, helmeted barbarians and gladiators, all dressed in the exuberant colors of pop art.

Jodelle is a combination of *James Bond*, *Barbarella* and *Astérix*, a Gallic freedom fighter who ends up battling the Imperial power of Rome. The Roman Proconsul looks like the Black Queen of Sogo and her Cardinals are caricatures of Pope Paul VI.

Publishing History:
Publisher Eric Losfeld's small publishing company *Le Terrain Vague* [*The Wasteland*], established in 1955, had already made a mark in literature by releasing a number of books that other, more mainstreams publishers would not

touch. Losfeld was a friend of André Breton, the founder of the Surrealist Movement, and was among the first to publish authors such as Arrabal, Topor, Ionesco, etc. In the early 1960s, Losfeld also published ground-breaking erotic fiction such as the world-famous classic *Emmanuelle*, which drew the ire of the French authorities and caused him to be prosecuted and fined. Losfeld was also a pioneer in publishing classics of French science fiction and fantasy by writers such as Gérard Klein, Jacques Sternberg, Louis Thirion, etc. Finally, in 1964, Losfeld became a pioneer in the field of adult comics by releasing the hardcover edition of *Barbarella* (1964).

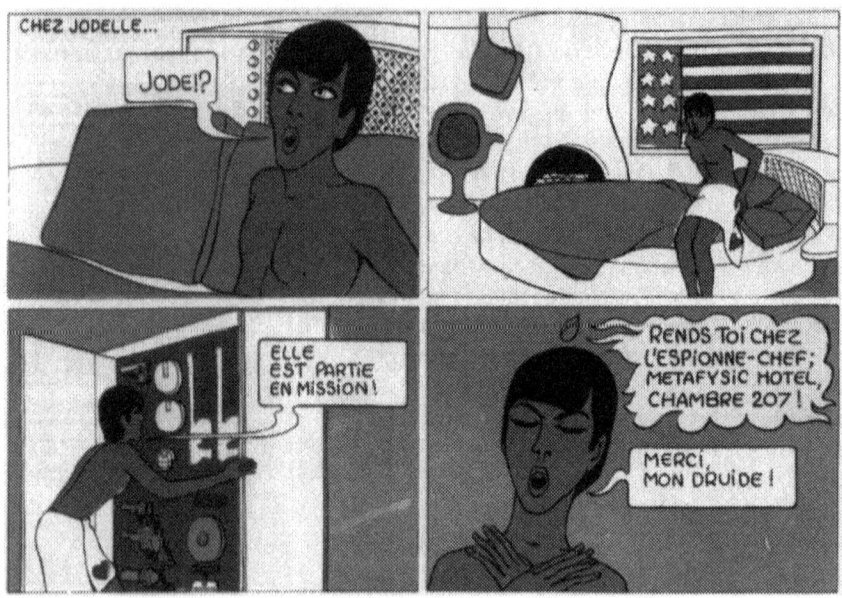

The success of *Barbarella* encouraged Losfeld to publish other mature comics, such as *Saga de Xam* (1967) by the collective of artists signing "Nicolas Devil," Philippe Druillet's *Lone Sloane* (1966), Pellaert's *Jodelle* and *Pravda* (1968) and later Jean Van Hamme & Paul Cuvelier's *Epoxy* (1968), Michael O'Donoghue and Frank Springer's *Phoebe Zeit-Geist* (1969) and Caza's *Kris Kool* (1970). Losfeld was not able to manage his success, his debts, and his troubles with the Law and was eventually driven into bankruptcy in 1971. Eric Losfeld died in 1979.

Website:
http://www.coolfrenchcomics.com/pravda.htm

Jodelle (1966)

La Planète de l'Angoisse (1969)

Luc Orient (1966)

"Orient of Earth, your name shall ever be preserved in the hearts of the people of Terango."
(Thar-Ojec to Luc Orient – *Le Maître de Terango*)

Created by:
Writer Greg and artist Eddy Paaape.

• One of the most prolific creators in French-language comics, Greg (pseudonym of Michel Regnier) (1931-1999) began his career as a writer-artist at age 16 with the humor series *Nestor & Boniface*. In the early 1950s, he wrote and drew a superhero series, *Le Chat* [*The Cat*] under the pseudonym of Michel Denys for *Heroic - Albums*. In 1954, Greg launched his own, short-lived magazine, *Paddy*. In 1958, he joined the editorial team of *Tintin* magazine, serving as its editor-in-chief from 1965  to 1975. At *Tintin*, Greg wrote and drew a number of humoristic adventure series such as *Rock Derby* and *Zig & Puce*, which he had taken over from their original creator, Alain Saint-Ogan. As a writer, he contributed scripts to Tibet's *Chick Bill*, André Franquin's *Modeste & Pompon* and Raymond Macherot's *Clifton*. As editor-in-chief, Greg co-created a number of cutting-edge, modern adventure heroes, such as *Bernard Prince* and *Comanche* with artist Hermann Huppen, *Bruno Brazil* with artist William Vance and *Luc Orient* with Eddy Paape. He also wrote the poetic series *Olivier Rameau* for artist Dany.

During the 1960s, Greg also wrote and drew the hugely successful humor series *Achille Talon*, briefly published in the U.S. as *Walter Melon*, created in 1963 for *Pilote*, and the juvenile adventure series *Les As* for *Vaillant*. Greg also penned some of *Spirou*'s best adventures, and after Franquin's death, took over the writing of its spin-off series, *Le Marsupilami*. In all, Greg's comics career totaled more than 250 graphic novels. Greg also penned several successful detective novels for publisher Fleuve Noir, and the film adaptations of two of *Tintin*'s animated features: *The*  *Temple of the Sun* and *The Lake of Sharks*.

• Eddy Paape (1920-) is a prolific Belgian artist who joined the editorial team of *Spirou* in 1946, first temporarily taking over the *Jean Valhardi* adventure series from fellow artist Jijé. In 1958, he and writer Jean-Michel Charlier created their own globe-trotting adventurer, *Marc Dacier*. In 1965, Paape moved to *Tintin* where he and Greg created the *Flash Gordon*-inspired popular science fiction series, *Luc*

Orient. More recent genre series by Paape include *Udolfo* and *Carol Détective* with writer André-Paul Duchateau, and *Les Jardins de la Peur* [*The Gardens of Fear*] with writer Jean Dufaux.

Eurocristal

Story:

Luc Orient, his mentor Professor Hugo Kala and Kala's lab assistant, the beautiful Lora, work for superlab Eurocristal located somewhere in western Europe, perhaps Switzerland. When the first volume opens, our heroes are drawn to the hidden valley of Sher-Dhang in the Far East, where meteor rocks have been found that may well be the remains of an ancient alien spacecraft. While investigating, Kala, Orient and Lora enlist the help of native guide Toba, who becomes the fourth member of the team. They also face the threat of rival evil scientist, Dr. Julius Argos.

Eventually, in Book 2, the heroes rescue a couple of white-skinned aliens from planet Terango, whose flying disks did crash in the valley long ago. They reanimate the crew of one of the disks, who had been placed in suspended animation. The Teranguians, led by the brave Galax-Ajh, return to their homeworld.

The next three books deal with the return of Galax-Ajh who now wishes to enlist Kala and Orient's help to free Terango from the tyrant Sectan. The Earthmen travel to Terango and destroy Sectan's invasion fleet. Then, Orient finds allies among the savage dragon folk and the winged people who inhabit Terango's backwater lands. Finally, the last battle pits the forces of Sectan and his newfound ally, Dr. Argos, whom he has brought from Earth, against the Terango rebels led by Orient. The rebels win.

Galax-Ajh warns Orient and his friends of Sectan's threat (1968)

After this *Flash Gordon*-inspired, five-book saga, the series settled into more Earth-based adventures. In Episode 6, Luc and Lora acquire temporary superpowers after being bathed in alien lights. Episode 8 deals with mutant children. Episode 9 has an alien blackmailing Earth. Episode 10 features a hidden human civilization patterned after insects *à la Hellstrom's Hive*.

Away from its *Flash Gordon* roots, *Luc Orient* lost its direction and uniqueness. Greg and Paape eventually returned Orient and his friends to Terango in Episodes 13 to 16, which began with a journey through time, then an attempt to find a world willing to take in three million Dartz, who had been wandering through the galaxy. But the Terango Luc, Lora and Kala found was that of its own future. Galax-Ajh and his friends were long dead, and the planet had reverted to savagery. Only the evil Argos still lived to threaten Orient. This wholesale trashing of the series' beginnings left a bitter taste for the readers.

Eddy Paape must have agreed for in the next book that he wrote and drew, *Caragal*, the action takes place in the Teranguian "past" with Galax-Ajh still very much alive. With both Greg and Paape nearing retirement age, *Luc Orient* was also allowed to retire gracefully.

Le Maître de Terango (1968)

Publishing History:

Luc Orient was originally serialized in the weekly comic magazine *Tintin*, beginning in 1966. It was one of the many series simultaneously launched by its then-editor-in-chief Greg to give the magazine a much-needed facelift. *Luc Orient*'s adventures were then collected as a series of graphic novels by Editions du Lombard, starting in 1969. The series continued regularly with one or two volumes per year until episode 13 released in 1978. After the cancellation of *Tintin* in 1978, the later episodes were released more sporadically.

Episode 16 was written by Paape himself, without Greg. Episode 17 was not a single new story but a collection of short stories previously published in the digest-sized *Tintin Pocket* in the early 1970s and reformatted for graphic novel publication. Episode 18, released in 1994, would seem to be the last in the series. *Luc Orient* is now being reprinted in omnibus editions, two volumes in one.

Bibliography:

1. *Le Dragon de Feu* [*The Dragon of Fire*] (*Tintin* Nos. 952-970, 1966; rep. Lombard, 1969)
2. *Les Soleils de Glace* [*The Ice Suns*] (*Tintin* Nos. 976-997, 1967; rep. Lombard, 1970)
3. *Le Maître de Terango* [*The Master of Terango*] (*Tintin* Nos. 1009-1029, 1968; rep. Lombard, 1971)
4. *La Planète de l'Angoisse* [*The Planet of Terror*] (*Tintin* Nos. 1040-1059, 1969; rep. Lombard, 1972)
5. *La Forêt d'Acier* [*The Steel Forest*] (*Tintin* Nos. 1082-1102, 1969; rep. Lombard, 1973)
6. *Le Secret des 7 Lumières* [*The Secret of the 7 Lights*] (*Tintin* Nos. 1118-1138, 1970; rep. Lombard, 1974)
7. *Le Cratère aux Sortilèges* [*The Crater*

of Spells] (*Tintin* Nos. 1183-1196, 1971; rep. Lombard, 1974)
8. *La Légion des Anges Maudits* [*The Legion of Fallen Angels*] (*Tintin* Nos. 1206-1221, 1971-72; rep. Lombard, 1975)
9. *24 Heures pour la Planète Terre* [*24 Hours for Planet Earth*] (*Tintin* No. 1258-*Tintin-Hebdo* No. 10, 1972-73; rep. Lombard, 1975)
10. *Le 6ème Continent* [*The Sixth Continent*] (*Tintin-Hebdo* Nos. 53-60, 1974; rep. Lombard, 1976)
11. *La Vallée des Eaux Troubles* [*The Valley of Murky Waters*] (*Tintin-Hebdo* Nos. 83-98, 1974; rep. Lombard, 1976)
12. *La Porte de Cristal* [*The Crystal Gate*] (*Nouveau-Tintin* Nos. 10-25, 1975; rep. Lombard, 1977)
13. *L'Enclume de la Foudre* [*The Anvil of Thunder*] (*Nouveau-Tintin* Nos. 96-107, 1977; rep. Lombard, 1978)
14. *Le Rivage de la Fureur* [*The Shores of Wrath*] (*Nouveau-Tintin* Nos. 233-246, 1980; rep. Lombard, 1981)
15. *Roubak, Ultime Espoir* [*Rubak: Ultimate Hope*] (Lombard, 1984)
16. *Caragal* (*Nouveau-Tintin* Nos. 447-457, 1984; rep. Lombard, 1985)
17. *Les Spores de Nulle Part* [*The Spores From Nowhere*] (includes the stories *Les Spores de Nulle Part* [*The Spores From Nowhere*] (1970); *La Vengeance* [*The Revenge*] (1980); *Les Rayons du Feu du Soleil* [*The Rays of the Sun*] (1981); rep. Lombard 1990)
18. *Rendez-Vous à 20 Heures en Enfer* [*Rendezvous in Hell at 20:00*] (Lombard, 1994)

Sectan and Argos

Website:
http://www.coolfrenchcomics.com/lucorient.htm

Les Soleils de Glace (1967)

Submerman – Glénat reedition (1976)

Submerman (1967)

"Did I just meet a member of an heretofore unknown race who lives at the bottom of the sea... Did I just meet an authentic Homo Aquaticus?"
(Captain Goujon – *Submerman*)

Created by:
Writer Jacques Lob and artist Georges Pichard (see *Ténébrax* entry).

Story:
The underwater explorer Captain Goujon, a Jacques Cousteau-like character and inventor of a new diving saucer-type of submarine, meets Submerman, a telepathic, water-breathing member of an undersea civilization who lives in the beautiful city of *Fond-Joli* [*Pretty Bottom*]. The other aquatics have been captured and taken away by a race of scaly, green humanoids dubbed "Hydrons" who reside at the bottom of an underwater abyss called the Great Cloaca. With the help of Goujon, Submerman frees his people, but they must first contend with the villainous trio of Hans Mudfer a.k.a. the Admiral, his henchman François Lebahu and the sinister Professor Plancton, creator of the deadly Black Submarine.

Captain Goujon comes face-to-face with Submerman (1967)

Submerman (1967)

In subsequent adventures, the hapless Lebahu becomes the subject of experimental surgery that turns him into an Aquatic—except that he hates living underwater (even though he ends up marrying the beautiful Paulette).

In a series of shorter stories entiled *Les Mémoires de Submerman* [*The Memoirs of Submerman*], Lob and Pichard explored the wonderful undersea world they created, and told stories of the Aquatic Civilization .

Publishing History:

Submerman was originally serialized in the weekly comic magazine *Pilote*, but it somehow never met with the success it so richly deserved. Publisher Glénat released two graphic novel collections, *Submerman* (1976) and *Les Peuples de la Mer* [*The Undersea People*] (1978). In 1979, publisher Dargaud released *Les Mémoires de Submerman* [*Submerman's Memoirs*], reprinting some further stories that initially appeared in the digest-sized *Super Pocket Pilote* from 1968-70. In 2001, young writer-artist Pierre LeGall obtained the permission of the estate of the creators and embarked on a redrawing of the Lob-Pichard stories.

The Admiral, Prof. Plancton and Lebahu

Bibliography:

1. *Submerman* (28 p.) (*Pilote* Nos. 377-390, 1967; rep. Glénat No. 1, 1976)
2. *Au-Dela du Grand Bouchon* [*Beyond the Great Stopper*] (28 p.) (*Pilote* Nos. 404-417, 1967; rep. Glénat No. 1, 1976)
3. *Les Peuples de la Mer* [*The Undersea People*] (28 p.) (*Pilote* Nos. 431-444, 1968; rep. Glénat No. 2, 1978)
4. *L'Aventure sans Retour* [*The Adventure of No-Return*] (28 p.) (*Pilote* Nos. 488-501, 1969; rep. Glénat No. 2, 1978)
5. *Le Péril Vert* [*The Green Peril*] (28 p.) (*Pilote* Nos. 520-533, 1970)

Super Pocket Pilote stories:
1. *Les Mémoires de Submerman* [*The Memoirs of Submerman*] (8 p.) (1968)
2. *L'Aventure Spongieuse* [*The Spongy Adventure*] (16 p.) (1968)
3. *Le Tour du Courant Doux* [*The Tour of the Soft Current*] (16 p.) (1969)
4. *La Faune des Profondeurs* [*The Fauna of the Depths*] (16 p.) (1969)
5. *L'Ambulant* [*The Travelling Salesman*] (16 p.) (1969)
6. *L'Aquarevarium* [*The Aquadreamarium*] (16 p.) (1969)
7. *Le Grand Ensemble* [*The Great Set*] (16 p.) (1970)
8. *Dans les Eaux Miroitantes des Fonds Mirageux* [*In the Mirror-like Waters of the Mirage-filled Depths*] (16 p.) (1970)
9. *L'Exilé des Fonds des Mers* [*Exiled in the Depths*] (16 p.) (1970)

Lebahu and Paulette

Website:
http://www.coolfrenchcomics.com/submerman.htm

Olympio & Vincent Larcher (1967)

"I shall never fear Olympio!"
(Prof. Spoliansky – *Olympic 2004*)

Created by:

Writer-artist Raymond Reding. Raymond Reding (1920-1999) was a Belgian comic book writer-artist who started his career writing and illustrating children's tales in *Bravo* in 1944. He then created the character of *Mr. Cro*, a detective, in 1947. In 1950, he joined the editorial team of *Tintin* for which, in 1957, he created the characters of tennis pro *Jimmy Torrent* and his young ward, *Jari*, followed by soccer pro *Vincent Larcher* in 1963. In 1972, Reding created *Section R*, about a trio of female crime solvers.
Jimmy Torrent, Jari, Vincent Larcher and the girls of Section R met in various adventures. Reding left *Tintin* in 1979 to go to *Super As*, for which he created *Eric Castel*, another soccer star.

Vincent Larcher meets Prof. Spoliansky (1967)

Story:

Vincent Larcher is a member of the French national soccer team. In the first story, Larcher rescues Olympio from the clutches of his father, Professor Spoliansky, a mad scientist who plans to create a new breed of supermen. Spoliansky has invited Larcher to be his technical advisor on *Olympic 2004*, a movie about the Olympics of the future which he purports to shoot on his private island, but it is only a cover for his experiments. Olympio's mother is Spoliansky's assistant, Sylvia.

Olympic 2004 (1967)

Olympio first emerges dazed and not in control of his great powers, but quickly befriends and trusts Vincent. Eventually, Spoliansky comes to realize his madness and seemingly dies helping fight an attack of giant mutated crabs accidentally released during Olympio's escape.

In the second volume, Larcher and Olympio, now friends, expose a conspiracy led by the mysterious Triangle, a dark-clad figure who ultimately is revealed to be Spoliansky (although a doubt remains). He and his eleven assistants hope to create world peace by making it look as if Earth is being threatened by alien invaders.

Olympic 2004 (1967)

Onze Gauchers pour Mexico (1968)

They do this by faking alien manifestations at global sports events. However, one of the eleven scientists, Professor Sato, turns out to be a traitor, who seeks revenge for the Hiroshima explosion which disfigured him and killed his family. (It is revealed that the eleven professors and their female assistants all benefit from a longevity drug originally discovered by Spoliansky.) Sato murders the Triangle and tries to gain control of Olympio and his powers, but is defeated. He then ages rapidly and dies. The ten remaining professors elect Olympio, the son of their late master, as their new leader. Jimmy Torrent and Jari guest-star in that story.

Olympio challenges Dr. Ketzal (1969)

Finally, in the third volume, Larcher and Olympio travel to Mexico for the 1968 Olympic Games. There, they battle the power-mad Doctor Ketzal, a Great Initiate who plans to rule the world using three powerful, magical, Aztec artefacts. Ketzal has found the way into a Mirror-Earth and gathered a large sect of followers, the Brotherhood of the Serpent, of which he is the leader. He succeeds in capturing the ten professors and experiments on them. Ultimately, they all sacrifice their lives rather than attack Olympio. Olympio manages to enlist the help of Ketzal's chief female assistant, Erica, and gains access to the Mirror-World, where Ketzal is forcing Vincent to go through a bloody Aztec sports ritual. Olympio confronts Ketzal and wins. The mad Doctor attempts to return back to our world but is disintegrated during the passage.

Publishing History:

Vincent Larcher was created by Raymond Reding for the weekly comic magazine *Tintin* in 1963. After a mundane, rags-to-riches origin story entitled *Vincent Larcher Avant-Centre* (serialized in *Tintin* Nos. 770-802), the character went on hiatus, but returned with a vengeance in 1967 with the superheroic *Olympio Trilogy* featured in this chapter. This, however, turned out to be a short-lived experiment, and Reding returned to telling more conventional, sports-themed stories.

Two more *Vincent Larcher* stories followed, *Le Condottiere* (serialized in *Tintin* Nos. 1088-1109, 1970) in which Olympio made a guest appearance but which otherwise featured no science fiction or fantasy elements, and *Mini-Jupes & Maxi-Foot* [*Miniskirts & Maxifoot*] (serialized in *Tintin* Nos. 1142-1157, 1970). Olympio was also the hero of a short story published in the digest-sized *Tintin Selection*.

The *Olympio Trilogy* was collected in the graphic novel format by publisher Lombard in their short-lived *Vincent Larcher* collection in the 1970s.

Bibliography:

1. *Olympic 2004* (*Tintin* Nos. 984-1004, 1967; rep. Lombard Vincent Larcher 1, 1969)
2. *11 Gauchers pour Mexico* [*11 Southpaws for Mexico*] (*Tintin* Nos. 1011-1030, 1968; rep. Lombard Vincent Larcher 2, 1970)
2b. *Le Nain Jaune et les Géants* [*The Yellow Dwarf and the Giants*] (*Tintin Selection* No. 7, 1970)
3. *Le Zoo du Dr. Ketzal* [*The Zoo of Dr. Ketzal*] (*Tintin* Nos. 1039-1059, 1969; rep. Lombard Vincent Larcher 5, 1973)

Website:
http://www.coolfrenchcomics.com/vincentlarcher.htm

Le Zoo du Dr. Ketzal (1969)

Wampus No. 1 (1969)

Wampus (1969) & L'Autre (1973)

"This is the beginning of the end, Mankind!
Wampus has come bearing a message of Doom!"
(Wampus – *Wampus*)

Created by:
Writer Franco Frescura and artist Lucanio Bernasconi.
- Franco Frescura (1934-) is an Italian writer, born in Venice, who began his career penning stories for various magazines and publishers such as Corriere della Serra, Mondadori and Alpe. For Editions Lug in France, Frescura co-created not only *Wampus* and its spin-off *L'Autre*, but also a number of other popular series such as *Dick Demon*, *Rakar*, *Mister Song* and *Waki*. In the 1980s, Frescura, who is also an attorney, returned to his legal practice in Milan.
- Luciano Bernasconi (1939-) is a renowned Italian artist. Born in Rome, Bernasconi first worked for Carlo Cedroni's Studio Barbato from 1959 to 1964. Then, from 1969 to the early 1980s, Bernasconi became the major artistic force working for Editions Lug, virtually co-creating all of their major series: *Wampus* and its spin-off *L'Autre*, *Bob Lance*, *Gladiateur de Bronze*, *Comte de Saint-Germain*, *Jeff Sullivan*, *Kabur*, *Kit Kappa*, *Phenix*, *Sibilla*, *Starlock*, *Waki* and many others.  After Lug discontinued the production of new stories, Bernasconi continued to draw comics for the Italian market. He returned to French comics in 2000 when Lug's successor, Semic, commissioned him to draw new stories featuring his old characters.

Story:
Wampus is an alien shape-shifer sent to Earth by an evil cosmic intelligence known only as the Great Mind to sow chaos and destruction. It will eventually be revealed that the Great Mind is one of the two super-intelligences that exist at the end of time. Its purpose in sending Wampus is to cull the strong from the weak in its billion year-evolutionary plan. Wampus is discovered, and opposed, by French secret agent Jean Sten; however, no one else believes him. Soon, Sten is pursued by his former colleagues.

In the course of several issues, Wampus causes havoc in France, then moves on to Germany, New York, Tokyo, and after a detour through the fourth dimension, to London, which he destroys with a tactical nuclear device. Then, with Sten ever hot on his trail, Wampus flees to Spain and, finally, Italy. And that is when the original series ended, without any resolution to the battle between Sten and Wampus.

Wampus faces Jean Sten in Japan (1969)

Four years later, the battle began again in the magazine *Futura*, but this time the adversaries were a less monstrous alien, known simply as *l'Autre* [*The Other*]. The Other has the same powers and eyes as Wampus (a downward arrow in their pupils), and also serves the Great Mind. His enemy is journalist Jean Vlad, who chases him all over the world. During a visit to the Other's native dimension, where all of Mankind has already begun to mutate into creatures like him, Vlad learns of the Great Mind's designs. He also discovers that the reason he (and presumably Sten as well) are the predestined adversaries of the Other (and Wampus) is that they are dopplegangers. It is also revealed that there is another god-like force opposing the Great Mind,  whom Vlad is unwittingly serving. Eventually, Vlad and the Other meet under Ayers Rock in the Australian Outback. Vlad kills the Other in hand-to-hand battle, but ends up confined to a lunatic asylum.

The saga of Wampus was picked up again in 2001. After a battle at the Vatican, Wampus is forced to travel back in time, in the process meeting other characters from Lug's comics universe (Dragut, Gallix, Kabur, Brigade Temporelle), affecting the history of Man for good and evil. Eventually, Sten and Wampus meet in a final battle held on Labyrinth, an artefact located at the End of Time, before the Great Mind and its opposite, the Universality. The stakes are the replay of the events that led to the destruction of London, with two possible futures hanging in the balance: one in which Wampus wins, London is destroyed, and Mankind becomes the Great Mind's playthings; the other in which he loses, London is saved, and Mankind lives on to a glorious future. By sacrificing himself, Sten wins the battle and kills Wampus.

In a postscript, it is revealed that the Other's sister, Mircea Vlad, escaped the fate of the Other-Earth and came to serve the Universality, which sent her to our Earth where she became known as Futura. She later witnesses the murder of Jean Vlad at the hands of the disciples of Wampus, and stays on to protect our world from further attempts by the Great Mind to alter its fate, joining a group called the Strangers.

Mircea (Futura) meets Jean Vlad (2003) (art by Pasarin)

Publishing History:
Wampus was originally published in 1969 by Editions Lug in six digest-sized magazines. The series was discontinued because of censorship problems. The final episode was eventually serialized in *Ombrax* in 1985. In the meantime, Lug published *L'Autre* [*The Other*] in *Futura* in 1973 and 1974.

Wampus made his reappearance in *Fantask* (2nd. Series) in 2001, before switching to *Mustang*. Futura appeared as part of a superhero group called *Strangers* in its eponymous title in 2002 and 2003. *Strangers* was released as a six-issue mini-series in the United States by Image Comics in 2003.

Bibliography:
Wampus (1st Series)
Writer: Franco Frescura.
Artist: Luciano Bernasconi.
1. *Wampus* (1969)
2. *Le Dernier Ricanement* [*The Last Laugh*] (1969)
3. *Et Vint le Chaos* [*And Chaos Came*] (1969)
4. *La Grande Explosion* [*The Great Explosion*] (1969)
5. *Vu du Pont* [*View from a Bridge*] (1969)
6. *Toilette du Bourreau* [*Executioner's Wash*] (1969)
7. *Le Ciel est Rouge* [*The Sky Is Red*] (drawn in 1969 but published in *Ombrax* Nos. 230-233, 1985)

Wampus No. 3 (1969)

L'Autre No. 8 (1974)

L'Autre
Writer: Franco Frescura.
Artist: Luciano Bernasconi.
1. *Je t'attendais Jean Vlad* [*I Was Waiting For You, Jean Vlad*] (*Futura* No. 11, 1973)
2. *La Grande Confrontation* [*The Great Confrontation*] (*Futura* No. 12, 1973)
3. *Au Bord de l'Abime* [*On the Edge of the Abyss*] (*Futura* No. 13, 1973)
4. *Un Monde Inconnu* [*An Unknown World*] (*Futura* No. 14, 1973)
5. *Saut dans le Vide* [*Jump into the Void*] (*Futura* No. 15, 1973)
6. *Gel, Feu, Soleil, Ténèbres* [*Frost, Fire, Sun, Darkness*] (*Futura* No. 16, 1973)
7. *Rampants et Volants* [*Crawling and Flying Things*] (*Futura* No. 17, 1974)
8. *Vainqueur et Vaincu* [*Victor and Vanquished*] (*Futura* No. 18, 1974)

Wampus (2nd Series)
Writer: Jean-Marc Lofficier.
Artist: Luciano Bernasconi.
1. *Le Sacrement du Mal* [*The Sacrament of Evil*] (guest-starring Mister Song) (*Fantask* No. 3, 2001)
2. *Dragut!* (guest-starring Dragut and Sibilla) (*Fantask* No. 4, 2001)
3. *La Chute de Camelot* [*The Fall of Camelot*] (guest-starring Bob Lance) (*Fantask* No. 5, 2001)
4. *Sous le Signe de Rome* [*Under the Mark of Rome*] (guest-starring the Count of Saint-Germain and Gallix) (*Mustang* No. 303, 2002)
5. *Le Pouvoir de Kabur* [*The Power of Kabur*] (guest-starring Kabur) (*Mustang* No. 304, 2002)

6. *La Fin des Temps: Labyrinthe* [*The End of Time: Labyrinth*] (guest-starring Brigade Temporelle and introducing Futura) (*Mustang* No. 305, 2002)
7. *La Fin des Temps: L'Ultime Confrontation* [*The End of Time: The Ultimate Confrontation*] (guest-starring Brigade Temporelle and introducing Futura) (*Mustang* No. 306, 2002)

Futura:
Writer: Jean-Marc Lofficier.
Artists: Various.
0. *Le Château de Cartes* [*The House of Cards*] (jam issue with various artists; dialogue by François Corteggiani) (*Planète Comics* No. 14, 2002)

1. *Les Anges à l'Oeil Fauve* [*Angels with Fiery Eyes*] (**art**: Manuel Garcia & Eduardo Alpuente) (*Strangers* No. 1, Semic, 2002 / Image, 2003)
2. *Les Ombres de la Nuit* [*Shadows of the Night*] (**art**: Manuel Garcia & Javier Pina & Eduardo Alpuente) (*Strangers* No. 2, Semic, 2002 / Image, 2003)
3. *Caresses de Serpent* [*Caresses such as Snakes Give*] (**art**: Javier Pina & Eduardo Alpuente) (*Strangers* No. 3, Semic, 2003 / Image, 2003)
4. *Le Matin Livide* [*The Livid Daylights*] (**art**: Fernando Blanco & Eduardo Alpuente) (*Strangers* No. 4, Semic, 2003 / Image, 2003)
5. *Au Soir, Il Fera Froid* [*Icy till the Evening*] (**art**: Fernando Blanco & Eduardo Alpuente) (*Image Comics* No. 1, Semic, 2003 / *Strangers* No. 5, Image, 2003)
6. *Régner par l'Effroi* [*To Rule with Fear*] (**art**: Fernando Blanco & Eduardo Alpuente) (*Image Comics* No. 2, Semic, 2003 / *Strangers* No. 6, Image, 2003)
7. *L'Autre Côté du Monde* [*The Other Side of the World*] (the origins of Futura) (**art**: Reed Man) (*Image Comics* No. 3, Semic, 2003)
8. *Où l'On Parle de Fins et de Débuts* [*Of Endings and Beginnings*] (death of Jean Vlad) (**art**: Fernando Pasarin) (*Yuma* No. 9, 2003)
9. *Le Pont sur les Etoiles* [*The Starbridge*] (**art**: Mariano De La Torre) (*Yuma* No. 10, 2003)

Note: *Strangers* is comprised of *Futura*, *Tanka*, *Homicron*, *Starlock*, *Jaleb the Telepath* and *Jaydee*. Cover art (*Futura*) by Gil Formosa.

Websites:

http://www.coolfrenchcomics.com/wampus.htm
http://www.coolfrenchcomics.com/autre.htm
http://www.lofficier.com/strangers.htm

L'Autre No. 8 (1974)

La Porte de Taï-Matsu (1973)

Thorkael (1971)

"The gods are thirsty for blood!"
(Thorkael – *La Porte de Taï-Matsu*)

Created by:
Writer Serge de Beketch and artist Loro.

• Serge de Beketch (?-) contributed numerous satirical and *National Lampoon*-like humor pages to the news section of *Pilote*, starting in 1969. *Thorkael* was his only regular adventure series. De Beketch left comics in the late 1970s and has, since then, become a noted right-wing commentator and journalist.

• Loro, a pseudonym of Jean-Marc Loreau (1943-1998), began his comics career in the pages of *Pilote* in the early 1970s with a series of humoristic horror pastiches collected as *Déboires d'Outre-Tombe* [*Misadventures From Beyond The Grave*] and *Thorkael*. Loro also contributed to the pages of the French edition of *Creepy* and illustrated an anthology of science fiction stories by Robert Sheckley. His later works included the cheesecake series *Sweet Delice*, also for *Pilote*, and the adventures of a zombie private eye, *Abe Dopeulapeul*. Loro eventually left comics in the 1980s to pursue a career as a commercial illustrator in the South of France.

Story:
Thorkael is a clever rogue, a valiant swordsman, an adventurer able to spin a yarn or bluff his way through any perilous situation. The character, obviously inspired by Jack Vance's *Cugel*, exists in a fantasy universe ruled by a small coterie of cruel, egotistical immortals who are revered as gods: Einar, bloodthirsty god of war, the beautiful Thiota, etc.

In his first adventure, Thorkael is sent by his master to find the so-called "Eye of God" which is supposed to give his people courage. He then runs afoul of the gods. In the second adventure, Thorkael becomes Thiota's champion in a mysterious challenge of the gods, and crosses a gate which sends him back into the past. The story was, sadly, left uncompleted.

Publishing History:
Thorkael first appeared in *Pilote* in 1971, when adult science fiction and fantasy made their first appearance in comics. Loro, like J.-C. Forest and Philippe Druillet before him, was a science fiction fan and was influenced by genre writers. He also contributed illustrations to books and magazines.

Because of its full-page spreads, bleeds and psychedelic montages, *Thorkael*, like *Lone Sloane*, made an impression. However, the premature ending of the series prevented it from gaining wider recognition.

Bibliography:
1. *L'Oeil du Dieu* [*The Eye of God*] (35 p.) (*Pilote* Nos. 588-603, 1971; rep. S.E.R.G., 1976)
2. *La Porte de Taï-Matsu* [*The Gate of Taï-Matsu*] (44 p.) (*Pilote* Nos. 720-730, 1973; rep. S.E.R.G. 1977; Dargaud, 1982)

Brigade Temporelle in Futura No. 24 (1974)

Brigade Temporelle (1972)

"Let's drink a toast–to the future!"
(Khanor – *Le Bouton Rouge*)

Created by:

Writer Claude-Jacques Legrand and artist Edmond Ripoll.

• Claude-Jacques Legrand (1928-) is the author of a science fiction novel, *Projet Nouvelle Vénus* [*Project New Venus*], published by Fleuve Noir in 1988, and numerous science fiction short stories published in the French edition of *F & SF* in the 1960s. Legrand also directed a documentary feature about comic books for French television, that led Editions Lug to entrust him with the creation of a number of superhero and science fiction series for their magazine *Futura* in the 1970s: *Jaleb the Telepath, Jeff Sullivan, Larry Cannon, Kabur, Gladiateur de Bronze* and *Brigade Temporelle*. He also translated *Conan*. When Lug stopped publishing new stories, Legrand left comics to go into advertising.

• Spanish artist Edmond Ripoll (1938-) (who sometimes simply signs "Edmond") began his comics career in 1960, working for various girls' magazines such as *Celia* and *Sissi*. Ripoll also adapted television series such as *Rin Tin Tin* and *Bonanza* into comics for the European market. In the 1970s, he worked for Editions Lug in France, co-creating *Brigade Temporelle*, and for the Dutch magazine *Tina*, drawing *Mimi* and *Astrid*. He also wrote and drew the popular *Jan Europe*, followed by *Doctor Impossible* and *Eva Star*. Ripoll has also worked as a book illustrator and movie poster designer.

Story:

The *Time Brigade* stories were clearly influenced by Poul Anderson's *Time Patrol*. When the series begins, 20th century archeologist Jason Spell on a dig in Mesopotamia is recruited to become a member of Delta Hand 28, a four-person operative unit of the Time Brigade, a time-travelling organization from the 40th century.

The Brigade is responsible for the monitoring and control of the pludimensionality of Earth, in a segment of the time-space continuum known as Sector Rhamno. This spans our galactic quadrant, six billion years from the creation of the Solar System to some unspecified date in the future, circa 1,000,000 years A.D., and all of its alternate timelines.

Brigade Temporelle No. 16 (1974)

While the origins of the Brigade are known, its ultimate destiny remains unchronicled. In the 40th century, the Brigade functions with teams of four operatives, called a "Hand" since it reports to an artificial superintelligence known as the Thumb. A Hand is comprised of one Coordinator and three Agents. While Coordinators tend to originate in the 40th century or later, Agents are recruited throughout time.

The members of Delta Hand 28 are Khanor Rhi, its coordinator, a former chronoprogrammer from the 40th century, the beautiful Varna Zelton, a time sensitive and former student of Khanor, and Spell. In the first series, the fourth member was Rock Klammers, who tried to kill Adolf Hitler, but his memory was erased and he was returned to his own time. He was replaced in the second series by Minus-3, an augmented ape. The first series of stories involved various missions through time, ending with a nuclear explosion that destroyed Sodom and Gomorrah. In the second series, the heroes discovered that the Brigade had been founded and was secretly controlled by a hidden group of immortals, inheritors of the science of Mu, the legendary fifth planet destroyed circa 65 million years BC. They tried to prevent the destruction of Mu by a lethal civil war, but failed.

The Time Brigade recently gueststarred in *Wampus* when they prevented the alien entity from creating an alternate dimensionality in which Earth would have belonged to the Great Mind.

Publishing History:

After the success of its Marvel Comics translations launched in 1969, Editions Lug decided to create their own brand of French superheroes and science fiction characters, which they did with *Wampus* in 1969 and *Futura* in 1972. *Futura* ran for 33 issues until 1975, and featured *Jaleb le Télépathe, L'Autre [The Other], Larry Cannon, Jeff Sullivan, Sibilla* and *Brigade Temporelle*, which was serialized in Nos. 1-10 and Nos. 19-26.

Bibliography:

1. *Les Policiers du Temps* [*The Policemen of Time*] (*Futura* No. 1, 1972)
2. *La Mission de l'Agent Brent* [*The Mission of Agent Brent*] (*Futura* No. 2, 1972)
3. *L'Incident de Venlo* [*The Venlo Incident*] (*Futura* No. 3, 1972)
4. *Les Statues Surgies du Passé* [*The Statues of the Past*] (*Futura* No. 4, 1972)
5. *Mister B* (*Futura* No. 5, 1972)
6. *La Nuit des Temps* [*The End of Time*] (*Futura* No. 6, 1972)
7. *Jason le Viking* [*Jason the Viking*] (*Futura* No. 7, 1973)
8. *Tyrannosaurus Rex* (*Futura* No. 8, 1973)

9. *La Mort Pourpre* [*The Purple Death*] (*Futura* No. 9, 1973)
10. *Les Temps Bibliques* [*Biblical Times*] (*Futura* No. 10, 1973)
11. *Le Naufragé du Passé* [*Castaway in the Past*] (*Futura* No. 19, 1974)
12. *Les Origines de l'Homme* [*The Origins of Man*] (*Futura* No. 20, 1974)
13. *Les Convicts de Botany Bay* [*The Convicts of Botany Bay*] (*Futura* No. 21, 1974)
14. *Depuis Combien de Millénaires* [*For How Many Millennia*] (*Futura* No. 22, 1974)
15. *Le Grand Maître du Temple* [*The Grand Master of the Templars*] (*Futura* No. 23, 1974)
16. *Le Souvenir du Néant* [*Memories of the Void*] (*Futura* No. 24, 1974)
17. *Mu... Le Continent Perdu* [*The Lost Continent of Mu*] (*Futura* No. 25, 1974)
18. *Le Bouton Rouge* [*The Red Button*] (*Futura* No. 26, 1974)
Also see *Wampus* entry.

Website:
http://www.coolfrenchcomics.com/brigadetemporelle.htm

Brigade Temporelle No. 12 (1974)

Frankenstein in Hallucinations No. 15 (1972)

Frankenstein (1972)

"Yes, he is dead. But what is death for one such as he?"
(Old Man Blessed to Helen Coostle – *La Tour de Frankenstein"*)

Created by:

Writer Jean-Claude Carrière based on the novel by Mary Shelley; artist unknown. In 1957, writer Jean-Claude Carrière (1931-) was approached by Editions Fleuve Noir to continue the adventures of Mary Shelley's immortal creature for their newly-started *Angoisse* imprint of horror novels. Carrière proceeded to write six *Frankenstein* novels in 1957 and 1958, which were initially released under the house name of Benoît Becker. Carrière is an award-winning French screenwriter  who has collaborated with such famous directors as Luis Buñuel, Jacques Deray, Jess Franco, Jean-Luc Godard, Louis Malle and Volker Schlondorff, to name but a few. His film credits include such masterpieces as *Belle de Jour* [*Beautiful by Day*] (1967), *Le Charme Discret de la Bourgeoisie* [*The Discreet Charm of the Bourgeoisie*] (1972), *Cet Obscur Objet du Désir* [*That Obscure Object of Desire*] (1977), *The Tin Drum* (1979), *Le Retour de Martin Guerre* [*The Return of Martin Guerre*] (1982) and *The Unbearable Lightness of Being* (1988).

In 1972, Carrière's *Frankenstein* novels, as well as Shelley's classic, were adapted into comics for Aredit by an unknown artist.

Story:

Carrière follows the footsteps of the Monster, christened Gouroull, one of the first words that he utters as he returns to life, and the meaning of which remains a mystery. Carrière's Monster is a ruthless, demoniacal thing, the very incarnation of evil. His yellow, unblinking eyes hide a cunning, inhuman intelligence. The Monster barely speaks, but uses his razor-sharp teeth to slit his victims' throats. Carrière emphasizes the inhumanity of the creature: the Monster does not breathe, his skin is white as chalk but strangely impervious to flames, his strength and speed are prodigious, what runs in his veins is not blood, and he has no normal heartbeat; even his thought process is shown to be alien.

La Tour de Frankenstein [*The Tower of Frankenstein*] opens in 1875 in the Ulster village of Kanderley. Young Helen Coostle meets Old Man Blessed who runs a Frankenstein Museum in his tower. Blessed was ten when Victor Frankenstein and the Monster briefly stayed in Kanderley after they left Scotland, following the scientist's failed attempt to create a Bride, and they became his life's obsession. Blessed eventually found the body of the Monster in the Arctic, and brought it back to his Museum. Eventually, the Monster is returned to life by the evil Vrollo, a local hobo who hates the villagers and lusts after Helen. Vrollo thinks he can control the Creature, but instead, it ends up killing him.

La Tour de Frankenstein – cover by M. Gourdon (1957)

La Tour de Frankenstein in Hallucinations No. 16 (1972)

Gouroull then escapes when Blessed arrives with reporter Gordon Mallorey and the police. He is believed to have perished in quicksand, but in reality has fled to the sea.

Le Pas de Frankenstein [*In the Footsteps of Frankenstein*] takes place a few years later in the Scottish village of Plosway on the Isle of Cround north of Scotland, which is where Victor Frankenstein tried to create the Bride. Percy, a resident witch doctor who knows how to create zombies, becomes the unwilling assistant of the mad Dr. Pilljoy who has come to Cround with Gouroull to create a new Bride and a race of monsters. When Percy finds out that Pilljoy plans to drain the blood of a local widow, Mary, he rebels and is savagely murdered by Gouroull. But the witch doctor eventually returns as a zombie, kills Pilljoy and with the help of other zombies he has created (including Mary's late husband), saves the widow and drives the Monster away.

La Nuit de Frankenstein [*The Night of Frankenstein*] takes place in 1895 in the village of Gottwohl in the Swiss Alps, near Ingolstadt, where the Monster had once found refuge. There, the misanthropic Pastor Schleger, obsessed with Nietzchean theories, comes across Gouroull and plans to mate him with a woman to create a superman. But the women Schleger kidnaps are terrified by the Monster and enraged, the Creature kills them. Gouroull eventually rapes Ingrid, Schleger's wife, and ends up killing the Pastor and driving Ingrid to her death in the icy mountains. A local poacher, Molli, hunts Gouroull who is attacked by wolves and falls into a chasm.

Le Sceau de Frankenstein [*The Seal of Frankenstein*] takes place in 1924 in Austria. Doctor Markus is taking care of Ingrid at the Lunatic Asylum of Hallshofen. She survived, found herself pregnant and went mad. (The book re-dates the events of the previous novel to 1904.) The Monster returns seeking his child. During a carnival, he is unmasked by Markus, and ends up killing him. The Monster breaks into the asylum. We are never told for certain, but his son may be a deformed woodsman and mass murderer interned there. The woodsman attacks the Monster, who kills him. Gouroull then frees the inmates, sets fire to the asylum and escapes. Ingrid hangs herself in her cell.

Frankenstein Rode [*Frankenstein Prowls*] takes place a year later, in 1925, in the Black Forest in Germany. Gouroull comes across an exiled Chinese doctor named Wou Ling and his blind ward, Nulla. The Monster, aware of his own hideous appearance, forces Wou-Ling to use acupuncture to alter his features, but in vain. Wou-Ling fails, and Gouroull kills them both.

The last novel, *La Cave de Frankenstein* [*The Cellar of Frankenstein*], takes place about 15 years later, just before World War II, in Antwerp, Belgium. The Monster is still seeking to transform his apperarance. He threatens an old Jewish junkman, Samuel Rohrbach, his young son Daniel,, and Samuel's friend, an alcoholic doctor named Mossart. Mossart is at first eager to complete Frankenstein's own work, but ultimately realizes it is hopeless. The Monster kills him and locks Samuel in a cellar infested with rats. After trying to kill Daniel, Gouroull vanishes back into the darkness.

Publishing History:
Carrière wrote six *Frankenstein* novels in 1957-59 for Fleuve Noir's *Angoisse* under the house pseudonym of Benoît Becker, with some plotting assistance from Guy Bechtel for the first novel. In 1972, comics publisher Aredit (see *Les Conquérants de l'Espace* entry) devoted seven issues of its digest-sized *Hallucinations* horror comic magazine to adapting them.

Bibliography:
The Novels:
1. *La Tour de Frankenstein* [*The Tower of Frankenstein*] (Fleuve Noir *Angoisse* No. 30, 1957)
2. *Le Pas de Frankenstein* [*In the Footsteps of Frankenstein*] (Fleuve Noir *Angoisse* No. 32, 1957)
3. *La Nuit de Frankenstein* [*The Night of Frankenstein*] (Fleuve Noir *Angoisse* No. 34, 1957)
4. *Le Sceau de Frankenstein* [*The Seal of Frankenstein*] (Fleuve Noir *Angoisse* No. 36, 1957)
5. *Frankenstein Rôde* [*Frankenstein Prowls*] (Fleuve Noir *Angoisse* No. 41, 1958)
6. *La Cave de Frankenstein* [*The Cellar of Frankenstein*] (Fleuve Noir *Angoisse* No. 50, 1959)

The Comics:
1. *Frankenstein* [adaptation of Mary Shelley's novel] (*Hallucinations* No. 15, 1972)

2. *La Tour de Frankenstein* [*The Tower of Frankenstein*] (*Hallucinations* No. 16, 1972)
3. *Le Pas de Frankenstein* [*In the Footsteps of Frankenstein*] (*Hallucinations* No. 17, 1972)
4. *La Nuit de Frankenstein* [*The Night of Frankenstein*] (*Hallucinations* No. 18, 1972)
5. *Le Sceau de Frankenstein* [*The Seal of Frankenstein*] (*Hallucinations* No. 19, 1972)
6. *Frankenstein Rôde* [*Frankenstein Prowls*] (*Hallucinations* No. 20, 1972)
7. *La Cave de Frankenstein* [*The Cellar of Frankenstein*] (*Hallucinations* No. 21, 1972)

Hallucinations No. 20 (1972)

Website:
http://www.coolfrenchcomics.com/hallucinations.htm

Frankenstein Rôde in Hallucinations No. 20 (1972)

Tiriel – Fernand Nathan (1974)

Tiriel (1974)

"Walk with us, Tiriel! With your help, we shall overcome!"
(Enion to Tiriel – *Tiriel, Héritier d'un Monde*)

Created by:
Writer Jean-Pierre Dionnet and artist Raymond Poïvet.

- Jean-Pierre Dionnet (1947-) began contributing several genre stories to *Pilote* in the early 1970s, including the classic, otherworldly *Jean Cyriaque*, drawn by Jean Solé. In 1973, Dionnet teamed up with Bernard Farkas and artists Moebius and Philippe Druillet to launch the genre magazine *Métal Hurlant*. For *Métal*, Dionnet created *Exterminateur 17* with Enki Bilal, *Arn* with J.-P. Gal and *Région Étrangère* [*Foreign Region*] with Bob Deum. After *Métal*'s first incarnation went out of business, Dionnet moved to radio and television where he became a local celebrity covering science fiction and comics.

- Raymond Poïvet (see *Les Pionniers de l'Espérance* entry).

Story:
An unnamed young man inherits a mysterious house from his uncle, Joseph Hermont. The house hides a dimensional gateway which takes him to another planet named Tirzah, in the Land of Har. There, old Enion, who knew his uncle, christens the yong man Tiriel, meaning Liberator, and asks him to take over his uncle's role as their leader. Tiriel's task is to lead a revolution against the beautiful but evil Queen Eno who lives in the City of Golgonooza and was once Tiriel's uncle's lover. A second story saw Tiriel's return to Golgonooza but was left uncompleted.

Tiriel, Héritier d'un Monde (1974)

Publishing History:

Tiriel was first serialized in the magazine *Lucky Luke* in 1974, then collected as a b&w graphic novel by publisher Fernand Nathan in 1975. It was then reprinted in color by Les Humanoides Associes in 1982. A new *Tiriel* story began in *Métal Hurlant* that same year, but was left unfinished.

Bibliography:

1. *Tiriel, Héritier d'un Monde* [*Tiriel, Inheritor of a World*] (*Lucky Luke* Nos. 5, 7, 9, 1974; Fernand Nathan; 1975 (b&w); Humanoïdes Associés, 1982 (color))
2. *Retour à Golgonooza* [*Return to Golgonooza*] (*Métal Hurlant* Nos.79-82, 1982-1983)

Website:

http://www.coolfrenchcomics.com/tiriel.htm

Kabur No. 1 (cover by Frisano) (1975)

Kabur (1975)

"Long before the destruction of fabled Mû, in an age of swords and sorcery, arose a great champion..."
(*The Saga of Kabur* – Kabur)

Created by:
Writer Claude-Jacques Legrand (see *Brigade Temporelle* entry) and artist Luciano Bernasconi (see *Wampus* entry).

Story:
The story of Kabur takes place during the time of Pangea, approximately 100 million years ago. Kabur was born the second son of King Sharon and Queen Damara of the Kingdom of Thule in the land of Hyperborea. His mother died in childbirth and his older brother perished in battle against the Shaikortin pirates. Kabur was educated by weapon-master Shaka and court minstrel Gorondur. His childhood sweetheart was Kimera, daughter of Duke Orande of nearby Commorion. Kabur was a boastful and rebellious adolescent.

Before Kabur reaches his legal majority, the traitorous General Sudryak and Oktar the Merchant conspire with the wizard Sham to turn a man-beast into Kabur's evil doppleganger. Accused of crimes he did not commit, Kabur is then banished by his father and forced to flee Thule with the slave-girl Lagrid. Eventually, Kabur discovers that Sham is trying to destroy him because his family are descendents of the powerful Danaian man-god Lug, sworn enemy of Shivar, Lord of the Abyss, whom Sham worships. The wizard Balthazar, who was once Moloch, weapon-maker of the Danaians, gives Kabur his inheritance, the magical Lance of Lug, after he recovers the Scepter of Moloch. Kabur then saves the city of Lorgash from his old enemy, Borg, Chief of the Nogol Hordes. Borg is allied to Balor of the powerful alien race, the Fomors, and who once killed Lug. Kabur later slays the man-beast who has impersonated him, and clears his name.

Kabur and Lagrid then return to Thule, escorting Tribhan's great merchant caravan. During the journey, they meet and reach a truce with the Reaper, a notorious bounty-hunter from the Brotherhood of Urajii.

Kabur No. 2 – drawn by Bernasconi (1975)

They fight alonside jungle lord Zembla (transported from the future) against the Demon Queen Mauve. Kabur also allies himself with the alien entity known as Wampus to fight the renegade Fomor Levan. In the city of Ilshanyi,

Kabur and Lagrid fight two ruthless mercenaries, Nevlak and Sebho. In Commorion, Kabur makes peace with Kimera who has become jealous of Lagrid. Kabur finally arrives back in Thule, and reconciles with his father.

Publishing History:

Kabur was launched in its eponymous magazine in 1975 by Editions Lug as an answer to Marvel's *Conan*, which was being successfully published by Lug. Despite its slick packaging, the magazine lasted only five issues. The character eventually returned in 2000 in *Special-Zembla* No. 152. A heretofore unpublished sixth episode was followed by a new series of adventures.

Bibliography:

Writer: Claude-Jacques Legrand.
Artist: Luciano Bernasconi.
1. *La Saga de Kabur* [*The Saga of Kabur*] (*Kabur* No. 1, 1975)
2. *L'Exil* [*The Exile*] (*Kabur* No. 2, 1976)
3. *La Cité des Araignées* [*The City of Spiders*] (*Kabur* No. 3, 1976)
4. *Les Jeux de Lorgash* [*The Games of Lorgash*] (*Kabur* No. 4, 1976)
5. *Moloch* (*Kabur* No. 5, 1976)
6. *Le Dieu-Démon* [*The Demon God*] (1976; first pub. in *Special-Zembla* No. 157, 2000)

Writers: Jean-Marc Lofficier & Thierry Mornet.
Artist: Luciano Bernasconi.
7. *Le Siège de Lorgash* [*The Siege of Lorgash*] (*Special-Zembla* No. 158, 2001)
8. *Le Pouvoir des Fomores* [*The Power of the Fomores*] (*Special-Zembla* No. 159, 2001)
9. *Le Duel des Dieux* [*The Duel of the Gods*] (*Special-Zembla* No. 160, 2001)
10. *La Vengeance de Shivar* [*The Revenge of Shivar*] (*Special-Zembla* No. 161, 2001)

Artist: Mike Ratera.
11. *Le Faucheur* [*The Reaper*] (*Special-Zembla* No. 162, 2001)
12. *La Voix des Sortakhi* [*The Voice of the Sortakhi*] (*Special-Zembla* No. 163, 2001)
13. *La Chair du Temps* [*The Flesh of Time*] (guest-starring Zembla) (*Special-Zembla* No. 164, 2002)

Kabur by Manuel Martin Peniche (2002)

14. *Le Destin de Zembla* [*Zembla's Destiny*] (guest-starring Zembla) (*Special-Zembla* No. 165, 2002)
Artist: Willy Hudic.
15. *Zothaqa* (guest-starring Wampus) (Special-Zembla No. 166, 2002)
16. *Les Intrigues d'Ilshanyi* [*Intrigues in Ilshanyi*] (Special-Zembla No. 167, 2002)
17. *Nevlak et Sebho* (*Special-Zembla* No. 168, 2002)

Writers: Jean-Marc Lofficier & J.-M. Lainé.
Artist: Manuel Martin Peniche.
18. *La Tour de Volodyane* [*The Tower of Volodyane*] (*Special-Zembla* No. 169, 2002)
Writer: Jean-Marc Lofficier.
Artist: Manuel Martin Peniche.
19. *La Colère de Kimera* [*The Wrath of Kimera*] (*Special-Zembla* No. 170, 2003)
Artist: Manuel Martin Peniche & Juan Roncagliolo Berger.
20. *Retour à Thulé* [*Back to Thule*] (*Special-Zembla* No. 171, 2003)
Artist: Juan Roncagliolo Berger (left).
21. *Les Démons d'Arkhanal* [*Demons of Arkhanal*] (*Special-Zembla* No. 173, 2003)
Artist: Manuel Martin Peniche.
22. *Je suis Arianrod...* [*I Am Arianrod...*] (*Special-Zembla* No. 174, 2003)
23. *Les Feux du Sessevar* [*The Fires of Sessevar*] (*Special-Zembla* No. 175, 2003)

Spin-Offs & Miscellaneous:
Writer: Jean-Marc Lofficier; **Artist**: Philip Xavier.
Lagrid, Princess de Mu [*Lagrid, Princess of Mu*] (*Special-Zembla* No. 164, 2001)
Writers: Jean-Marc Lofficier & Thierry Mornet; **Artist**: Patrice Lesparre.
Le Retour du Combat des Titans [*The Return of the Clash of the Titans*] (*Special-Zembla* No. 168, 2002)
Writer/Artist: Ange Sierra de la Mar.
La Fontaine [*The Fountain*] (*Special-Zembla* No. 172, 2003)

Writer: Jean-Marc Lofficier; **Artist**: Marta Bonfill.
Au Fond de la Mer Glauque [*At the Bottom of the Dim Sea*] (*Special-Zembla* No. 175, 2003)
Writer: Jean-Marc Lofficier; **Artist**: David Lafuente.
La Jeunesse de Kabur [*Young Kabur*] (*Special-Zembla* No. 175, 2003)
Writer: Jean-Marc Lofficier; **Artist**: Mike Ratera.
King Kabur 1: Les Seigneurs Blêmes [*King Kabur 1: The Pale Lords*] (graphic novel, Semic, 2003)

Website:
http://www.coolfrenchcomics.com/kabur.htm

Kabur by Mike Ratera (2002)

Kabur vs. Zembla – cover by Gil Formosa (2002)

Felina (1979)

Felina (1979)

"I will avenge you Wilbur, my love! From now on I shall know no mercy! I shall be like the furies! Like a panther!"
(Felina – *Felina*)

Created by:
Writer Victor Mora and artist Annie Goetzinger.

• Victor Mora (1931-) is a renowned Spanish writer who created *El Capitan Trueno* in 1956 under the pseudonym of Victor Alcazar. His best-known series is the science fiction sagas of *Dani Futuro* and *Delta 99* with artist Carlos Gimenez, *Doctor Niebla* with Francisco Hidalgo and the Western *Sunday* with Victor de La Fuente. He is also responsible for the following series: *Chroniques de l'Innommé* [*Chronicles of the Unnamed*] with Luis Garcia, *Supernova* with José Bielsa, *Gigantik* with José Maria Cardona, *Les Inoxydables* [*Stainless Steel Gang*] with Antonio Parras, *Arcane* with Brocal Remohi, *Les Anges d'Acier* [*Steel Angels*] with Victor de La Fuente, *Tequila Bang* with Alfonso Font and many more. He has recently returned to *El Capitan Trueno* with Jesus Blasco.

• Annie Goetzinger (1951-) is a student of Georges Pichard. *Felina* was among her first major works in comics. She went on to write and draw a series of realistic graphic novels, such as *Barcelonight* (1990). With writer Pierre Christin, she produced *La Demoiselle de la Légion d'Honneur* (1980), *La Diva et le Kriegspiel* (1981), *La Voyageuse de Petite Ceinture* (1985) and is now working on the series *L'Agence Hardy*.

Felina (1979)

Felina (1979)

Story:
Felina was born of a liaison between Spanish anarchist Carlos Rocca and French nun Hermine de Broutignol a.k.a. Sister Camille of the Sacred Chalice, both killed in tragic circumstances. Orphaned in 1878, Marie-Madeleine is adopted by the Sabot family but left home and runs away to join a circus. She grows up as a panther trainer and trapeze artist nicknamed Felina, and eventually falls in love with and marries American millionaire Wilbur Kholderup. Kholderup is later killed by the criminal sect of the Kriss. Felina then becomes a black-cloaked heroine, using her circus skills to avenge her husband. She is ably assisted by Lobjak, a Tibetan wizard, and Colonel Pembroke, two of her husband's friends. Her arch-enemy is Touan Naga, the mysterious leader of the Kriss.

Publishing History:
Felina was published in the magazine *Circus* in 1979, then in *Pilote* in 1982. The first two stories were initially published as graphic novels by Glénat. Dargaud then reprinted them, and published the third and last graphic novel.

Bibliography:
1. *Felina* (Glénat, 1979)
2. *Les Mystères de Barcelone* [*The Mysteries of Barcelona*] (Dargaud, 1982)
3. *L'Ogre du Djébel* [*The Djebel Ogre*] (Dargaud, 1986)

Website:
http://www.coolfrenchcomics.com/felina.htm

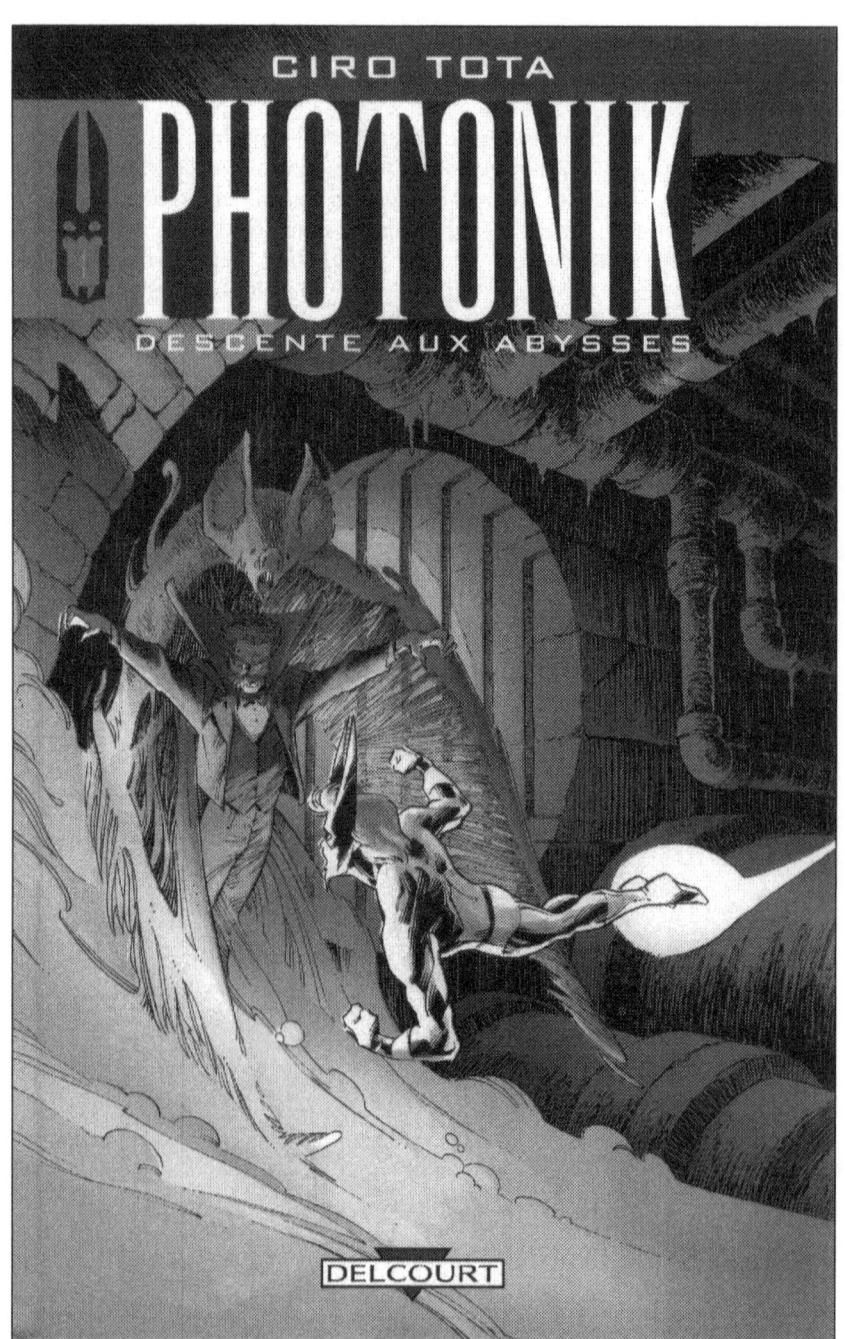

Photonik (1980)

"What I feared the most is happening... I'm changing...
Changing back into puny, weak Thaddeus..."
(Photonik – *La Nuit des Dupes*)

Created by:
Writer-artist Cyrus Tota. Cyrus Tota (1954-) was born in Italy, and began working for Editions Lug in the 1970s. He contributed to the long-running Italian series *Blek* produced by the studio Essegesse from 1977 to 1980, before creating *Photonik*. More recently, Tota has contributed several volumes to the popular *Aquablue* and *Etoile Blanche* science fiction series.

Story:
Thaddeus Tenterhook, an alienated, hunchbacked teenage orphan, is accidentally transformed by the explosion of a luminotron into the golden, super-powered "Man of Light" known as Photonik. With the help of neuropsychologist and super-powered mentalist, Dr. Nazel Ziegel, and the street urchin nicknamed Tom Thumb, Photonik fights a variety of colorful super-villains, from the space-born invader, the Minotaur, to Maelstrom, Lord of the Lower Depths, and Count Wampyr, the Vampire of New York. He is pursued by Lt. Wilcox of the NYPD who wants to arrest him for breaking the law.

Publishing History:
Photonik was launched in the magazine *Mustang* in 1980 as part of Editions Lug's effort to create a universe of characters to compete with Marvel's. Other characters included *Wampus*, the various characters launched in the magazine *Futura* such as *Jaleb*, *Sibilla*, *Jeff Sullivan*, *Kabur* and *Phénix*.

Initially, editor-in-chief Marcel Navarro had planned to launch a new title called *Sup-Héros* but, for business reasons, at the last minute, he decided instead to revamp one of Lug's existing Western magazines, *Mustang*. With No. 54, *Mustang* therefore became a full-fledged superhero comic, starring *Photonik*, Native American mystic *Ozark* and *Mikros*.

Unfortunately, the new *Mustang* was not profitable enough, at least compared to the relatively inexpensive purchase of American material, and was cancelled with No. 70 in 1981.

Seventeen episodes of *Photonik* were originally serialized in *Mustang*. After its cancellation, *Photonik* returned in the Marvel-based magazine *Spidey*, starting with No. 22 in 1982 and continuing until No. 83 in 1986. In 1999, episodes originally published in *Spidey* Nos. 55-58 and Nos. 80-83 were reprinted in two hardcover editions by publisher Delcourt.

Bibliography:
Mustang:
Writer-artist: Cyrus Tota.
1. *Black Out* (*Mustang* No. 54, 1980)
2. *La Nuit des Dupes* [*The Night of the Dupes*] (*Mustang* No. 55, 1980)
3. *David et Goliath* [*David and Goliath*] (*Mustang* No. 56, 1980)
4. *Pièges* [*Traps*] (*Mustang* No. 57, 1980)
5. *Le Bulbe* [*The Bulb*] (*Mustang* No. 58, 1980)
6. *Panique à Central Park* [*Panic in Central Park*] (*Mustang* No. 59, 1980)
7. *La Souricière* [*The Mousetrap*] (*Mustang* No. 60, 1980)
8. *Lachez les Fauves!* [*Unleash the Wild Beasts!*] (*Mustang* No. 61, 1981)
9. *Petit-Homme-Blanc* [*Little-White-Man*] (*Mustang* No. 62, 1981)

10. *Et l'Empire s'effondra!* [*And the Empire Collapsed!*] (*Mustang* No. 63, 1981)
11. *Cauchemar* [*Nightmare*] (*Mustang* No. 64, 1981)
12. *Resurrection* [*Rebirth*] (*Mustang* No. 65, 1981)
13. *African Devil* (*Mustang* No. 66, 1981)
14. *Sur la Piste du Sorcier* [*On the Trail of the Witch Doctor*] (*Mustang* 67, 1981)
15. *À l'Ombre des Volcans* [*In the Shadow of the Volcano*] (*Mustang* 68, 1981)
16. *Dans l'Oeil du Volcan* [*In the Eye of the Volcano*] (*Mustang* 69, 1981)
Writer-artist: Jean-Yves Mitton.
17. *Maelstrom* (*Mustang* No. 70, 1981)

Spidey:
Writer-artist: Cyrus Tota.
1. *Le Veilleur de Pierre* [*The Stone Watcher*] (*Spidey* No. 22, 1981)
2. *La Malédiction* [*The Curse*] (*Spidey* 23, 1982)
3. *Le Vampire de New-York* [*The Vampire of New York*] (*Spidey* 24, 1982)
4. *Horreur à l'Aurore* [*Horror at Dawn*] (*Spidey* No. 25, 1982)
5. *Echec et Supermat* [*Check & Supermate*] (*Spidey* Nos. 26-27, 1982)
6. *Le Hasard et la Violence* [*Hazard and Violence*] (*Spidey* No. 28, 1982)
7. *Photonik contre Photonik* [*Photonik vs. Photonik*] (*Spidey* No. 29, 1982)
8. *Le Rachat* [*The Buy-Back*] (*Spidey* No. 30, 1982)
9. *La Gemme* [*The Gem*] (*Spidey* Nos. 31-32, 1982)
10. *Prisonnier des Étoiles* [*Prisoner of the Stars*] (*Spidey* Nos. 33-34, 1982)
11. *Le Mystère du Pueblo Maudit* [*The Mystery of the Cursed Pueblo*] (*Spidey* Nos. 35-36, 1982)
12. *Les Origines du Docteur Ziegel* [*The Origins of Dr. Ziegel*] (*Spidey* Nos. 37-38, 40, 1983)
13. *Le Casse du Millénaire* [*The Break-In of the Millennium*] (*Spidey* Nos. 41-42, 1983)
14. *Bas les Masques* [*Masks Off*] (*Spidey* Nos. 43-44, 1983)
15. *La Saga de Photonik* [*The Saga of Photonik*] (*Spidey* No. 55, 1984)
16. *Descente aux Abysses* [*Descent into the Abyss*] (*Spidey* Nos. 56-58, 1984; rep. Delcourt No. 1, 1999)
17. *Les Enfants de l'Apocalypse* [*Children of the Apocalypse*] (*Spidey* Nos. 80-83, 1986; rep. Delcourt No. 2, 1999)
Writer-artist: Jean-Yves Mitton.
18. *L'Ombre* [*The Shadow*] (*Spidey* Nos. 84-86, 1987)

Website:
http://www.coolfrenchcomics.com/photonik.htm

Photonik (1980)

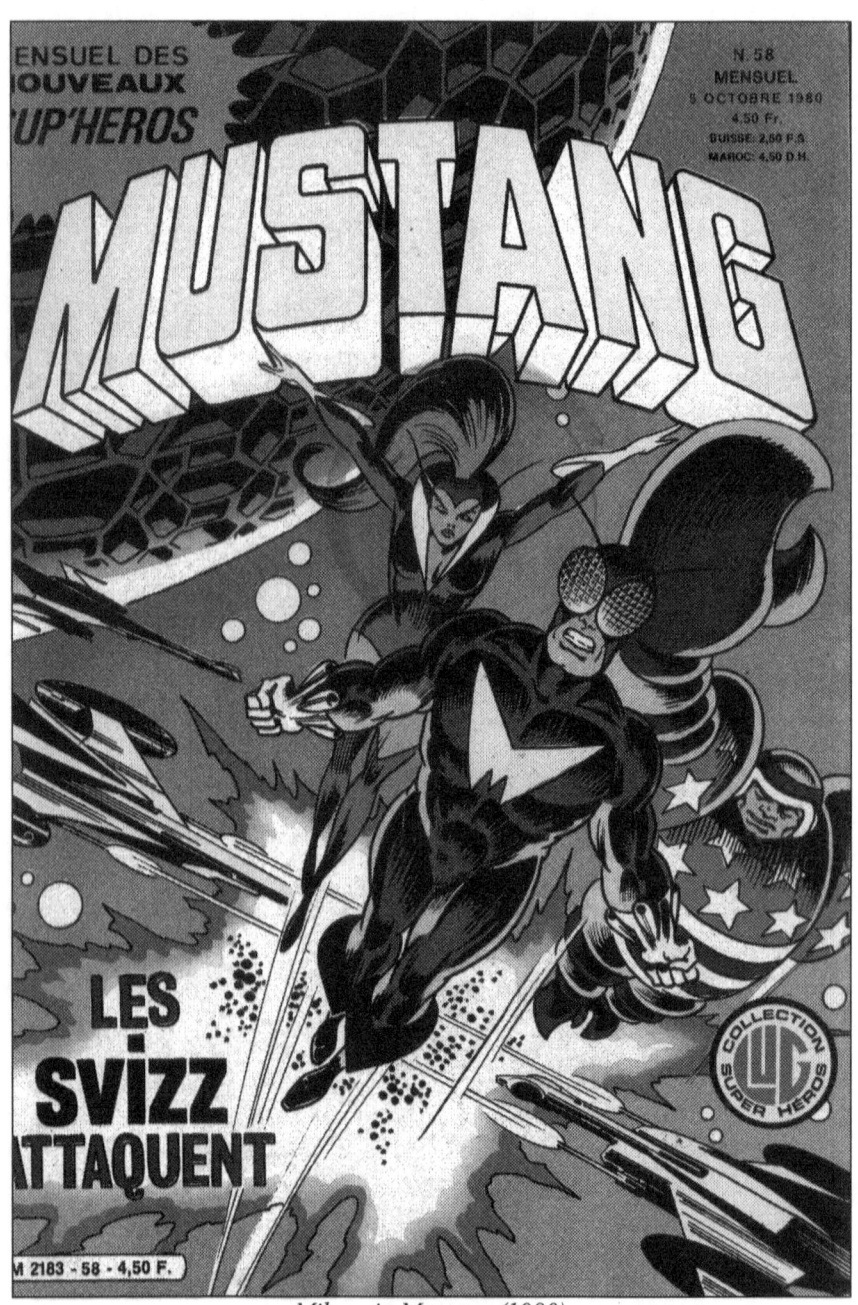
Mikros in Mustang (1980)

Mikros (1980) & Epsilon (1986)

"The Svizz have made us into mutants... monsters..."
(Mikros – *Mikros, Titan Microcosmique*)

Created by:
Writer-artist: Jean-Yves Mitton. Jean-Yves Mitton (1945-) joined Éditions Lug as a staff artist in 1964 and, after working on a number of digest-sized magazines, including a notorious stint on *Blek*, wrote and drew *Mikros*, *Epsilon*, *Photonik*, *Cosmo* and *Kronos* for Editions Lug. Also for Lug, he drew a special episode of Marvel's *Silver Surfer* written by Marcel Navarro for the French market. Mitton then worked with writer François Corteggiani on *L'Archer Blanc* [*The White Archer*]. In the 1990s, he produced *Vae Victis*, a series about the Roman conquest of Gaul, *Les Survivants de l'Atlantique* [*The Survivors of the Atlantic*] about pirates and *Chroniques Barbares* [*Barbarian Chronicles*] about the Vikings.

Story:
Mikros is the story of three Harvard entomologists and Olympic athletes, Mike Ross (Mikros), Priscilla Conway (Saltarella) and Bobby Crabb (Crabb), who are unwillingly mutated into insect-sized humanoids by the alien insectoid race called the Svizz. The Svizz plan to use armies of insect-sized slaves to conquer Earth, but Mikros and his friends defeat their plans and overthrow their ruler, Super-Termitor.

Later in the series, the heroic trio is forced to move to France, where they encounter their arch-nemesis, the power-mad mentalist Raoul de Roquemaure, Count of Monsegur, a.k.a. Psi, who turns Saltarella into his queen.

Epsilon's story takes place in the year 2086. Epsilon is told that he is the teenage son of Psi, Mikros' old arch-enemy, now the despotic ruler of the self-dubbed Eden, a futuristic Pan-European city-state. But the super-powered Epsilon revolts against Psi and becomes a rebel.

Mikros (1980)

He teams up with Foxie and the robot Mentor to fight Psi and search for his unknown mother. It eventually turns out that Epsilon is, in reality, the son of Mikros and Saltarella.

Publishing History:

Mikros was originally serialized in 1980 in Editions Lug's superhero magazine *Mustang* alongside *Photonik*. After *Mustang*'s cancellation in 1981, the series was continued in *Titans*, which also published French translations of *Star Wars*, *Iron Fist* and *New Mutants*. At Mitton's behest, the series, which had originally taken place in the United States, moved to Southern Europe, first to Venice and then to France.

Mitton eventually created a sequel to the saga of *Mikros* with *Moi, Epsilon, 15 Ans, Fils du Néant* [*I, Epsilon, 15-Year Old, Son of No One*], which also featured the return of the nefarious Psi. Two volumes of *Mikros* were reprinted by Editions Sang d'Encre in 2000.

Bibliography:
Mustang:
Writer-artist: Jean-Yves Mitton.
1. *Mikros, Titan Microcosmique* [*Mikros, Microcosmic Titan*] (*Mustang* Nos. 54-55, 1980)
2. *Quelque part une Étoile...* [*Somewhere A Star...*] (*Mustang* No. 56, 1980)
3. *Rush sur la Ruche* [*Rush to the Hive*] (*Mustang* No. 57, 1980)
4. *Eternel Retour* [*Eternal Return*] (*Mustang* No. 58, 1980)
5. *Super-Termitor* (*Mustang* No. 59, 1980)
6. *Le Grand Fléau* [*The Great Plague*] (*Mustang* No. 60, 1980)
7. *Le Conte d'Hoffmann* [*Hoffmann's Tale*] (*Mustang* No. 61, 1981)
8. *Terrific!* (*Mustang* No. 62, 1981)
9. *Alerte Rouge!* [*Red Alert!*] (*Mustang* No. 63, 1981)
10. *CIA, KGB and Co.* (*Mustang* No. 64, 1981)
11. *Métamorphoses* [*Metamorphoses*] (*Mustang* No. 65, 1981)
12. *Le Vaudou!* [*Voodoo!*] (*Mustang* No. 66, 1981)
13. *Le Vaudou est toujours debout* [*Voodoo Lives*] (*Mustang* No. 67, 1981)
Writer: Jacques Lennoz; **Artist**: Andre Amouriq.
14. *La Bête de Nulle Part* [*The Beast from Nowhere*] (*Mustang* No. 68, 1981)

15. *Illitha Joue et Gagne* [*Illitha Plays and Wins*] (*Mustang* No. 69, 1981)
16. *Crabb Ecartelé* [*Crabb Pulled Apart*] (*Mustang* No. 70, 1981)

Titans:
Writer-artist: Jean-Yves Mitton.
1. *Voir Venise et Mourir* [*To See Venice And Die*] (*Titans* Nos. 35-40, 1982)
2. *Microbios* (*Titans* No. 41-43, 1982)
3. *Descente aux Enfers* [*Descent into Hell*] (*Titans* Nos. 44-46, 1982)
4. *Peste Noire* [*Black Plague*] (*Titans* Nos. 47-49, 1983)
5. *Adieux du Troisième Type* [*Good-Byes of the Third Kind*] (*Titans* No. 50-52, 1983)
6. *Pour que Règne le Mal* [*Let Evil Reign*] (*Titans* No. 53, 1983)
7. *Psi* (*Titans* Nos. 54-56, 1983)
8. *La Beauté du Diable* [*The Devil's Beauty*] (*Titans* Nos. 57-58, 1983)
9. *Le Beau, La Belle... et les Bites* [*Handsome, Beauty... and Bytes*] (*Titans* Nos. 59-61, 1984)
10. *Destination Néant* [*Destination Void*] (*Titans* Nos. 62-64, 1984)
11. *Psiland* (*Titans* Nos. 65-68, 1984)
12. *Piège pour un Insecte* [*Insect Trap*] (*Titans* Nos. 69-71, 1984)
13. *Punch* (*Titans* Nos. 72-74, 1985)
14. *Outre-Monde* [*The World Beyond*] (*Titans* Nos. 75-78, 1985)
15. *Le Mur de la Lumière* [*The Light Barrier*] (*Titans* Nos. 79-81, 1985)
16. *Passeport pour l'Infini* [*Passport for Infinity*] (*Titans* Nos. 82-87, 1986)

Epsilon:
Writer-artist: Jean-Yves Mitton.
1. *Enfer en Eden* [*Hell in Eden*] (*Titans* Nos. 88-90, 1986)
2. *Evasion – Le Secret d'Eden* [*Escape – Eden's Secret*] (*Titans* Nos. 91-93, 1986)
3. *Hors d'Eden, Point de Salut* [*Outside of Eden, No Salvation*] (*Titans* Nos. 94-95, 1986)
4. *Underground* (*Titans* Nos. 96-99, 1987)
5. *Jeux Barbares* [*Barbarian Games*] (*Titans* No. 100, 1987)
6. *Cité Haute* [*High City*] (*Titans* Nos. 101-102, 1987)
7. *Zyklon* (*Titans* No. 103, 1987)
8. *Déportation* (*Titans* No. 104, 1987)
9. *Rebellion* (*Titans* No. 105, 1987)
10. *Retour vers Eden* [*Return to Eden*] (*Titans* Nos. 106-108, 1987)

Mikros (1983)

Phénix in Strangers – cover by Gil Formosa (2002)

Phénix (1980)

"You, Dr. Carter, know everything there is to know about bodies, and you, Father Brown, about souls. But I know what connects the two–money!"
(Phénix – *La Boîte Rouge*)

Created by:
Writer Corsini and artist Luciano Bernasconi (see *Wampus* entry).

Story:
When she was in college, Patricia Hope, the daughter of a Chicago billionaire couple, was raped by an assailant who remains unknown. She slipped into a deep coma that lasted nine months, and emerged like a phoenix from the ashes, miraculously transformed, with both body and mind optimized to superhuman levels. After inheriting her parents' fortune and charitable foundation, Patricia became a leading socialite by day, and the black-clad, bike-riding crime fighter known as Phénix by night.

Phénix occasionally helps Father Brown's local church; after breaking up with young Dr. Bobby Carter, Patricia shares her life with Dr. Douglas Sullivan, head of the E.R. at Saint Justin's Hospital. Phénix also teams up on a semi-regular basis with Sibilla, another superheroine.

In her most recent saga, Phénix runs afoul of a criminal organization called "Phantom." She is believed to have been killed. Her head is transplanted on a chimera-like body built by mad scientist Désirée Landru, while an android in her likeness designed by Professor Quanter becomes jealous of Doug Sullivan's romance with super-model Babette.

Publishing History:

Phénix was originally published in 1980 by Editions Lug as a mini-series in *Special-Rodeo* Nos. 74 to 78. The character returned in 2001 in *Fantask*, then *Yuma*. Phénix and Sibilla were featured in a crossover with American superheroine Witchblade published by Semic in 2003.

previous pages: Phénix by Juan Roncaglio Berger (2002), Luciano Bernasconi (1980) and Fernando Pasarin (2003).

Bibliography:
Special-Rodeo:
Writer: Corsini; **Artist**: Luciano Bernasconi.
1. *La Dernière Chance* [*The Last Chance*] (*Special-Rodeo* No. 74, 1980)
2. *L'Adieu au Ring* [*Farewell to the Ring*] (*Special-Rodeo* No. 74, 1980)
3. *Le Rapt* [*The Kidnapping*] (*Special-Rodeo* No. 75, 1980)
4. *Le Secret de Gonzalo Morales* [*The Secret of Gonzalo Morales*] (*Special-Rodeo* No. 75, 1980)
5. *Les Iroquois* (*Special-Rodeo* No. 76, 1980)
6. *La Vieille Dame* [*The Old Lady*] (*Special-Rodeo* No. 76, 1980)
7. [Untitled] (*Special-Rodeo* No. 77, 1980)
8. *Les Diables Volants* [*The Flying Devils*] (*Special-Rodeo* No. 78, 1980)
Writer: Jean-Marc Lofficier.
Artist: Frédéric Grivaud.
L'Ombre du Phénix [*The Shadow of the Phoenix*] (guest-starring Sibilla) (*Fantask* No. 5, 2001)
Artist: Stéphane Louis (cover above).
Le Chat et la Souris [*Cat and Mouse*] (*Planète Comics* No. 14, 2002)

Artist: Edouard Cop (cover right).
La Sanction Vega [*The Vega Sanction*] (*Strangers* No. 1, 2002)

Yuma:
Writer: Jean-Marc Lofficier.
Artist: Mariano De La Torre.
1. *La Nuit du Léopard* [*The Night of the Leopard*] (*Yuma* No. 1, 2002)
Artist: Juan Roncagliolo Berger.
2. *Mon Diner avec Babette* [*My Dinner with Babette*] (*Yuma* No. 2, 2002)
3. *L'Assassinat du Père Fouettard* [*The Murder of the Evil Santa*] (*Yuma* No. 3, 2002)
4. *Ma Nuit Chez Quanter* [*My Night at Quanter's*] (*Yuma* No. 4, 2002)
5. *Le Pacte des Loufoques* [*The Lunatic Legion*] (*Yuma* No. 5, 2003)
6. *Un Phénix sur le Toit* [*A Phoenix on the Roof*] (*Yuma* No. 6, 2003)
7. *La Belle et Babette* [*Beauty and Babette*] (*Yuma* No. 7, 2003)
Artist: Luciano Bernasconi.
Le Rire de la Nuit [*The Laughter of the Night*] (*Yuma* No. 8, 2003)
Artist: Fernando Pasarin.
La Boîte Rouge [*The Red Box*] (*Yuma* No. 8, 2003)

Phénix-Sibilla-Witchblade:
Writer: Jean-Marc Lofficier.
Artist: Stéphane Roux.
Serment de Sang [*Blood Oath*] (*Top Cow Universe* Nos. 8-9, 2003)

Websites:
http://www.coolfrenchcomics.com/phenix.htm
http://www.coolfrenchcomics.com/sibilla.htm

Stany Beule

Index

13, Rue de l'Espoir 201
À Suivre 11, 197
Abe Dopeulapeul 259
Ache, Jean **100-105**
Achille, Lastuce & Cremolet 101
Achille Talon 229
Adam Strange 110, 147
Adventures of Mr. Obadiah Oldbuck 8
Against the Fall of Night 21
Agence Hardy, L' 289
Aggie 131
Aigle d'Or 209
Aigle des Mers, L' 145
Akewa 175
Akim 175
Alain Cardan 138
Alain Landier 169-173
Alan Bruce 209
Albator 137
Albin Michel 222
Albo Gioiello 175
Alexandre, Gérard 131
Alpuente, Eduardo 194, 256
Alvignac, Jean d' 90-95
Amanda 101
Amouriq, André 301

Anacleto 175
Andax 69, 70
Anderson, Poul 263
Andrevon, Jean-Pierre 197
Anges d'Acier, Les 289
Angoisse see Fleuve Noir
Annaud, Jean-Jacques 213
Anticipation see Fleuve Noir
Anton Marcus 209
Apex 99
Aquablue 293
Aquaman 110
Arabelle 100-105
Arak 138
Arcane 289
Arc-en-Ciel 209
Archer Blanc, L' 299
Archibald 101
Ardan 110
Aredit 10, 66, 69-73, 106-120, 268-275
Ariel see Auger, Raoul
Arn 277
Arrabal 226
Artima see Aredit
As, L' 73
As, Les 229

Astérix 7, 225
Astrid 263
Atome Kid 110
Atomos 110
Attali, Jacques 213
Attila 121
Audax 70, 107, 110
Auger, Raoul 82, 83
Autre, L' see ***Wampus***
Avenger, The 49
Aventures & Voyages 45, 175
Aventures Fiction 110
Bagage, Robert 45, **81-85**, 145
Balzac, Honoré de 7
Barbara Tiger 47
Barbarella 11, **158-168**, 220, 222, 225
Barbe-Rouge 137
Barcelonight 289
Barrichella, Thomas 194
Bartier, Pierre 225
Bastard, René 33, 137
Batman 47, 66
Batmax 197
Bébé Cyanure 159
Bécassine 8
Bechtel, Guy 273
Becker, Benoit see Carrière, J-C
Beketch, Serge de **258-261**
Belle de Jour 269
Benoît Brisefer 121
Berger, Juan Roncagliolo 285, 308, 309
Bernard Prince 229
Bernasconi, Luciano 9, 10, **248-257**, 280-287, 304-310
Bevere, Maurice de see Morris
Bibi Fricotin 66, **130-135**
Biddle Wood, Clement 167
Bielsa, José 197, 289
Biffignandi, Alessandro 191
Big Bill le Casseur 45
Big Boy 110
Big Boss 110
Bignon, Alain 159
Bilal, Enki 277
Billon, Daniel 166, 167
Bison Noir 209
Black Boy **44-58**
Blake & Mortimer 10, 29-31

Blanche-Epiphanie 197
Blanco, Fernando 256
Blasco, Jesus 289
Blek 293, 299
Blondin & Cirage 169
Bob Lance 249, 255
Bob Morane 138
Bobo 121
Bonanza 263
Bonfill, Marta 286
Bonicelli, Vittorio 167
Bordelet, Rémy 47, 51, 53, 54, 57
Bornéo Jo 197
Bouquet, Cyril 194
Bowie, David 225
Branner, Martin 8, 16
Brantonne, René **64-71**
BraveStarr 138
Breton, André 226
Brick Bradford 66
Brigade Temporelle 251, 255, **262-267**
Brik 45
Bravo 29, 241
Brétécher, Claire 10
Brick Bradford 9
Bringing Up Father 16
Brouyère, Jean-Marie 25, 26
Brulant 110
Brule, Claude 167
Bruno Brazil 229
Buck Danny 169
Buffalo Bill 66
Buffolente, Lina 137
Buñuel, Luis 269
Burroughs, Edgar Rice 175, 223
Cabanes, Max 159
Callaud, Gaston 134
Calone 110
Canard en Ciné 65
Caniff, Milton 10
Cap 7 209
Capitaine Fantôme 73
Capitaine Nemo 34, 165
Capitaine Pat'Folle 73
Capitan Trueno 289
Captain America 107, 110
Captain Fulgur 137
Caran d'Ache 8

Cardona, José Maria 289
Carol Détective 230
Carrière, Jean-Claude **268-275**
Castex, Pierre **137**, 141-144
Caza 226
Cebe, Dominique 194
Cendres, Martial see Thévenin, René
Cendrillon 81
Césarin Pitchounet 73
Cet Obscur Objet du Désir 269
Chaplin, Charlie 131, 159
Chapuys-Montlaville (Baron de) 7
Charlas, Bertrand 191, 192
Charlier, Jean-Michel 33, 137, 138, 229
Charlot see Little Tramp
Charme Discret de la Bourgeoisie 269
Chasseur de Monstres, Le 73
Chasseurs d'Hommes, Les 19
Chat, Le 229
Chateau, Denis 221
Chéret, André 33, 137
Chevallier, Roger see Kline
Chick Bill 229
Chott see Mouchot, Pierre
Chouchou 33, 197, 199, 202, 205, 206
Christin, Pierre 289
Christophe 8
Chroniques Barbares 299
Chroniques de l'Innommé 289
Circus 291
Clameurs 110
Clarke, Arthur C. 21
Clifton 229
Coelho, E.T. 137
Coeurs Vaillants 81
Cohl, Emile 8, 65
Colliard, Robert see Lortac, R.
Colonel X 33, 73, 79
Comanche 229
Commander, Le 110
Comte de Saint-Germain, Le 249, 255
Conan 110, 220, 223, 263, 283
Conquérants de l'Espace, Les 10, 66, **106-120**
Constantine, Eddie 49
Cop, Edouard 309
Coplan FX-18 110, 138
Coq Hardi 73, 77, 79

Coraline 101
Cormoran, Le 201
Corsini 305
Corteggiani, François 194, 255, 299
Cosmo 299
Cosmos 110, 111
Costo Chien Policier 73
Creepy 259
Croc Blanc 137
Cugel 259
Culliford, Pierre see Peyo
Cuvelier, Paul 226
Dama di Picche, La 175
Dan Cooper 169
Dandy, Jim 194
Dani Futuro 289
Dany 229
Dargaud 222, 239, 261, 291
Davy Crockett 79, 137
Dazergues, Max-André 50, 54
DC Comics 11, 49, 110, 147
Déboires d'Outre-Tombe 259
Défenders, The 110
Degas, Brian 167
De La Torre, Mariano 256, 309
De Laurentiis, Dino 167
Delcourt 295, 296
Deliège, Paul 121
Deligne, Michel 80
Delporte, Yvan 121, 138
Delta 99 289
Demoiselle de Légion d'Honneur 289
Demon 110
Démonax 66
Demuth, Michel 213
Denoël 105
Deray, Jacques 269
Derib 121
Dernière des Salles Obscures, La 201
Desberg, Stephen 128, 129
Deum, Bob 277
Devil, Nicolas 226
Deynis, René **138**, 141-144
Diavolo 45
Dick Demon 45, 249
Dimanche Illustré, Le 8, 15
Dinamite Kid 175
Dineur, Fernand 121, 128

312

Dionnet, Jean-Pierre 11, 33, 213, **276-279**
Disney, Walt 10, 66
Diva et le Kriegspiel, La 289
Doc Savage 81
Docteur Justice 137
Doctor Impossible 263
Doctor Niebla 289
Doom Patrol, The 147
Dossiers Soucoupes Volantes 197
Dragut 251, 255
Druillet, Philippe 10, 11, **212-223**, 226, 259, 277
Dubos, Dannie 197
Duchateau, André-Paul 230
Ducray, Camille 13
Dufaux, Jean 230
Dumas, Jacques see Marijac
Dupuich, J.A. 107
Dupuis (Editions) 25, 26, 128-129
Dupuis, Pierre 137, **208-211**
Durga Rani 19, **59-62**
Dut 73, 75, 77, 107
Duteurtre, Pierre see Dut
Dynamic 110
Dzialowski, Jean-Jacques 194
Echo des Savanes, L' 10, 201
Eclair 110
Eclipso 110
Electropolis 19, 21
Elric 213, 223
Emmanuelle 226
Enfants, C'est l'Hydragon... 159
Epatant, L' 8, 134
Epervier Bleu, L' 10, **23-27**
Epoxy 226
Epsilon see **Mikros**
Eric Castel 241
Erik le Viking 209
Espiègle Lili 8
Essegesse 293
Etoile Blanche 293
Etranges Aventures 110
Eva Star 263
Exterminateur 17 277
F & SF see *Fiction*
Face d'Ange 110
Fafhrd & the Gray Mouser 213, 223

Falk, Lee 49
Fantasia 50, 57, 58
Fantask 255, 308
Fantax 10, **44-58**, 81
Farkas, Bernard 277
Felina **288-291**
Fernand Nathan 279
Féval, Paul 7
Fiction 159, 197, 263
Fillette 8, 62, 79, 99
Fils de Chine 33, 201
Fils du Dragon 137
Five Stars Studio 137, 138
Flash Espionnage 110
Flash Gordon 9, 10, 29, 30, 49, 73, 79, 229
Flaubert, Gustave 219, 220
Flèche Noire 159
Fleuve Noir 65, 66, 107, 110, 229, 268-275
Fluide Glacial 11
Fonda, Jane 167
Font, Alfonso 33, 289
Forest, Jean-Claude 11, **158-168**, 200-207, 225, 226, 259
Formosa, Gil 193, 256, 287, 304
Forns, Jaime 148
Forton, Gérald 33, **138**, 140
Forton, Louis 8, 131, 134, 138
Forzano, Gilbert 18
Foster, Hal 10
France-Dimanche 101
France-Soir 101, 103-105, 138, 159, 201, 205
Francis, Les 66, 107
Franco, Jess (Jesus) 269
François Veyrac 73
Frankenstein **268-275**
Franquin, André 10, 121, 229
Frescura, Franco 10, **248-257**
Frisano, Jean 280
Fromage 37
Fulgor 110, 175
Fulguros **64-71**, 110
Futura 249, 252-256, 262-267, 293
Futuropolis (publisher) 16, 37-39
Futuropolis **19-22**
Gal, J.P. 277

Galaor 175
Galax 33
Gall 201
Gallet, Georges H. 166
Gallix 251, 255
Gamba, Pietro 181
Garcia, Luis 289
Garcia, Manuel 194, 256
Garry 145
Gates, Tudor 167
Gaty, Christian 33, 137
Gavroche 66, 137
Gelin, Xavier 221
Gigantik 289
Gigi, Robert 197
Gillain, Joseph see Jijé
Gillon, Paul 33, 159, **200-207**, 209
Gimenez, Carlos 289
Giordan, R. & R. 10, 66, **106-120**
Gladiateur de Bronze, Le 249, 263
Glénat 17, 21, 77, 105, 211, 239, 291
Godard, Jean-Luc 269
Goetzinger, Annie **288-291**
Gotlib, Marcel 10, 197
Gourdon, M. 271
Gouroull see **Frankenstein**
Greffiere, Pol see Legoff, Pierre
Grêlé 7/13, Le 33
Greg 12-18, 103, **228-235**
Grivaud, Frédéric 308
Guerre à la Terre 72-77
Guerre du Feu, La 19, 213
Guingla Bill 175
Gulliver's Travels 66
Guy Lebleu 33, 138
Habits Noirs, Les 7
Hachette 16, 17, 203, 205, 206
Hallucinations 110, 268-275
Hammett, Dashiell 49
Hara-Kiri 197, 225
Hardy 110
Heart of Juliet Jones, The 201
Hemmings, David 167
Hellstrom's Hive 231
Henneberg, Nathalie Ch. 161
Hergé 8, 13, 16, 29
Héritiers d'Orphée, Les 145
Hermann 229

Heroic-Albums 169, 229
Hidalgo, Francisco 289
Histoire de M. Vieuxboix 8, 65
Hitler, Adolf 81, 84, 265
Hogarth, Burne 49
Homicron 256
Homme au Landau, L' 197
Hourman, The 49
Howard, Robert E. 220, 223
Hubinon, Victor 169
Hudic, Willy & Jonathan 194, 285
Huet, Jean see Ache, Jean
Hulk 110
Humanoides Ass. 205, 206, 222, 279
Hurrah 138
Hypocrite 159, 166
Ici Même 159
Il Faut y Croire pour le Voir 159
Illustré du Dimanche, L' 105
Image Comics 252, 256
Imperia 10, 45, 81-85, 145-157
Inattendu, L' 110
Inoxydables, Les 289
Insolite, L' 110
Intrépide, L' 138
Ionesco, Eugène 225
Isabelle 121
Jacobs, Edgar P. 10, **28-32**
Jacques Flash 136-144
Jaleb 256, 263, 265, 293
James Bond 225
Jan Europe 263
Jardins de la Peur, Les 230
Jari 241, 245
Jaydee 256
Jean & Jeanette 137, 138
Jean Bolide 175
Jean Cyriaque 277
Jean Valhardi 10, 229
Jeff Sullivan 249, 263, 265, 293
Jeremie 201
Jeunesse Illustrée, La 8
Jeunesse Joyeuse 134
Jeunesses & Vacances 140
Jijé 10, 121, 169, 229
Jim Boum 73
Jim et Joe 73
Jimmy Torrent see *Jari*

Jodelle 11, 220, **224-227**
Johan 10
Johnny Speed 66
Jonah Hex 138
Jonque Fantôme..., La 159
Journal de Bibi Fricotin, Le 134
Journal de Mickey, Le 101, 137, 138
Journal du Dimanche, Le 105
Joy, André 137
Jules Bariboule 73
Jumbo 81
Junior 19, 21
Kabur 11, 45, 194, 249, 251, 255, 263, **280-287**, 293
Kangourou 37
***Kaza le Martien* 78-80**
Kazhann 221
Keirsbilk, Emile 110
Kid Meteora 175
Kim Devil 138
Kit Kappa 249
Klein, Gérard 226
Kline **78-80**, 96-99, 137
Kris Kool 226
Kronos (Dupuis) 209
Kronos (Mitton) 299
Lacroix, Pierre 66, **130-135**
La Fontaine, Jean de 65
Lafuente, David 286
La Fuente, Victor de 289
La Hire, Jean de 66
Lainé, Jean-Marc 194, 285
Lang, Fritz 22
Lapière, Denis 128
Larry Cannon 263, 265
Law, John Philip 167
Lawrence, Don 209
Lazo Jim 175
Leblanc, Raymond 29
Lecureux, Roger **33-43**, 137
Lefrancq 138
Lefrancq, Claude 111
Le Gall, Pierre 239
Legoff, Pierre 138, 144
Legrand, Benjamin 221
Legrand, Claude J. **262-267**, 280-287
Le Guen, Pierre **137**, 139, 140
Leiber, Fritz 213, 223

Lemmy Caution 49
Lennoz, Jacques 301
Lenvers, Max **138**, 144
Leonid Beaudragon 159
Leroux, Gaston 138
Lesparre, Patrice 285
Léviathans, Les 201
Liebermann, Rolf 213
Lilia entre l'Air et l'Eau 159
Liquois, Auguste **72-77**, 86-95
Linus 197, 199
Little Tramp 131, 159
Lob, Jacques **196-199**, 219, 220, 222, 236-240
Lofficier, J.-M. & Randy 138, 194, 255, 256, 283-286, 308, 309
Lombard 16, 17, 31, 229-235, 241-247
Lone Sloane 11, 197, **212-223**, 226, 260
Loreau, Jean-Marc see Loro
Loro **258-261**
Lortac, R. 10, **64-71**, 106-120, 130-135
Losfeld, Eric 166, 213, 220-227
Louis, Stéphane 308
Louk Chien Loup 138
Loup 172
Loup Noir 79
Lovecraft, H. P. 213
Luc Condor 169
***Luc Orient* 228-235**
Lucky Luke 279
Lug 10, 45, 47, 81, 110, 174-195, 248-257, 262-267, 280-287, 292-310
Lynx 33
Lynx Blanc 201
Mac Gallan 207
Macherot, Raymond 121, 229
Magda 79
Malgrain, Christophe 194
Malices de Plick et Plock, Les 8
Malle, Louis 269
Maltaite, Willy see Will
Mandryka, Nikita 10
Mange-Bitume, Les 197
Manuel, L'Enfant-Rêve 213
Marc Dacier 138, 229
Marceau, Marcel 167
Marcello, Raphael 137

Marco Polo 45
Marijac 33, **72-77**, 79
Marsupilami, Le 229
Martian Manhunter 110
Marvel Comics 11, 110, 265
Maskar 51
Masters of the Universe 138
Mayeu, Max see Sirius
McCay, Winsor 65
McManus, George 16
Mazzanti, Attilio 175
Melwyn-Nash see Navarro, Marcel
Mémoire des Celtes, La 137
Mendez, Rafael 148
Métal Hurlant 11, 205, 213, 219, 220, 222, 277, 279
Meteor 66, 70, 106-120
Metropolis 22
MGM 66
Mickey Mouse 9, 131
Mikros 11, 45, 293, **298-303**
Mimi 263
Minguez, Jean-Marie 194
Mission: Impossible 121
Mister Song 249, 255
Mitton, Jean-Yves 45, 295, 296, **298-303**
Modeste & Pompon 229
Moebius 10, 213, 277
Molinari, Félix **145-157**
Mondiales 49, 93
Mon Journal 101
Monsieur Choc 121-129
Monsieur Poche 13
Moorcock, Michael 213, 223
Moore, Catherine L. 159, 160, 213
Mora, Victor **288-291**
Mornet, Thierry 194, 283
Moron, Tomas 194
Morris 121
Motoman 175
Mouchot, Pierre 10, **44-58**, 81
Mozam 194
Mr. Cro 241
Mustang 252, 255, 293, 301
Mystérieuse Matin, Midi et Soir 159, 165, 166
Mystic 110

Name of the Rose, The 213
Nasdine Hodja 33, 137
Naufragés du Temps, Les 159, **200-207**
Navarro, Marcel **45-46**, 51, 52, 81, 175, 293, 299
Nestor & Boniface 229
Nic et Mino 101
Nic Reporter 137
Northwest Smith 160, 213
Nosferatu 213
Nouvelles Littéraires, Les 159
Nuit, La 213
Nuit Barbare, La 137
Nyctalope, Le 66
O'Donoghue, Michael 226
Offenstadt 21
OK 79, 101, 137
Olac le Gladiateur 209
Olivier Rameau 229
Olivier, Thierry 194
Ollivier, Jean **137**
Olympic 110
Olympio see **Vincent Larcher**
Ombrax 252
Onésime Pellicule 73
Oneta, Fausto 175
Oneta, Franco 10, **175-195**
Opera Mundi 29, 138
Opta 213
Ortiz, José Maria 148
Oscar Mittoman 138
O'Shea, Milo 167
OSS 117 110
Other, The see **Wampus**
Ouragan 110
Outer Limits, The 147
Ozark 175, 194, 293
Paape, Eddy **228-235**
Paddy 229
Pallenberg, Anita 167
Pallino 175
Paris Monde Illustré 49, 50, 51
Parras, Antonio 289
Pasarin, Fernando 252, 256, 308, 309
Pat'apouf 101
Pedrazza, Augusto **175-195**
Péguet, Francis 51, 56, 57

316

Pélerin, Le 101
Pellaert, Guy 11, **224-227**
Pellarin, René see Pellos
Pellos **19-22**, 59-62, 131
Pellucidar 223
Pemberton 23
Peniche, Manuel Martin 284, 285
Petit Journal Illustré, Le 8
Petit Illustré, Le 134
Petit Vingtième, Le 8
Peyo 10, 121
Pham Minh Son 137
Phantom, The 49
Phénix (magazine) 31
Phénix 11, 45, 249, 293, **304-310**
Phoebe Zeit-Geist 226
Photonik 11, 45, **292-297**
Pic-Nic 69
Pic & Nic 81
Piccolo Corsaro 175
Pichard, Georges **196-199**, 236-240, 289
Pieds Nickelés, Les 8, 19, 131, 134, 138
Pierino 175
Pierrot 73
Pif see *Vaillant*
Pilote 10, 11, 23, 33, 101, 138, 197, 212-223, 229, 236-240, 258-261, 277, 291
Pina, Javier 256
Pinchon, Joseph P. 8
Pionniers de l'Espérance 10, **33-43**
Pirates de l'Infini, Les 209
Planète 197
Planète Comics 255, 308
Poche 105
Poïvet, Raymond 10, **33-43**, 276-279
Popeye 9
Praline 66
Pravda la Survireuse 225
Presses de la Cité 110
Prifo 89, 93
Prince Valiant 9
Principe Nero, Il 175
Processus de Survie 201
Projet Nouvelle Vénus 263
Proust, Marcel 7
P'tit Gus 33

P'tit Joc 137
Quest for Fire see *Guerre du Feu*
Rabier, Benjamin 8
Radar 81
Radarex 66
Ragnar le Viking 137
Rahan 33
Rakar 45, 249
Rancho 50, 54, 55, 56, 57
Ratera, Mike 194, 195, 283, 286
Ratier, Bernadette 45
Raymond, Alex 10, 49, 79
Rayon Fantastique, Le 159, 161, 166
Rayon U, Le 10, **28-32**
Reding, Raymond **241-247**
Reed Man 194, 256
Région Étrangère 277
Regnier, Michel see Greg
Remohi, Brocal 289
Remparts 66
Renzi, Robert 175
Reportages Sensationnels 50, 54
Retour de Martin Guerre, Le 269
Ric Hochet 138
Rieux, Georges **137**
Rin Tin Tin 263
Ripoll, Edmond **262-267**
Robba see Bagage, Robert
Robida, Albert 8, 13
Robin Hood 45
Robinson 29
Robinsons de la Terre, Les 33
Rob-Vel 8
Rocca, Robert 47, 48, 52
Rochette 197
Rock Derby 229
Rock Dreams 225
Roc Meteor 169
Roger Fringant 197
Rollin, Georges 18
Rolling Stones, The 225
Roman de Renart, Le 159
Ronald-Wills see Dazergues, M.-A.
Roos, E. 56
Rosny Aîné, J-H 19, 161
Rosset, Gérard 18
Rosy, Maurice **121-129**
Rouletabille 138

Rouletabosse Reporter 73
Roux, Stéphane 309
R.T.P. 31
S.A.E.T.L. 69
S.A.G.E. 45, 81
Saga de Xam 226
Saint, The 49
Saint-Ogan, Alain 8, **12-18**, 229
Salammbo 219, 220
Salvator 73, **86-89**
Sam Spade 107
Sang d'Encre 301
Satanax 73, **90-95**
Savant Cosinus, Le 8
Savant Microbus..., Le 65
Savard, Didier 159
Schlondorff, Volker 269
Schtroumpfs, Les 10
Schwarz see Bagage, Robert
Scooby-Doo 175
Scugnizzo 175
Secret Agent Z.302 81
Section R 241
Semaine de Suzette, La 8
Semic see Lug
S.E.R. 45, 50
S.E.R.G. 62, 199, 261
S.F.P.I. 209, 211
Shambleau 160
Shadow, The 49
Sheckley, Robert 259
Shelley, Mary 268-275
Sibilla 249, 255, 265, 293
Sidéral 107, 110
Siècle see Imperia
Siegel, Jerry 49
Sierra de la Mar, Angele 285
Sikorski, Alain 128
Silver Surfer, The 45, 299
Sim, Bob 33
Simon le Danseur 23
Sirius 10, **23-27**
Sitting Bull 73
Sloane, William 159
Smurfs see *Schtroumpfs*
Snorky 175
Soleil 37, 40
Solini, Cesare 175

Souriau 137
Southern, Terry 167
Space Family Robinson 107
Space Gordon 107
Space Ranger 110
S.P.E. 62
Special-Kiwi 179
Special-Rodeo 308
Special-Zembla see *Zembla*
Spectral 110
Spectre 110
Spider, The 49
Spider-Man 138
Spidey 295, 296
Spiritello 175
Spirou 7, 8, 10, 11, 23-26, 121-129, 138, 169, 209, 229
Spoutnik 110
Springer, Frank 226
Sprint 81
Stany Beule dans la Lune 79, **96-99**
Starlock 249, 256
Starlog 166, 168
Star Trek 35, 107, 109
Steiner, Kurt 219
Sternberg, Jacques 226
Strangers 252, 256, 309
Submerman 197, **236-240**
Sunday 289
Super Boy 81, **145-157**
Super Dupont 197
Superman 147
Supernova 289
Sur l'Autre Face du Monde 19, 21
Survivante, La 201
Survivants de l'Atlantique, Les 299
Sweet Delice 259
Sylvie 69, 70
Tabor 175
Tangor 137
Tanka 178, 256
Tarawa 169
Tardi, Jacques 159
Targa 81
Tarou 110
Tarzan 9, 33, 49, 73, 89, 166, 175
Teddy Ted 33, 138
Tele-Junior 138

Téméraire 110
Téméraire, Le 33, 73
Tempest 110
Ténébrax 196-199
Tequila Bang 289
Terrain Vague, Le 66, 225
Tetar-Zan 66
Thévenin, René **19-22**, 59-62
Thirion, Louis 226
Thorkael 258-261
Tibet 229
Tif & Tondu see Monsieur Choc
Tigres Volants, Les 145
Tillieux, Maurice 121, 128
Tim Tyler's Luck 81
Time Patrol, The 263
Timour 23
Tin Drum, The 269
Tintin 7, 8, 10, 15-18, 29, 31, 103, 105, 131, 138, 169-172, 229-235, 241-247
Tiriel 33, **276-279**
Titan 208-211
Titans 301
Tognazzi, Ugo 167
Tom Tempest 107
Tom X 81-85
Tonton Molécule 101
Tony Comet 175
Top Cow 309
Topffer, Rodolphe 8, 65
Topor 226
Torelli, Maurizio 175
Tota, Cyro **292-297**
Transperceneige, Le 197
Trois Mousquetaires du Maquis 73
Trottolino 175
Tumak 33
Twilight Zone, The 147
Udolfo 229
Ulysse 197
Unbearable Lightness of Being 269
Universal Pictures 66
Urm le Fou 213
Vadim, Roger 167
Vae Victis 299
Vaillant 10, 33, 37-43, 79, 137-144, 201, 209, 229
Vaisseau Hanté, Le 159

Valérie, André see Thévenin, René
Vallet, A. 8
Vance, Jack 259
Vance, William 229
Vander, Stéphane 18
Van Hamme, Jean 226
Van Vogt, A.E. 159, 161
Vartan, Sylvie 225
Velter, Robert see Rob-Vel
Vengeur 110
Ventura, Lino 49
Verne, Jules 13, 159, 165
Vers les Mondes Inconnus 73
Vicky 169
Vigor 73, 107, 110
Vincent Larcher 241-247
Vingtième Siècle, Le 8
Virgola 175
Vistel, Auguste 45
V-Magazine 160, 166, 197
Voyageuse de Petite Ceinture, La 289
Vuzz 213, 220
Waki 45, 249
Walter Melon see Achille Talon
Wampus 9, 10, 45, **248-257**, 265, 285
Weinberg, Albert **169-173**
Wild Wild West 138
Will 10, **121-129**
Williamson, Jack 159, 161
Winkler, Paul 29
Winnie Winkle 8, 16
Witchblade 309
Witches of Thessalia, The 197
Wolfs, Roger 225
Wul, Stefan 219
Xavier, Philippe 285
X-Files, The 36, 169
Yak 45
Yatan 175, 178
Yogi Bear 175
Yragaël 213
Yuma 308, 309
Yvain de Kanheric 138
Yves Le Loup 137
Yvon et Toni 81
Zembla 10, 45, **174-195**, 282-285, 287
Zig et Puce 8, **12-18**, 229
Zorro 138, 209

www.ingramcontent.com/pod-product-compliance
Lightning Source LLC
Chambersburg PA
CBHW022051160426
43198CB00008B/191